Cultural Theory in the Films of Alfred Hitchcock

Cultural Theory in the Films of Alfred Hitchcock

Gary McCarron

ANTHEM PRESS

Anthem Press
An imprint of Wimbledon Publishing Company
www.anthempress.com

This edition first published in UK and USA 2023
by ANTHEM PRESS
75–76 Blackfriars Road, London SE1 8HA, UK
or PO Box 9779, London SW19 7ZG, UK
and
244 Madison Ave #116, New York, NY 10016, USA

British Library Cataloguing-in-Publication Data
A catalogue record for this book is available from the British Library.

Library of Congress Control Number: 2023933055
A catalog record for this book has been requested.

ISBN-13: 978-1-83998-846-2 (Hbk)
ISBN-10: 1-83998-846-0 (Hbk)

Cover Credit: Image Courtesy of the bioscope.net, Silhouette Thriller Film director graphy, PNGWING.

This title is also available as an e-book.

CONTENTS

ACKNOWLEDGEMENTS

I want to thank the many colleagues and friends from the School of Communication and the Graduate Liberal Studies Program at Simon Fraser University who offered their support and advice during the writing of this book. In particular, I want to express my gratitude to Richard Smith for his generous counsel and the exceptional pleasure of co-teaching a course on social theory and film with him. These classes provided me with opportunities to try out some of my developing ideas regarding Hitchcock's work, with several of these ideas landing a place in this book. There is no greater pleasure than working with friends.

I am also grateful to Jerry Zaslove from Graduate Liberal Studies for the unparalleled excellence of the observations he made, the questions he asked, and the problems he raised. Jerry passed away without seeing the manuscript in a complete form, yet his memory is recorded in passages too numerous to mention.

I am also indebted to the staff and editors at Anthem Press for their encouragement and hard work. As I point out in Chapter 7, there are times when things do not turn out exactly as expected, and the people at Anthem were extraordinarily accommodating when plans went temporarily awry. Their patience and good humour were greatly appreciated.

No one has been a more important source of guidance and inspiration than Cathy Hill. She tolerated my long-winded disquisitions, prodded me with sharp-eyed critique, encouraged me beyond what I deserved, and managed to maintain her good humour even while handling her own demanding workload. I owe her everything.

INTRODUCTION: RE-VIEWING HITCHCOCK'S FILMS

Two Questions

During the time that I worked on this book, two questions occasionally cropped up when I spoke to friends and colleagues about what I was writing. The first question was beguilingly simple while the second was rather more challenging. These were also questions I had addressed to myself periodically as I moved on to fresh ideas in the development of my position on Hitchcock's work. I don't believe that I ultimately arrived at satisfactory answers in every instance, but in the effort to appease my interlocutors I travelled part of the way toward eliminating most of my self-doubt. So, I will start with these questions – and with my attempts to answer them – to draw a frame around the text that follows.

The first question, which I initially took to be simple, asked what the book was going to be about. More specifically, people wanted to ask me about my method. How did I plan to approach Hitchcock? Was the book going to be an original series of analyses of Hitchcock's films, analyses that until now no one had attempted? And if so, which of Hitchcock's films would I be examining? Was I writing about Alfred Hitchcock with the plan of rescuing a filmmaker from the void of forgetfulness into which popular icons are sometimes swallowed up? Was the book to be a fresh take on Hitchcock's already well-covered biography in consequence of recently unearthed material that showed him to be quite different from traditional accounts of his life?

Questions concerning my approach did not stop there, for I was also asked if my book was to be an account of Hitchcock's role in the history of cinema, the enduring influence of his work on contemporary filmmakers, or possibly a demonstration of the latest film studies trend – I don't think that a particular trend was ever specified – in the task of explicating the master's works. One colleague wanted to know if I was writing a book that used some new psychological theory to make sense of Hitchcock's infamously enigmatic personality, while another asked if I would be arguing against the conventional interpretation of Hitchcock as an important and inspirational figure in cinema. If that was the case, she said, was my Hitchcock book actually an anti-Hitchcock book? That is, was I going to present a critique of Alfred's misogyny, his tendency to demonize gays and lesbians, or his tragically myopic view of people of colour? In short, was my intention to celebrate or condemn Hitchcock?

These were all good and interesting questions which certainly led me to reflect critically on my purposes. I was also moderately distressed by these questions, for they opened a door to the realization that perhaps I was being inattentive to the sorts of concerns that naturally arose when Hitchcock's name was mentioned. It seemed I wasn't always engaged by the same sorts of issues a good many viewers of Hitchcock's films were naturally drawn to. Perhaps I was pushing my own interests more to the forefront of the work than was justified? Suddenly, I had my own questions.

That the present work deals with some of the issues just mentioned will be plain enough to the reader, but it is equally true that my treatment of these matters is not my primary focus. I concentrate on other themes in addition to history, influence, biography, and legacy. However, to explain my approach properly, I need to address the second question I frequently encountered on my way to completing the text. As I have said, this second question was of a more challenging nature even though it was in other ways a more down-to-earth question: Why? Why are you writing this book?

"Why" can be practical or metaphysical. It can also be a serious blow to one's ego in that it challenges basic assumptions of value and significance. Something thought to be worth considering can be thrown into doubt when the why question is presented. However, to be asked why also presents an opportunity for self-reflection. What soon became clear to me is that some colleagues and friends asked me 'why' because they ultimately wanted to know how I could I defend a book about the films of Alfred Hitchcock. What reasons did I have for writing a book about a popular filmmaker who died in 1980, a filmmaker whose life has been the subject of multiple biographies, and whose films, though enduringly popular with audiences and clearly influential on other filmmakers, are broadcast infrequently, and usually on specialty channels? What was the point, especially given the large body of literature already available on Hitchcock? What is left to say?

What and *why* often form an intellectual alliance to the extent that purpose must be directed to a narrowly circumscribed subject matter. However, whereas the 'what' question was ordinarily casual, I sometimes felt a latent hostility in the second question – indeed, I occasionally thought that the second question really came in the interrogatory form by happenstance, and that it constituted something of a demand for justification. This might be overreaction on my part, though I am confident that in at least a few instances my judgement is correct. In any event, there is a logic to the second question, and that logic I believe constitutes an imperative it would be advisable to obey.

First, it is certainly true that there are many fine volumes about Alfred Hitchcock, some biographical, others theoretical, many rather popular. There are so many articles about virtually every facet of Alfred's life including his childhood, education, early filmmaking influences, and perversities that we have reached the point that the word *Hitchcockian* can be found in several dictionaries. There is even an academic field known as Hitchcock Studies to which I hope this volume will make a modest contribution.

None of this is surprising with the benefit of hindsight. As someone who contributed a good deal to the development of cinema in the twentieth century, Hitchcock rightly deserves to be one of the most written about filmmakers – indeed, he is usually described as the filmmaker about whom more books and articles have been written than any other director, though I am unsure about the empirical measures that have used to support that claim. Still, I imagine that it is probably accurate, and it is therefore tempting to simply point to these numbers as a justification for my own contribution. On the other hand, one could suggest the opposite point of view and argue that we have had enough about Hitchcock, especially if he is, as just noted, the most widely written about director in cinema history. Given that Hitchcock has inspired so many studies, articles, treatises, doctorates, and books, it seems perfectly fair to ask what more remains to be said. So, the second question is an important one, for how could anyone justify another book about Hitchcock? This is my answer.

Justifying Hitchcock

I fear that there is really no excuse for this book. I don't mean that the present volume is without merit, or that the arguments I raise lack originality. Rather, I am suspicious about the broader issue, the idea that scholarship of any sort requires some form of justification. Moreover, I am apprehensive about some of the ways in which scholarly work can end up being justified. This isn't because I think people are overtly deceptive in respect of their intentions, though it is certainly true that authors are not always to be trusted when lining up the reasons for their work in the effort to defend their labours. Rather, I am concerned about the common presumption that one inherits an obligation to explain things merely because one's subject is thought to stand in a particular and somewhat dubious relationship to utility.

There are many ways to respond to the question concerning the usefulness of a book in the grand scheme of things. For instance, an argument can be made based on the sheer pleasure of writing, the beauty of how we connect apparently disparate ideas in wonderful and sometimes moving ways. Personally, I like this argument chiefly because I sometimes find myself captured by the beauty of the passionate; I am enchanted by Hitchcock's work for reasons that are not easily reduced to the status of skeletal accounts of mere preference. The logic that underlies my appreciation is more complex than can be expressed in the formulas that traditionally satisfy a desire to know why. I have great appreciation for the aesthetics of the mise en scène in *The Lodger*, the chiaroscuro lighting of *Psycho*, the abruptness of the camera's ricocheting movements in *The Birds*, the sweeping revelations of subjectivity in *Marnie*, and the attenuated crispness of the dialogue in *Shadow of a Doubt*. Of course, none of these cinematic moments is unique to me or to my perception, and many other films deserve to be added to the list. Familiarity with an artist or an art form usually reveals hidden depths and dimensions that preliminary encounters are unable to detect. In the case of Alfred Hitchcock, it is commonly pointed out that he famously claimed that none of his films could be viewed only once, that the richness of the narrative had to unfold over multiple viewings. Not every one of Hitchcock's films is a masterpiece, yet even in insubstantial works like *To Catch a Thief* (1955) there are still moments of cinematic ingenuity and witty dialogue to make the viewing experience pleasurable. And multiple viewings of Hitchcock's films are certainly one of the ways to come to these sorts of realizations, especially as the airiness and outright improbability of some of his stories can distract from his works' deeper and more satisfying pleasures. And pleasure is important. Indeed, while pleasure is not an inconsiderable thing, citing pleasure as a reply to *why* might seem more evasive than analytic. Regardless, there was a good deal of pleasure at the foundation of my impulse to undertake this work. Much of that pleasure was more scholastic, perhaps, than purely aesthetic, but for me, that has been one of the main reasons I enjoy Hitchcock's work: it forces me to think beyond the usual cinematic categories of good and evil, truth and falsity, innocence and guilt, and to contemplate instead the viability of those very categories. Hitchcock's work can push us to question the ontological security of our conventional ways of thinking.

If I put aside my instinctive defence at being asked to explain *why*, and focus instead on the nature of the question, I can't help but notice that there are other questions, and questionable assumptions, that lie back of that deceptively simple query. Charles Tilly has argued that when pressed to explain why, people tend to give reasons which fall into one of the four categories: (1) Conventional accounts, which generally rely on truisms and folk wisdom; Narrative accounts, which seek to order things in a scheme that shows how they are related elements of a comprehensible story; Technical cause-and-effect accounts, which rely on mechanistic principles; and Codes, which appeal to legal or extrajudicial procedures or inventories of proper conduct.[1] Of course, Tilly is largely re-visiting and expanding on Aristotle, but his categories serve to show that in being asked *why* it is important to know the intellectual interests that motivate the inquiry.[2] Thus, according to Charles Tilly, there is no simple answer to *why*, for you need to know why you are being asked *why*, you need to examine what sorts of responses will be considered relevant – or perhaps appropriate – in responding to the question, and what kinds of political, ideological, cultural, or ethical frames have prompted the question in the first place. Multi-levelled, and hopelessly contextual, the *why* question is neither innocent nor simple. But it is also a question whose driving force is important to the point that it should probably not be ignored.

Other authors have dealt with precisely this question: why write about Alfred Hitchcock. One of the more notable Hitchcock scholars, Robin Wood, used the question to frame his analysis of Hitchcock's films and to suggest an important link between cinema and art, suggesting that Hitchcock's contribution to this relationship was one of the more important in film history. Hence, I will begin with a close reading of how Robin Wood sought to justify his interest in, and his analyses of, the films of Alfred Hitchcock.

Seriously Hitchcock

Robin Wood began his 1965 book, *Hitchcock's Films*, by asking readers, "Why should we take Hitchcock seriously?" (Wood, p. 55).[3] With this opening query, Wood employed a common rhetorical manoeuvre wherein the author

---

1 Tilly, Charles. *Why? What Happens When People Give Reasons … And Why*. Princeton and Oxford: Princeton University Press, 2006.

2 Jürgen Habermas's ideas are relevant here. See *Knowledge and Human Interests* (orig. 1968), translated by Jeremy Shapiro. Boston: Beacon Press, 1972.

3 Wood's revised edition of *Hitchcock's Films* appeared in 1989 and re-examined some of the positions he adopted in his 1965 text. Some critics, as Wood himself noted, had responded negatively to this later edition, though Wood saw the second edition of his book as a personal "awakening." The main concern his critics raised was that Wood had left behind the clarity and perhaps the innocence of his 1965 book in favour of more political readings of Hitchcock's films. Wood said that some critics saw the analyses in the second edition as "constricting," "limited by ideological concerns," and compromised by his "adopted political position" [Marxism] (p. 3). For my part, I do not find the second edition to be burdened with ideological baggage or compromised by Wood's forays into cultural politics. I agree with Wood that the second edition is more sensitive to cultural context, and that the analyses transcend the theory of auteurism on which Wood had previously relied.

presents a proposition in the guise of a question, and he does this to circumvent possible opposition to the implicit claim he is making. In this case, that proposition is simply that we *should* take Hitchcock seriously rather than otherwise. The strategy upon which this operation relies is that by embedding the proposition within the question, resistance to that argument will be weakened while searching for the answer as opposed to denying the putative claim. The question, *why should we take Hitchcock seriously*?, is an invitation; the proposition, *we should take Hitchcock seriously*, is a provocation. Robin Wood's strategy was to solicit his readers' interest in finding answers to his question while cleverly sidestepping the potential disapproval of those who thought Hitchcock's work didn't warrant thoughtful attention.

Of course, time and context are important in explaining Wood's decision. As Hitchcock was principally seen as an entertaining filmmaker in 1965 – and is still "the master of suspense" for many casual film viewers today – Wood likely thought that at least some readers would be disinclined to accept that the director's work was anything other than diversionary, and that his efforts therefore required some measure of justification. The common prejudice against Hitchcock's films, in other words, was the same as we find in the case of many popular texts and artefacts today: such things exist for purposes of amusement and mere entertainment, and these purposes militate against the idea that they warrant serious contemplation or study. Wood's proposal, therefore, makes that prejudice apparent in being framed as a question, and thus the interrogation it initiates is ultimately broader than the sphere of Hitchcock's work.

The strategy was interesting though possibly unnecessary in some ways, for it is unlikely that anyone interested in reading Wood's book required convincing of Hitchcock's relevance. In the first place, it is doubtful that Wood would write a book decrying the filmmaker's work, and the supposition that an argument could be made for not taking Hitchcock seriously was not apt to be a feature of Wood's text. Second, it seems reasonable to presume that most of the book's readers tended to be self-selected for their interest in Hitchcock's films, and while their interest was guaranteed to be at least somewhat uneven, it is improbable that readers picked up Wood's volume to find new reasons for disliking Alfred Hitchcock. The principal strategy behind the question, as I have suggested then, was more rhetorical than anything else. Putting the presumed suspicions of certain members of the viewing public front and centre gave Wood an opportunity to play the role of cultural theorist and to propose a series of reasons for regarding the director's work with an appropriate level of seriousness. Hence, asking 'why we should take Hitchcock seriously' allowed Wood to intimate that Hitchcock was both a legitimate auteur and a symbol of the way cultural criticism was being brought around to embracing the so-called lower arts. Moreover, his book also offered readers the opportunity to engage in the task of rethinking the high art/low art tradition by answering an important question concerning the politics of popular culture.

Wood's *Hitchcock's Films* appeared one year after the publication of Marshall McLuhan's *Understanding Media* and thus it entered a world of readers coming to grips with the idea that popular entertainment – and popular culture, especially – was a worthwhile subject for academic exegesis. Hitchcock was and remains popular, and to some extent Wood's task consisted of taking on the job of convincing his readers that there is nothing wrong with being popular – that pleasure cannot always be reduced to diversion. That this was a challenge is apparent when we consider that among the synonyms the *Oxford English Dictionary* offers for the word "popular," we find "base," "vile," and "riff-raff." The job of rescuing Hitchcock from the stigma of popularity was a more serious undertaking than one might first imagine.

These considerations take us to the response Wood offered to the question that framed his analyses of Hitchcock's work. Given the influence Robin Wood has exerted on the countless Hitchcock scholars who followed him, it is important to know how Wood responded to his own question. How did Wood explain why filmgoers should take Hitchcock seriously?

Although Wood covers a lot of ground in his list of justifications for being a serious viewer of Hitchcock's work, there was rather little in what he said that today's reader would find especially innovative or surprising. He mainly focused his attention on the usual suspects, citing among other possible reasons for treating Hitchcock respectfully such issues as thematic unity, the pursuit of pure cinema, and the claim that the director's films, taken as a collection, made evident the presence of an overarching moral vision. Of course, Wood cited other factors as evidence of Hitchcock's greatness, some more incidental than substantive. However, among the considerations he raised in respect of the need to regard Hitchcock with due seriousness, there was one which clearly stood out for Wood, one particular reason that ultimately seemed to cinch the argument. According to Robin Wood, we should take Hitchcock seriously because Hitchcock's films were a form of art.

This sounds rather important, but what did Wood mean with this argument? The answer is a bit complicated in part because of the problem of circularity that attends this designation. In other words, to claim that Hitchcock deserves serious analysis because his films constitute a form of art is to appeal to an unstated proposition concerning the value and purpose of art. This might have seemed obvious to Wood, and probably seems likely to many readers today, but in falling back on the idea that art is the answer to his question, Wood was implicitly asking us to start over again and deal with a separate question: Why should we take art seriously? This is a bigger and more challenging query than asking why Hitchcock should be taken seriously, and for the moment I am going to forestall the investigation that asks after the value of art. Instead, I am going to trace the line of reasoning that Wood followed in reaching his conclusion and spell out as plainly as I can some of the consequences that I believe follow from the connections he elucidates. Because the notion of art was foundational in Wood's thinking, it will be worth our time to look more closely at how he makes his case for the argument that Hitchcock's films merit serious consideration because they are a form of art.

The Disturbance of Art

First, Wood argued that the most notable feature of Hitchcock's work justifying a serious study was the "disturbing" quality of the films, and it was precisely this quality that Wood saw as fundamental to making Hitchcock's films synonymous with art. Hence, the essential argument explaining why we should take Hitchcock seriously is because he produced cinematic art, not merely movies, and the notion of art was concerned chiefly with effects of a specific kind. More important, the aesthetic quality of the films was apparent not because of their fidelity to other visual arts, but in their being disturbing and disruptive.

This notion of the aesthetic impulse is controversial but not unique. As Wood says, "it is one of the functions of art to disturb, to penetrate and undermine our complacencies and set notions, and bring about a consequent readjustment in our attitude to life" (Wood, p. 67). The tendency of art to produce disequilibrium and thereby encourage critical reflection, Wood said, was also an essential component of Hitchcock's films owing to their "disconcerting moral sense" and the way they force us to recognize "the impurity of our own desires" (Wood, p. 67). According to Wood, therefore, the capacity for thoughtful provocation was the way in which Hitchcock's movies, like all good art, affected their viewers.

Wood's claim that desires can be impure is potentially misleading if left unqualified, for desire's potential for impurity (whether defined in legal or moral terms) is not essential but is consequent upon social and cultural circumstances and concrete behaviour. Rather than refer to "the impurity of [...] our desires," then, it would be more correct to say that desire can be put to ends that may be regarded as impure within a larger institutional or societal setting. Sexual desire, for instance, can be regarded as being in thrall to an impure intention if directed at particular persons (children, for instance), but this is far different than the claim that sexual desire per se is impure.

Wood does not specifically state that desire in its essential and unmediated condition is impure. But it is important to stress the active and intentional structure of desire to avoid lapsing into a more intransitive interpretation.

Still, the central point is clear enough: we should take Hitchcock seriously owing to the fact that his films are not merely amusing diversions but challenging social and moral texts that force us to confront the dangerous and unsavoury side of the human condition. If art is disturbing, and if Hitchcock's films are disturbing, then his films are art.

Wood's argument, which might seem self-contained (if not outright schematic) at first reading, is based on an interesting enthymeme, the unstated premise being that art should be taken seriously. But had Wood started his book by inquiring about the value of art, I imagine that his question would have seemed unnecessary, perhaps naïve. Framing his text by asking why we should take Hitchcock seriously rather than why we should take art seriously showed that Wood was aware of an underlying problem in the presumption that cinema could be considered a subject for serious intellectual investigation; it also provided him with the opportunity to assert that the resolution to this problem was to draw a direct line of descent from serious art to mainstream film. Carrying the argument further, then, Wood argued that Hitchcock's films were linked to serious art by consideration of the effect that both have on their audiences. The "disconcerting moral sense" of Hitchcock's movies that compelled us to confront "the impurity of our own desires" joined film and art together in respect of a mutual purpose: the unmasking of false consciousness. By this line of reasoning, critical reflection was the telos of Hitchcock's work, and a disturbed moral sensibility was important in this scheme as kind of method if not part of the actual goal. Moreover, it appeared that Wood intended his readers to understand that the sorts of disturbances to which art was said to contribute were of a political nature.

Wood was not content with arguing a strictly functional lineage between Hitchcock's films and art, however, and so he suggested a morphological connection as well, explaining that "what distinguishes a work of art" is the manner in which "theme should be seen [...] to inform the whole" (Wood, p. 66). Here his point is more straightforward, namely that in the case of the artwork, content is manifested in style, and this relationship is characteristic of Hitchcock's movies. This is neither a controversial nor original claim, though it is certainly important. The essential point, I take it, is that Hitchcock's work influences viewers in the same way in which the artwork moves its patrons, and his films were formed according to the principles of organic completeness that were characteristic of art. It was this sense of organic singularity to which Wood appealed in suggesting that Hitchcock's films, both for their disturbing themes and stylistic wholeness, were constitutive of art. Indeed, in Hitchcock's films Wood detected a profound intertextuality that gave evidence of the dialectical quality of true art. The kinship of Hitchcock's work with the artist's work was thus complete.

The consequence of Wood's ruminations was the proposition that we should take Hitchcock seriously because his films, as works of art, are characterized by an interest in universal themes that explore the precarious condition of human nature. Equally important, Hitchcock's films engage questions about the human predicament without separating style from substance, and thus give visual evidence of the dialectical union of theory and praxis. And in their exposé of our moral failings, they invite critical reflection on the social mechanisms at work in the task of understanding the complex nature of the cultural order. Indeed, considering the gravity of the considerations Wood associates with Hitchcock's work – and the gravity of the issues explored in those works – the question as to why the director's films merit serious analysis would seem moot: How could anyone, having watched even one of his films, refuse to take Hitchcock seriously?

Low and High Hitchcock

In 1965, however, the question was probably worth asking, and Wood was one of the first English language authors to make the case that Hitchcock's films merit serious attention, whatever the reasons one might cite in support of that contention. The argument was persuasive, and Wood's book became a kind of expedition into unexplored territory where art and cinema appeared to have formed a harmonious union. Indeed, so much subsequent scholarship on Hitchcock has descended from Robin Wood that it would be difficult to overstate the influence his original volume has had in the field of Hitchcock scholarship.

That influence has generally been productive insofar as it helped to christen an era of international Hitchcock studies. However, the premises upon which Wood inaugurated his analyses are not necessarily constitutive of the firmest of foundations. I agree with Wood that we should take Hitchcock seriously and, alongside Wood, I recognize that there may be certain tendencies among select viewers to resist doing so. Some film scholars continue to see Hitchcock as too limited in his approach to filmmaking and too commercial to be regarded as an artist or an auteur, a social role he sought to play especially in later life. Hence, I agree with Wood both on the point of the value of studying Hitchcock's films as well as the resistance one encounters from certain commentators on film history. But to accept Wood's main argument that Hitchcock's work should be taken seriously *because it is art* is to embark upon a potentially confusing line of reasoning: If we are enjoined to take Hitchcock's films seriously, are they, in the spirit of Marcel Duchamp's playfulness, transformed by that attention into legitimate art? Or are they art in need of an interpreter who can guide the masses to an appreciation of their artistic merits? Perhaps we need to recast Hitchcock's films as art in order to elevate them to the plateau of serious debate? In short, do we take Hitchcock's films seriously because they are art, or do the films become art in consequence of our taking them seriously?

These questions follow a line of inquiry first set down by Plato in the dialogue, *Euthyphro*, where Socrates and Euthyphro debate the nature of piety. The problem I am examining here is certainly different in substance, but similar in that it deals with the relation between process and outcome. Such procedural tautologies are always troubling, especially when the point is to get beyond the circular logic in order to penetrate it once again with a cleverly organized series of arguments. In the present case the troubles are magnified because any argument meant to convince readers (and viewers) that a film they regard as a popular cultural artefact is actually a work of art would likely only be persuasive to those already inclined to accept that the film in question should be taken seriously. And for such aficionados the idea that Hitchcock's work is legitimate art will be easy to accept – largely because such a proposition would confirm their predilection for being interested in Hitchcock's films in the first place. On the other hand, for viewers coming to Hitchcock's work for the first time, or for those for whom Hitchcock's appeal has never included the proposition that his work is serious art, Wood's central point is likely to be unpersuasive.

So, is our problem with the definition of art? If we can find a way to gain widespread agreement as to what constitutes art, and then convince a majority of the interested public that this definition applies in the case of Hitchcock's films, have we solved our dilemma? I do not think so. Fundamentally, I think that there is a problem in the idea that an aesthetic transformation is required at all in order to justify the film text as meriting more than casual attention. In other words, although I include myself among those who take Hitchcock seriously, I do not do so on the basis that the work he produced is art. One reason for my reluctance is the obvious contentiousness in asserting that his films are art. This does not mean I deny that Hitchcock's work is art. It simply means that I regard any such proposition as ultimately unprovable. A second reason is the controversy that is invoked when we attempt to state precisely what we mean when we say 'art,' particularly in a discussion of so popular a medium as film.[4] Naturally, I regard these as important issues, and my comment is not intended as a simple critique of Hollywood's commercial aesthetic in respect of its capacity to monetize great art. In fact, my argument is more limited than that, and deals only with the suggestion that to merit serious consideration a cultural artefact such as a film requires a specific form of justification, which Wood says is dependent upon our capacity to reframe the artefact in question as an instance of art.

Let me make this point clearer. I take many things seriously without claiming that they are actually art. In fact, I sometimes take them seriously believing that they are not art. Perhaps if I restrict my appreciation to the conditions of an aesthetic process, then the artfulness of the object would be of particular importance in explaining why I take the thing in question seriously. This is possible but it is unclear what might be gained with this strategy. Moreover, with Hitchcock's films there are many other reasons I might cite other than their status as art as constituting motives for taking the films seriously.

One of the pitfalls in searching out a reason to justify one's interest in a cultural text by transforming it into a different (and ostensibly higher) cultural form is that this tactic risks diminishing the very object it is intended

4 Max Horkheimer once railed against those writers (Mortimer Adler, in particular) who insisted on defending movies against the charge that they were not art because films were a "collective" product and not the result of an individual, creative genius – a strongly anti-auterist argument. Horkheimer rejected this reasoning, arguing that "the discrepancy between art and film, which exists despite the potentialities of the motion picture, is not the result of the surface phenomenon of the number of people employed in Hollywood as much as of the economic circumstances. [...] What today is called popular entertainment is actually demands evoked, manipulated and by implication deteriorated by the cultural industries. It has little to do with art, least of all where it pretends to be such." Thus, for Horkheimer, the problem with equating films with art was that the machinery of capitalism lay back of cinematic production, and the consequent commodities the film industries produced could therefore make no claim to being art as they represented nothing more than the naked pursuit of money. Horkheimer's position, unfortunately, invoked a binary opposition whose poles were film as art or film as business, a pseudo-resolution at best. Of course, commercial success has frequently been seen as fatal to the ascription of art, especially in conversations about film. Indeed, commercial films have long been seen as different from so-called *art films*, an argument that has helped sustain the high-culture-/low-culture dichotomy. I refuse this binary opposition by focusing not on the historical debate about art as film (or not), but on the question of *why we would take Hitchcock seriously*, and whether the only answer to that question is to reply that we take his work seriously because his work is art. As should be apparent, this is the specific response I am trying to problematize (see Horkheimer, Max. "Art and Mass Culture." In *Critical Theory: Selected Essays*, translated by Matthew J. O'Connell. New York: Continuum Books, 1968. p. 250).

to defend and thereby contradicts the process in which one is engaged. After all, if a conceptual transformation is necessary for us to accept the value of the text in question, this implies that in its pre-transformational state the text is undeserving of serious consideration. Yet if we transform the artefact into a representational mode of a different order, so the argument seems to go, the text will then warrant consideration appropriate to its new status. If we can say that Hitchcock's films are art, then we are justified in treating them seriously.

One reason this strategy is problematic is because it is difficult to determine whether this transformation relies on transcending the object's initial limitations or whether this transformation is the recognition of qualities immanent in the object. In other words, does the argument that Hitchcock's films are actual art amount to a modification of those films through some act of addition or augmentation, or is the argument meant to help us realize and appreciate the presence of latent qualities previously hidden in the works? In the former case, which we might call *transformation as transcendence*, an everyday cultural object is reformulated as art principally through discursive practice. This might be a subject for speech act theorists interested in how the performative powers of language initiate cultural transformation. That is, certain stakeholders and experts pronounce the work as a mode of art and thereby bring about an ontological transformation. In the latter case, that of *transformation through artistic immanence*, the object's latent artistic qualities will be manifested in audience reaction and in the subsequent construction of an interpretive community whose members share a common point of view concerning the aesthetic worth of the object. This could become an exclusionary project, leaving those who reside outside the interpretive community doomed to lower, voyeuristic pleasures, while proclaiming that those who can recognize artistic attributes dormant in the object are privy to loftier aesthetic experiences. In both cases, however, this act of reframing shifts our perception of the value of the object from an appreciation of its intrinsic merits to a more exalted understanding ostensibly based on its potential value. In other words, we end up dealing not with the cultural object as it is but as *we imagine it could be*.

This brings me to my main disagreement with Wood, for though it may seem counterfactual, I want to take Hitchcock seriously because his films, very often, are not art. Or, to put that in different terms, I want to take Hitchcock seriously irrespective of whether his films are or are not art. One reason for this position is obvious: a lack of irrefutable criteria by which the assessment Wood provides could be proven. Therefore, whether Hitchcock's films constitute artistic achievements as determined by expert evaluation is a matter of indifference to me, mainly because I am not prepared to say that I know with certainty whether an individual film warrants the label "art." It is perhaps unnecessary to say that I am unprepared to move further with this point because I also refuse to claim the privilege of being able to separate art from non-art. It is enough for me to repeat what I have said above regarding my suspicion of any strategy that claims for a cultural product – such as a Hitchcock film – the right to be taken seriously because, in some secular kind of transubstantiation, that cultural product can be re-designated as a member of the class of art objects. It is possible that Hitchcock's films are art, but I do not really know whether this is so. Furthermore, I am unsure if this is a problem about which I should deeply care.

I prefer to avoid the conditional proposition implied in Wood's analysis: *if* art deserves to be taken seriously, and *if* Hitchcock's films are art, *then* Hitchcock deserves to be taken seriously. This syllogistic approach burdens my appreciation of Hitchcock with the instrumentalism of an intrusive inferential logic. On many points, Wood is correct, but is it necessary to recast Hitchcock's films as art as a precondition for treating his work seriously? I believe not. It is preferable in my view to remain free of the constraints that are imposed by framing reactions to, and conceptions concerning, the value of Hitchcock's films solely in terms of their alleged kinship with – or status as – art. Naturally, this does not mean that I deny the artistic qualities of Hitchcock's work against those who justify their interest in Hitchcock on those grounds. For that matter, questions concerning my interest in Hitchcock are difficult to address without resorting to the kind of tactic Wood adopted, and for that reason his remains an attractive strategy. In the end, however, I believe there is no ironclad justification for taking Hitchcock seriously that can be proven with an airtight syllogism.

Overview of the Book

My approach to Hitchcock's films involves a movement between cinema, social theory, and philosophy, with the aim of showing that it is possible to produce important analyses of Hitchcock's work without having to make artistic merit the centrepiece of such critiques. In other words, I use Hitchcock's films as a jumping off point for discussions of ideas, theories, and philosophical concepts that follow from a focused analysis of a particular feature of Hitchcock's work. This sometimes means avoiding the more conventional interpretations of the director's work by a form of critical rhetoric to that enables a more focused analysis of the presuppositions that constitute the broader cinematic themes. For example, it is rather common to read in works about Alfred Hitchcock that he was constantly striving to achieve what he famously called "pure cinema," but what could he have meant by this phrase, and how did the quest for filmmaking free of possible impurities lead him to certain decisions? Or consider Hitchcock's alleged fondness for situations that dealt with a wrongly accused man. How did Hitchcock conceptualize the idea of guilt, and how closely does it come to current ideas about the socially constructed nature of guilt and innocence? For that matter, what does Hitchcock tell us about the phenomenological condition of suspicion in his appropriately titled film of 1941, *Suspicion*? This book, then, is neither biography nor conventional film critique. Rather, my text explores aspects of Hitchcock's work in relation to theories drawn from the social sciences and philosophy.

Individual chapters do not necessarily focus on specific films, then, but on larger constellations of ideas central to Hitchcock's work. Broadly speaking, the book uses Hitchcock's films to illustrate ideas in the social sciences and philosophy and uses those same ideas to illustrate aspects of Hitchcock's films. This dialectic movement is the central principle in the analyses that follow. In order to indicate how these ideas fit together, I round out the introduction with a brief overview of the book.

Chapter 1: The Incidental **MacGuffin***: Equivalence and Substitution*

In this chapter I look at one of Alfred Hitchcock's most incidental concepts: the thing that he referred to as the film's *MacGuffin*. To start with the MacGuffin may seem a curious decision given that Hitchcock said that the MacGuffin is a largely inconsequential part of the story, suggesting at one point that the MacGuffin, if developed correctly, would really be nothing. In this chapter, however, I aim to show that if we examine the concept of the MacGuffin more closely – and examine in detail the work Hitchcock did to develop a MacGuffin appropriate to the film's circumstances – we can come to a more fulsome appreciation of the architecture of many of his films. At the same time, the MacGuffin raises several interesting philosophical issues such as equivalential logic and ultimate substitutability, issues to which I turn near the end of the chapter. I spend some time discussing Hitchcock's political thriller, *Notorious* (1946), which is well known for its 'uranium MacGuffin.' It is also a film about which Hitchcock spoke at some length in terms of how he and his screenwriter, Ben Hecht, came to settle on uranium as the film's MacGuffin, a discussion that reveals a good deal about Hitchcock's working practices. The perfect MacGuffin may indeed be nothing, but it is a substantial kind of nothing.

Chapter 2: The Myth of Ideal Form and Hitchcock's Quest for **Pure Cinema**

In this chapter I take a close look at Hitchcock's notion of pure cinema. I also examine in detail how Hitchcock scholars down the years have used the concept as a productive tool for analysing the director's work despite the obvious absence of a universally agreed upon definition. What is pure cinema? Hitchcock offered several different definitions over the decades, though he appears to have had a certain set of criteria in mind. On the other hand, Hitchcock scholars have ranged more widely in their use of the concept, applying it to mean visuality, montage, and even poetry. No matter how we divide Hitchcock's various expressions of pure cinema, however, it is plain that the concept can be expressed in artistic, technical, and even psychological terms. Such elasticity can make pure cinema problematic for the film scholar, yet its flexibility also underscores the value of cinematic purity in relation to the way we understand and analyse Hitchcock's work. To ask what Hitchcock meant by pure cinema is to ask a question which, as we will see, can be answered from a surprising range of viewpoints.

Chapter 3: Ambiguity and Complexity in **The Birds**

The Birds (1961) can be a difficult film to interpret, a fact that forms the essential principles upon which this chapter is based. However, rather than try to answer the challenge of interpreting *The Birds*, I am more interested in discussing *The Birds* in the context of what I call the problem of meaning. That my discussion of the film has very little to do with explaining what the film means frees my analysis from the usual problems commentators have in trying to prove the value of a particular interpretation. I have considerable respect for such approaches. However, framing my approach to the film by a consideration of interpretive practice rather than cinematic content allows me to show the inherent value of the film's undecidability as this impacts viewer experience. I do not rely on traditional structuralism in this chapter, but I do focus on how meaning can be constituted from specific modes of interpretive activity. I rely in particular on the work of philosopher Wilhelm Dilthey to sort out several of the philosophical issues raised by *The Birds.*

Chapter 4: Telling the Truth and **The Wrong/ed Man**

Throughout his life, Alfred Hitchcock told interviewers about the time he was locked in a jail cell at his father's request because of some childish act of disobedience. The story is typical Hitchcock in that it shows the police in an unflattering light even as it depicts a stock Hitchcockian character: the innocent man wrongly accused by unfeeling and bureaucratic social institutions. Unsurprisingly, perhaps, the story makes an appearance in virtually all Hitchcock biographies since it appears to capture aspects of his subsequent films so neatly. However, many of these same biographers doubt that the incident ever occurred, and in exploring this apparent contradiction, I try to blend the biographical with the cinematic, showing how aspects of the incarceration narrative fit into a reading of Hitchcock's film, *The Wrong Man* (1956). Though the comparison is far from exact, Hitchcock's childhood story and his 1956 film can be drawn together in terms of their mutual concern with questions of what is true and false. More important, these issues are explored in the context of judicial reasoning. Alfred Hitchcock's and Manny Balestrero's situations are representative of a cultural predicament in which an innocent person is interpellated by the law and provided with a criminal identity that is ultimately a product of social construction.

Chapter 5: Alfred Hitchcock's **Blackmail** *and the Problem of Moral Agency*

This chapter takes up one of the most common issues raised in Hitchcock scholarship: his persistent interest in ethical problems. My goal in this chapter, however, is to raise several questions regarding some of the conventional readings of Hitchcock's ethical preoccupations by focusing on the subject of moral agency in his 1929 film, *Blackmail*. In looking at *Blackmail* I believe that we can expand our understanding of the relevance of Hitchcock's work not only in traditional film studies, but also as it has been taken up by feminism, communication theory, and moral philosophy. Whereas the theory of retributive justice often figures prominently in Hitchcock scholarship, I want to avoid the usual tendency to divide Hitchcock's moral universe into the usual categories of good and evil, or guilty and innocent. These are, of course, significant motifs in Hitchcock's films. However, in this chapter I want to focus on an often-unnoticed element of moral theory Hitchcock explored rather often, the idea that his films frequently represent moral agency in the context of concepts like indeterminacy, undecidability, and anti-foundationalism. In other words, Hitchcock frequently showed moral agency to be complex, ambiguous, and indeterminate. These themes are depicted with stunning clarity in *Blackmail*, whose ending is a powerful rebuke of the belief that justice is achieved simply by being faithful to a socio-ethical code. Hitchcock's moral theorizing moves us well beyond the hegemony of ethical certitude.

Chapter 6: Hitchcock's Debt to Silence: Time and Space in The Lodger

This chapter differs from the others in this book in being a scene-by-scene analysis of Hitchcock's 1926 film, *The Lodger.* The analysis focuses mainly on the film's mise en scène with the goal of demonstrating how one can work from the structural configurations of the players, the sets, the lighting, the camera work, and so on, to come a deeper understanding of the thematic elements at work in the production. In other words, while the approach in this chapter stands apart from the others, the focus is still with developing an analysis of broader sociological and philosophical issues. For instance, in the use of the motif of triangular forms, Hitchcock suggests important comments about the interpersonal connections between the three principal players even as he establishes resonance between these characters and the never seen villain of the film, the notorious serial killer, the Avenger. A detailed scenic analysis like this is certainly far easier to accomplish with earlier, silent, black-and-white films. For one thing, films of the 1920s had shorter running times, and the number of sets was far fewer. Nonetheless, there is a richness to *The Lodger* that belies the assumption that it is a simple story, easily told with theatrical facial expressions and complemented with copious intertitle cards. In fact, while the film demonstrates how thoroughly Hitchcock had mastered the mechanics of camera movement, lighting, and character choreography, it also proves how well he had come to realize the figurative potential of the mise en scène as necessary in establishing psychological motivation, personality, and even emotional longing.

Chapter 7: Hitchcock's Deferred Dénouement and the Problem of Rhetorical Form

This chapter provides a critical rhetorical approach to the question of Hitchcock's willingness to contradict cinematic conventions. I am particularly interested in the way our expectations of film narratives derive from our familiarity with cinematic conventions and genres, and on a narrative strategy that Alfred Hitchcock used in several of his films. Hitchcock would occasionally disrupt or destabilize his film's narrative form by deviating from the customary 'happy ending,' a process that I refer to as the *deferred dénouement.* In a general sense, as the rhetorical scholar, Kenneth Burke argues, forms demand completion, and completion is ordinarily taken as a kind of affective and epistemological satisfaction. The question I pursue in this chapter, then, is what happens when the satisfaction promised in the anticipatory nature of the form is denied. In the course of this analysis, I provide an analysis of

Lloyd Bitzer's famous notion of the rhetorical situation, showing how this concept applies in the case of cinema, and more particularly in the case of Hitchcock's work.

Chapter 8: Moralizing Uncertainty: Suspicion and Faith in Hitchcock's **Suspicion**

In this chapter I argue that suspicion can be understood as an interpretive framework, that by adopting a suspicious attitude we ultimately try to bring order to circumstances that otherwise would remain confounded by uncertainty. Of course, the relation between the practices of textual demystification and cultural interpretation has been argued by a range of commentators who focus on the role of suspicion as an underlying analytical principle. Thus, suspicion can be viewed as integral to the modernist project of a rational, deconstructive understanding. However, even in everyday life, people can be driven by suspicion, as they try to discover the hidden truths behind their relationships, for example. Hence, suspicion has two sides to it: on the one hand, it is a form of uncertainty motivated by unclear, equivocal, or doubtful perception; on the other, it is a form of certainty that draws its subject onward by the seductive allure of what is already suspected. In short, suspicion is a curious state in which the subject balances uncertainty and faith, and this is the argument I present by way of a close reading of Alfred Hitchcock's 1941 film, *Suspicion*. My central point is that suspicion is represented in this film as an interpretive strategy that can help us make sense of situations that appear ambiguous or uncertain. For this reason, I argue that suspicion and faith are actually related interpretive experiences, a point that is made powerfully in Hitchcock's film although it is generally overlooked. Faith and suspicion may be equally paradoxical conditions, but they are essential strategies by which the world is interpreted, and uncertainty is domesticated.

In taking the eclectic approach I pursue in this book I hope to provide readers with both insight and pleasure in the experience of Hitchcock's films. Although much of what is to be found in these pages is related to a course on Hitchcock that I have taught over the past decade, the form of these chapters differs considerably from the way that I present the material in the classroom where I expect my students to contribute to our seminar discussions and offer their own views and observations. Indeed, if there is one thing that I wish I could replicate in the written text it is the enthusiasm my students have shown for Alfred Hitchcock's work, and the passion with which they attack and defend him. I suspect that for teachers, nothing is more exciting than having your own enthusiasm confirmed by a new generation of scholars.

Chapter 1

THE INCIDENTAL *MACGUFFIN*: EQUIVALENCE AND SUBSTITUTION

> What seems beautiful to me, what I should most like to do, would be a book about nothing, a book without any exterior tie, but sustained by the internal force of its style [...] a book which would have almost no subject, or at least in which the subject would be almost invisible, if that is possible. The most beautiful works are those with the least matter.
>
> – Gustave Flaubert[1]

> The MacGuffin: The talismanic object that provides the pretext for every thriller, leading to battles between the heroes and villains who struggle to find and possess it.
>
> – Thomas Leitch[2]

> The spies must be after *something.*
>
> – Alfred Hitchcock[3]

Introduction

I begin with one of Alfred Hitchcock's most incidental concepts: the thing, notion, or motive that he referred to as the film's *MacGuffin.* To spend any

1 Cited in Burke, Kenneth. *Counter-Statement* (orig. 1931). Berkeley and London: University of California Press, 1968, p. 6.

2 Leitch, Thomas. *The Encyclopedia of Alfred Hitchcock.* New York: Checkmark Books, 2002, p. 191. As this definition suggests, the MacGuffin may have been more common in spy films and thrillers than in other Hitchcock films, a point to which I return later (the point is that spy films are based on the idiocy of foreign affairs, and thus the MacGuffin can itself be supremely idiotic as a way of criticizing international espionage, state secrets, military ventures, and so on).

3 Cited in Adair, Gene. *Alfred Hitchcock: Filming Our Fears.* Oxford and New York: Oxford University Press, 2002, p. 51.

time at all on the subject of the MacGuffin may seem an odd decision given that Hitchcock said that when properly realized in the film's narrative the MacGuffin is an inconsequential cinematic element, a nonentity even. But as there are times when rejecting authoritative pronouncements can result in modest dividends, I want to demonstrate that looking at the MacGuffin more closely than is the case in most Hitchcock scholarship will help to reveal the way that Hitchcock prioritized affect over material essences even as it enables a deeper appreciation of the architecture of many of his films. The MacGuffin also raises some interesting philosophical issues to which I turn near the end of the chapter. The perfect MacGuffin may indeed be nothing, as Hitchcock suggested, but it is a substantial kind of nothing.

When the matter of the MacGuffin arose in interviews, or when he discussed the MacGuffin in pieces he wrote for publication, Hitchcock's usual strategy was to offer comments tinged with bemused indifference. However, a careful look at this material shows that Hitchcock was equally inclined to speak about the MacGuffin with a certain fondness, and, despite asserting its relative unimportance on many occasions, he also conceded his concern with prioritizing his search for the appropriate MacGuffin, the one that would be helpful in setting his story on its way. Hence the first challenge is accepting that Hitchcock's own descriptions of the MacGuffin render it both incidental and important. To speak about the MacGuffin, therefore, we would be wise to remain mindful of Hitchcock's own equivocal assessment. In fact, recognizing Hitchcock's relative ambivalence leads me to suggest that my first approach to the MacGuffin is to see it as *consequentially inconsequential.* As we will see, the MacGuffin emerges as something of a contradiction.

The challenge presented by this contradictory understanding may be less daunting than it first appears, for while Hitchcock's characterizations suggest that the MacGuffin is generally understood to have an object-like status, I believe that we fall into error if we confine ourselves to thinking that the MacGuffin's value can be discerned in its material essence. That is, we will fail to grasp the nature of the MacGuffin's significance if we regard it strictly as a thing or an object; reification must be avoided. Hence, I suggest at the outset that the importance of the MacGuffin is distinguished in the function it serves, and not in the actual thing in which that function is manifest. This part of my argument is certainly simple, and while it doesn't totally deny the significance of the materiality of the MacGuffin in every instance, neither does it dispute the fact that the MacGuffin retains crucial significance in the narrative. Indeed, my argument will lead in precisely the opposite direction in reclaiming some measure of significance for the MacGuffin in terms of what it says about the relation between objects and people. Thus, I propose that the MacGuffin has a transcendental quality that owes to its being eminently substitutable, and that this helps explain why, in the context of Hitchcock's work, the MacGuffin's value is determined principally by its purpose and has little meaningful relation to its essence. I believe that the MacGuffin's insignificance is more alleged than absolute.

The MacGuffin and Arbitrary Value

That Hitchcock proclaimed indifference as to what particular thing constituted a film's MacGuffin may help to explain why the MacGuffin usually turns out to be something that is forgettable, inconsequential, and – some might argue – sometimes ridiculous. What are the *39 steps*? Could a ring really constitute decisive proof of murder, or could finding a lost cigarette lighter prove that someone is *not* a murderer? Can we be sure the avenger was ever caught? Were Marnie's emotional and sexual troubles finally resolved? How could a melody contain the clause of an international peace treaty and still be a melody? The characters in Hitchcock's films – spies or otherwise – invariably must be seeking *something* simply because the narrative requires a necessary thing to initiate the action, provide motivation, and suture the disparate events into a cohesive narrative. So, although Hitchcock said that the MacGuffin is inconsequential at the level of spectatorship, he acknowledged that it plays an important role in the film narrative: setting the travellers on their journey, providing a purpose for their quest, and suggesting a reason for their efforts to resolve the film's underlying problematic. In its own way, then, the MacGuffin is humble, but as with many humble things, it is not without value.

Indeed, value is such a central feature of the MacGuffin that I should acknowledge an important point implicit in what I have said thus far, namely, that the reason the MacGuffin has value is because it is valued. In addition to thinking of the MacGuffin in non-essentialist terms, so too we must be cautious in addressing the question of value as it applies to the MacGuffin as a part of the narrative. Perhaps in some cases an argument can be made in favour of the essential value of the MacGuffin (it may be made of gold or platinum, for instance), but stopping here would miss the point concerning the arbitrary construction of value that underpins the MacGuffin's narrative significance, for the narrative value of the MacGuffin – which is ultimately its principal value – is unvaryingly formed from non-essential considerations. The MacGuffin speaks to the fact that human relations are often driven by things, which, to the outside observer, may seem incidental, and hardly worth the time to fight over. But noting how the MacGuffin can rise to the level of a formal obsession is important in the context of the characters' attributions of value. The MacGuffin is nothing of fundamental (denotative) value but something of symbolic (connotative) value in the immaterial currency of human relations. Thus, the MacGuffin highlights the process by which value is ascribed rather than inferred.

As the MacGuffin is insignificant for the audience because it is conspicuously lacking in everyday material value, can we say that this is what Hitchcock meant when he referred to it as inconsequential? The simple answer is yes, but our assent must be provisional, for some further detail is clearly required. The MacGuffin is unimportant because it lacks in the way of exchange value; more crucially, the MacGuffin is inconsequential because it is an arbitrary thing. This is an important matter, for in this context, arbitrariness is made evident in the fact of the MacGuffin's fundamental substitutability. To draw a provisional conclusion then, we can say that the MacGuffin is a thing of consequential inconsequentiality, and that this paradoxical condition arises from the fact of its necessary substitutability. Furthermore, we must recognize the MacGuffin as something that is important in respect of what it does and not in terms of what it is. In speaking of the MacGuffin, we are speaking of relations rather than of things.

The MacGuffin: Ontologically Nothing

These opening remarks possibly have left some readers asking an obvious question: What is a MacGuffin? And almost immediately this is where we run into some difficulties. As Sidney Gottlieb observed, Hitchcock offered "endless definitions of the MacGuffin" throughout his career, a fact designed to generate troubles. Nonetheless, I believe we can reasonably distil Hitchcock's various comments to something approaching a basic definition.[4]

Hitchcock conceptualized the MacGuffin as an object or an idea, which, necessary to the storyline in a functional sense, is usually incidental to the narrative's genuine purpose. Thus, the MacGuffin has two sides: it is unimportant to the viewer in respect of its essential nature, but enormously important to the characters in the story insofar as it is the reason for undertaking the actions that constitute the narrative. These points warrant elaboration.

First, the MacGuffin is unimportant to viewers because it is a transitory thing that could just as easily have been something else. It is also rarely comprehensively explained. It is frequently presented a-historically and can be something of a cliché, a hackneyed convention or trope that merely "works" insofar as it is sufficient to the purpose of sending the story on its

---

4 Gottlieb, Sidney, ed. *Hitchcock on Hitchcock: Selected Writings and Interviews*. Berkley and London: University of California Press, 1995, p. xix.

way. Therefore, as long as this object serves the purpose of motivating the characters, its actual composition is incidental. As Hitchcock told Truffaut, "boiled down to its purest expression" an effective MacGuffin will turn out to be "nothing at all."[5]

Second, the MacGuffin is important in the context of the film's logic where its primary function is to provide motivation for the characters and serve as a rationale for the onscreen action. Thought of in this way, one could say that the MacGuffin is a prop, the mystery that Hitchcock's characters seek to unravel, the truth they labour to reveal, the treasure chest marked by an X on an ancient map. But because the MacGuffin has this dual articulation – incidental at one level of interpretation and crucial at another – it can be difficult to ascertain how the MacGuffin should be regarded cinematically, for it would appear to be serving both diegetic and extra-diegetic functions simultaneously. Perhaps the most productive solution is the idea that the MacGuffin is a kind of bridge, uniting the two perceptual points of view by which it is constituted: that of the audience and that of the film's characters. These perspectives coalesce in the way that the MacGuffin is constructed as an object of arbitrary importance. Moreover, this dual structure is valuable in the way the MacGuffin anchors the primary themes of the film in an accessible form of cinematic practicality, a fact that is made clear in the way the MacGuffin's dual structure expresses a surface interpretation set off from, but never entirely separated from, the principal subject of the film. Let me explain this point.

Taking Hitchcock at his word, we can say the MacGuffin constitutes the *nominal* but not the *principal* reason for the story, for although it is largely incidental in respect of the deeper motives at work in the film, it must reasonably account for the story unfolding as it does. For instance, we can seek the reason behind the murderous behaviour of our avian neighbours in *The Birds* (1960), but this search risks taking us into a frenzy of endless speculation and textual posturing. *That* the birds attack puts everything in play; *why* they attack never interested Hitchcock.[6] One might also say that the MacGuffin is the *proximate* but not the *ultimate* cause of the main themes around which the film is constructed. Thus, while it is rational to seek an object of interest, this object can become the rationale that holds the narrative together. We might say, then, that the MacGuffin must have sufficient substance to be meaningful even as if the film's end it often turns out to have been largely incidental.

5 Truffaut, François. *Hitchcock* (Revised edition). New York: Simon & Schuster, 1983, p. 139.

6 I develop several of these points further in Chapter 3.

An example from one of Hitchcock's better-known films helps make some of these observations clearer, the 1959 spy thriller, *North by Northwest.* A government agent by the name of George Kaplan is being sought by a group of enemy spies operating in the United States. These agents believe that Kaplan is close to exposing them to American intelligence agencies and thwarting their plans to smuggle an object of national interest out of the United States. However, in their efforts to find and eliminate Kaplan they have misidentified an advertising executive by the name of Roger Thornhill as their presumed enemy, George Kaplan. How Thornhill comes to be confused with Kaplan is comedic in a typically Hitchcockian fashion, and the way the mistake occurs serves larger thematic concerns developed in the film. However, these details won't delay us here. Suffice it to say that the enemy spies' dreadful mistake of misidentification leads to Thornhill being thrown into a world of trouble.

Convinced that Thornhill is Kaplan, the spies kidnap him and spirit him away to a secluded mansion for interrogation. They are anxious to know what information he has gathered about their plans to smuggle the still unidentified object of national importance out of the country. Because Thornhill is not Kaplan he understandably refuses to talk – indeed, he cannot talk, for his ignorance regarding their identities or their scheme means he legitimately has nothing to tell them. Disappointed and frustrated by their failure to gain any useful information from Thornhill (and still operating under the mistaken belief that he is Kaplan) they devise a ludicrous scheme to eliminate him by forcing liquor down his throat, bundling him behind the wheel of a car, and directing the vehicle down a treacherous mountain highway. That the scheme fails owing to the conversion of Thornhill's alcoholism into a saving talent as he successfully navigates the perilous road despite his inebriation foreshadows Thornhill's ability to wend his way through a maze of confusing events looming on his future horizon. It also slyly winks at the viewer in terms of the role that fate has played in landing Kaplan into enemy hands.

Having survived the murder attempt and regained his liberty, Thornhill begins his own search for Kaplan in order to confront him and clear up the predicament into which fate has landed him. Of course, as most readers know, George Kaplan does not exist, his identity merely the creation of a clandestine American espionage agency. The enemy spies and Thornhill are seeking an object (Kaplan) that does not exist.

Now, some film analysts regard the fictional Kaplan as a MacGuffin in that the search for Kaplan sets much of the action of *North by Northwest* on its way. This interpretation makes sense, of course, and I would not dispute the view that Kaplan is *a* MacGuffin. But I believe that *North by Northwest* is built around a more obvious MacGuffin than the imaginary George Kaplan: the previously mentioned item of national security that the spies intend to smuggle out of the country. This object is a higher order MacGuffin, one might argue, since it is also the thing that even the non-existent Kaplan is supposed to be chasing. We can, in other words, argue that among the potential MacGuffins in *North by Northwest*, the object to be smuggled out of the United States is the central thing of concern. It is literally the *something*, as Hitchcock would have it, that the spies are after, the very reason they have come to the United States. This object explains why the spies have kidnapped Thornhill in their effort to abduct Kaplan. Moreover, the quest for this unidentified object sets two groups of political foes against one another to the point of encouraging murderous plots on both sides. And, once it has at last been discovered, it is this object that sutures the film's events into an understandable whole. In other words, it is plainly the thing that motivates the film's principal action. Even the quest to discover the fictional Kaplan's identity is driven by the value both parties have placed in this object. The Americans are trying to recover the object even as the enemy spies are intent on spiriting it abroad. Everything that happens in the film including the eventual apprehension of the enemy spies happens because of this object. So, what is it?

Throughout the film, the audience has no idea what this object might be, and when it is finally revealed to be a strip of microfilm, this disclosure is unlikely to be met with surprise, pleasure, or even satisfaction. Indeed, had it turned out to be something else, would we really care? For one thing, we learn nothing of the national secrets involved in this espionage caper since nothing about the information contained on the microfilm is ever revealed. Further, the reason the spies are trying to smuggle this information out of the country is never explained. There may be some significance to the fact that the microfilm is to be removed from the country hidden inside a pre-Columbian statue purchased (rather unaccountably) at a public auction, but too little information is provided by Hitchcock to do more than speculate whether this fact has particular significance within the drama.[7] In other words, we have here a MacGuffin in the classic sense: it is unimportant to us as viewers what the spies are trying to acquire and why the American government is so intent on blocking their plans; and we have no idea what the enemy agents intend to do with this thing, nor what sort of national emergency would ensue should it fall into the wrong hands. But this object's acquisition is as important to the enemy agents as it is to their American counterparts. So, despite the narrative significance of this object, it is an utterly indifferent and arbitrary thing for

7 Of course, one might argue that the unimportant MacGuffin (the microfilm) is contained inside something recognizably important (the artwork). Hence, it functions as an inconsequential thing contained within the more consequential wrapping – the film.

the viewer, easily substitutable by stolen jewellery, pilfered artwork, or a one-of-a-kind manuscript. Nonetheless, it is the bridge that connects the American and foreign spies, the mechanism that brings the audience to understand the manic preoccupations of the characters in the film. We can accept that the MacGuffin has tremendous value for the film's characters because we are drawn into the story by the considerable emotional energy both sides invest in trying to acquire this object. By contrast, we are not especially drawn into the maelstrom of *North by Northwest* by the MacGuffin-as-thing. And this emotional investment is key: the MacGuffin is compelling to us insofar as it signifies human longing. But what the thing consists of is *essentially* unimportant.

As film viewers, then, what is important to us? It becomes evident early in the story that what *is* important to the viewer is that Roger Thornhill and one of the American spies working as a double agent, Eve Kendall (Eva Marie Saint), will fall in love, and that their relationship will survive interference from spies both nefarious and friendly. The production of the romantic heterosexual couple is what marks *North by Northwest* as a classic Hitchcock thriller. It makes little difference whether the enemy agents are trying to remove microfilm, advanced weapon designs, or a secret cocktail recipe out of the country. The plausibility of the MacGuffin's motivational impetus does not reside in its materiality, but in the reasons for the actions people undertake in its pursuit. Hence the significance of the MacGuffin is a feature of how it is valued by those who have an interest in it as a means of resolving a problem. What is engaging and real to us are the emotions displayed by the film's characters, and not the thing in which they have become passionately and even obsessively interested. The key feature of the MacGuffin is not the thing that it is, but the purpose that it serves; it is ontologically poor, but semantically rich.

Consequentially Inconsequential

The importance of the MacGuffin does not consist in that of which it consists, then, for it is much closer to a totem than to a commodity charged with a symbolic value justified by the context of the story. This explains why Hitchcock was steadfast in maintaining that the MacGuffin "not be or mean anything at all, except of course to the characters who are chasing it."[8] Because the characters in the film care about this thing – and whether they are motivated by politics, greed, criminal ambition, or self-protection is largely unimportant – the MacGuffin overcomes the cynical critique determined by

8 Leitch, pp. 191–192.

essentialist thinking. The MacGuffin shows people doing what people have always done: attaching cultural value to an object that exceeds its material worth. The MacGuffin may be insignificant, but as Derrida might say, it is excessively insignificant.

We should also note that the MacGuffin's inconsequential nature is sometimes revealed when the social relations that hold it in a collective embrace of valuation are dissolved. In other words, once the MacGuffin is uncovered – once the object the spies are pursuing is revealed – the inconsequential nature of the object becomes evident. This means that the MacGuffin can reveal its inconsequential core in consequence of becoming a known thing, for to unravel the mystery of its identity is to destroy the aura of its value. Of course, this occurs chiefly in the mind of the spectator who is liberated from the mystery of the MacGuffin's nature following its revelation. And once this occurs, the viewer can focus on the real issues that constitute the heart of the film's purpose. For this reason, the narrative disclosure of the MacGuffin often forms the first part of a two-part dénouement: first, the revelation of the MacGuffin's identity – what the spies have been after, for instance – and second, the resolution of the human drama contingent upon the successful search for the MacGuffin. This is, of course, a sleight of hand on Hitchcock's part, for the point of the film is never really the search for the MacGuffin in the first place. The MacGuffin becomes history so that the story's ending can indicate the possibility of a new future.

An illustration of this double dénouement can be found in the classic 1933 film, *The 39 Steps*. As the film nears its conclusion, the heroes and villains converge on a theatre during a stage act featuring Mr Memory, a performer who uses his enormous powers of recall to amaze and entertain audiences. The film's hero, Richard, is familiar with Mr Memory's act and aware that Mr Memory is somehow involved in the enemy agents' plans. So, in an inspired moment he calls from the audience during a performance to ask Mr Memory to reveal the meaning behind the phrase, "the 39 steps." The enemy agents who have followed Richard to the theatre have previously forced Mr Memory to memorize the design details of a new aircraft engine, their plan being to smuggle this information out of the country by forcing Mr Memory to accompany them to their homeland. In an age without memory chips, Mr Memory himself will have to suffice as a recording device. And owing to their having brainwashed him to respond with automaton-like compulsion, Mr Memory is unable to resist the question Richard shouts at him. Hence, he commences to answer Richard's query, explaining that "The 39 Steps is an organization of spies [...] collecting information on behalf of the foreign office of [...]" But here Mr Memory's answer is cut short by a bullet fired by one of the enemy agents. The shooter is immediately apprehended, and as the authorities gather about Mr Memory, carefully lifting him into a chair as his life ebbs away, he continues his revelation regarding the meaning behind the film's eponymous MacGuffin. But his explanation is truncated and halting, little more than gibberish to which viewers likely pay little if any attention. And the reason for this relative lack of interest in Mr Memory's revelation is twofold. First, it is difficult to care to any great extent what constitutes the meaning of the 39 steps given that the film has virtually ended, the antagonists having been either shot or arrested. In addition, Mr Memory simply drones on about mechanical designs and mathematical formulae that are utterly meaningless. Second, and more important, the narrative offers the second dénouement as it segues from the disclosure of the meaning of the film's MacGuffin to a different and more consequential revelation: the fact that the hero and heroine have discovered (and are prepared to acknowledge) their mutual affection despite a litany of obstacles having been raised against the prospect of their falling in love. This emblem of romantic coupling happens in a signature Hitchcock moment.

As the camera moves to frame Mr Memory slouched in his chair, Richard and Pamela, with their backs to the camera, move into the foreground completely blocking our view of Mr Memory as he gasps his final breaths. And as their bodies converge directly in front of Hitchcock's camera, Mr Memory is hidden from sight, pushed into the background. In other words, Mr Memory, who symbolizes the film's MacGuffin – and who is the bridge between the audience and knowledge of the MacGuffin – is subordinated to the central purpose of the film in the realization that Richard and Pamela are at last romantically linked. And all of this is effectively realized for the audience as their formerly manacled hands clasp together willingly to signify the consummation of their romance – heterosexual union once again comprising the principal point of the film. Hence Mr Memory's account of the 39 steps is also an account of its insignificance for the audience, a fact that is visually symbolized in the way that Hitchcock arranges his players in the scene. In being made known, the MacGuffin of *The 39 Steps* is also shown to be inconsequential. Even as the MacGuffin is removed from the shadows and brought into the light, viewers are unlikely to bother inspecting it with any degree of interest. The details of a new aircraft engine design are simply too technical, too boring, and too unimportant for viewers to really care about. Indeed, the philosopher Irving Singer puts this rather well, saying that "Hitchcock's entire effort as a filmmaker consists in arousing our curiosity about something that hardly matters to us."[9] This is certainly true, particularly if we keep in mind that the MacGuffin is the vehicle and not the destination.

9 Singer, Irving. *Three Philosophical Filmmakers: Hitchcock, Welles, Renoir.* Cambridge, MA: MIT Press, 2004, p. 77.

Substitutability and the MacGuffin

Earlier I said that the MacGuffin has a transcendental quality owing to its being eminently substitutable; here I want to consider the issue of substitutability in greater detail. I specifically want to consider how Ernesto Laclau's notion of equivalential substitution might apply in the case of the MacGuffin.[10] Because Hitchcock says that the MacGuffin could be one thing, or it could be another, the question of *what* constitutes the MacGuffin is immaterial and even to some extent, indeterminate. But is there more to this ideal of essential or unconditional substitutability, the idea that in choosing a particular MacGuffin Hitchcock does little more than engage in random selection? Does Laclau's logic of equivalential substitution suggest that something more consequential than ethically inconsequential substitution is in play? In other words, to say "this or that" suggests indifference, but how is this indifference structured in the case of equivalential substitution?

One way we can examine the relation between substitutability, equivalential substitution, and the MacGuffin is to consult Hitchcock's reflections on how he came to choose a particular MacGuffin for a particular film. For this purpose, let us consider comments Hitchcock offered in his interviews with François Truffaut concerning his 1946 war thriller, *Notorious*. Film scholar and Hitchcock biographer Donald Spoto has said that *Notorious* contains Hitchcock's most famous MacGuffin: wine bottles filled with uranium ore.[11] Spoto is particularly enthusiastic in his assessment of *Notorious*, calling it "Hitchcock's most complex and compelling romance up to his great masterpiece *Vertigo*," and praising the film's use of an inverted parallel structure to balance the opening and closing sequences. These are both valuable observations deserving detailed attention, but for the present moment I am going to focus only on Hitchcock's decision to use uranium ore as the film's MacGuffin, and how that choice is framed by Laclau's theory of the equivalential logic of association. Indeed, in his conversations with Truffaut about *Notorious*, Hitchcock straightforwardly revealed the degree to which his pre-production practices were defined by an acceptance of this logic of equivalence. *Notorious* thus provides us with one of Hitchcock's most sustained commentaries concerning the MacGuffin, alongside a detailed account of the principle of substitutability.

---

10 Laclau, Ernesto. *The Rhetorical Foundations of Society*. London and New York: Verso Press, 2014.

11 Spoto, Donald. *The Art of Alfred Hitchcock: Fifty Years of his Motion Pictures*. New York: Doubleday Books, 196, p. 152.

The Ore MacGuffin

The fact that uranium ore is the MacGuffin in *Notorious* would seem to counter my earlier claim that in its physical manifestation, the MacGuffin is largely inconsequential, and that the significance of the MacGuffin is a product of its being valued by the film's characters independent of its material nature. It might be argued that uranium ore is hardly an inconsequential thing at a time when atomic weapons had shown their awesome, catastrophic powers. However, uranium's use value is never properly developed in *Notorious* (1946). Indeed, Hitchcock and his screenwriter, Ben Hecht, had no interest in exploiting or explaining to their audience uranium's actual military potential. Moreover, neither Hitchcock nor Hecht knew until the final draft of the script that the film's MacGuffin would involve an effort by expatriate Nazis living in Brazil to collect uranium in preparation for building an atomic bomb.[12] Hence uranium ore is a perfectly insignificant MacGuffin in that it is used in the film as a largely meaningless object. As with Mr Memory's revelation of the MacGuffin in *The 39 Steps*, the disclosure of the MacGuffin in *Notorious* ultimately serves to undermine its motivational force. For even though uranium is unquestionably an important thing, it is important in *Notorious* only in relation to the part it plays in the film's emplotment, and its functional value denies any gesture to its real-world military implications. Whereas uranium ore is clearly important in certain contexts, the world of *Notorious*, ironically, is not one of those contexts.

The inconsequential nature of uranium ore, and its ultimate substitutability as a MacGuffin for the film, was made clear by Hitchcock himself during his discussion with Truffaut. Hitchcock related that he and Hecht started by "looking for a MacGuffin, and as always, we proceeded by trial and error, going off in several different directions that turned out to be too complex."[13] In fact, Hitchcock says that he and Hecht initially imagined they would base their story on the discovery of a clandestine army of German refugees being trained at a secret military facility hidden away in a South American jungle, but they rejected this plan because it was too complicated. Hitchcock also

---

12 Following their decision to use the atomic bomb as the raison d'être for the Nazi gang, Hitchcock and Hecht visited physicist Robert Millikan at the California Institute of Technology to make inquiries about the feasibility of their narrative device. Although Millikan found the idea ridiculous, he purportedly placed a phone call to the FBI who put the two men under surveillance for several months (Thomas Leitch says Hitchcock and Hecht were under government surveillance for six months, but Hitchcock told François Truffaut he and Hecht were followed by agents for three months).

13 Truffaut, p. 167.

worried that though it would be exciting to base his story on the assembly of a secret Nazi military force it was hard to imagine "what they were going to do with the army once it was organized."[14] Their decision to find a simpler MacGuffin was therefore explained by their wish to find an object that would be affectively compelling but materially inconsequential, a MacGuffin, Hitchcock explained, that was "simpler, but concrete and visual."[15]

The film's producer, David O. Selznick, met Hitchcock's idea of the "uranium MacGuffin" with confusion: "What in the name of goodness is that?" Selznick allegedly asked when told that the MacGuffin would be uranium ore.[16] As Hitchcock explained:

> The producer was skeptical, and he felt it was absurd to use the idea of an atom bomb as the basis for our story. I told him that it was not the basis for the story, but only the MacGuffin, and I explained that there was no need to attach too much importance to it. Finally, I said, "Look, if you don't like uranium, let's make it industrial diamonds, which the Germans need to cut their tools with." And I pointed out that if it had not been a wartime story, we could have hinged our plot on the theft of diamonds, that the gimmick was unimportant.[17]

Hitchcock refers to the MacGuffin as a "gimmick," revealing that it is a shallow and substitutable thing in its relation to the principal trajectory of the story.[18] However, Hitchcock was still concerned to get it right, to fit the MacGuffin to the times, and to choose something that would also be sufficiently negligible so as not to distract the audience nor tax the script. He also makes plain that the MacGuffin is not the basis of the story, but merely the thing upon which the story will be "hinged." The notion of hinging is synonymous with articulation, and in Hitchcock's account of the object for which he and Hecht were searching – a plausible and workable MacGuffin – he shows

14 Truffaut, p. 167.
15 Truffaut, p. 167.
16 Truffaut, p. 168.
17 Truffaut, p. 168.
18 The word *gimmick* is linked etymologically to *magic*, a connection that makes sense in the present case. Like the mechanism involved in a conjurer's trick, the MacGuffin/gimmick can be used for purposes of misdirection, for like a magician's sleight of hand the MacGuffin can distract from the narrative's larger purposes, especially in the initial stages of the film. For instance, in *North by Northwest*, audiences can be forgiven for assuming that discovering the whereabouts of George Kaplan will be the primary focus of the film. But, of course, Kaplan is a non-entity.

how they sought an object that would be doubly articulated, speaking both to the audience's need for an inconsequential device and the characters' need for something that could be cathected with genuine human emotions. In other words, the plot demands that the "something" that Hitchcock identifies as the motivational source be an object about which passionate engagement will be reasonably elaborated in the characters' actions. And yet, the importance of this thing, whatever it might ultimately consist of, must play a secondary role to the drama of human relations and personal intrigue. Hence, we see Hitchcock telling Selznick that it is vital that not "too much importance" be attached to the MacGuffin since this would take away from the more important issue, the unfolding of the human drama that is played out in *Notorious* in the complicated relationship between Alicia and Devlin. And finally, the MacGuffin is eminently substitutable. Though uranium-as-MacGuffin fits the time frame perfectly, there is no need to elect this particular object as the sole possibility for the narrative. Industrial diamonds, Hitchcock says, would have served just as well. Indeed, we can easily see that even industrial diamonds could be changed out for some other object. In the world of the Hitchcockian MacGuffin there is nothing unique about uranium.

Hitchcock's account of his search for a MacGuffin for *Notorious* amplifies the idea that the MacGuffin is a structural element serving a special function in the process of the narrative's development. But in serving this role, the MacGuffin does not convey the specific meaning ordinarily attached to that object owing to its status as a thing of indefinite arbitrariness. That it could be something other than what it is suggests that *it is other than what it is.* The uranium ore could have been industrial diamonds, Hitchcock says, and because diamonds and uranium would be functionally equivalent in this context, either would serve the same narrative purpose. They are in a sense, then, the same thing, for according to Ernesto Laclau, the equivalential logic of substitution renders the (literal) meanings of both things inconsequential. They mean the same insofar as they provide the same motivation, serve the same function, and direct the plot in the same way. They are like synonyms in that they are substitutable, although, as also with synonyms, the choice of one or the other results in slight differences in nuance (that *Notorious* is a war picture makes uranium more apropos, for instance, than, say, a sought-after blackmail note). However, the differences are minor because the specificity of their connotative implications is tied up entirely with the mythic world of the cinema narrative.

To put this another way, the substitutability of the MacGuffin cancels out the meaning of the object as a thing-in-itself and replaces that meaning with something entirely different: an object of interest that has mythic value. The object itself is unimportant (consequentially inconsequential), for its import is its capacity to motivate the interests of the story's characters. The matter of the object doesn't matter; what matters is that the object matters. The MacGuffin provides the opportunity for the self-discovery that lies at the heart of the narrative by framing the relationships among the characters.

Ernesto Laclau says that when you have terms that can "replace each other because they all, within the enumerative arrangement, express the same thing," these terms will be contained within a relation of equivalence. And this equivalential enumeration, he writes, "destroys the particularized meanings of its terms."[19] This claim certainly applies in the case of the MacGuffin. Because the MacGuffin is an eminently substitutable concept, an empty container that can be filled with anything so long as the resulting weight serves the necessary purpose, it follows that the MacGuffin is part of an "enumerative arrangement" in which each possible term is shorn of its particularized meaning. The MacGuffin is not this particular thing; instead, it is the thing that is the MacGuffin, for the priority is found in the function and not the object. Hitchcock alleges that we are disinterested in the MacGuffin, that as viewers it doesn't matter to us what it is. However, as we have seen, the MacGuffin is deeply important in respect of its purpose. What is unimportant, then, is the particularity of this or that thing playing the part of the MacGuffin.

This doesn't mean that 'uranium ore' lacks signification, but that its dual articulation includes, alongside its literal meaning, an additional sense or interpretation arising from its being valued as an article with motivational power.[20] As Laclau says, "the contents of the myth are substitutable by each other [...] as they all symbolize an absent fullness, and their efficacy has to be measured by their equivalential mobilizing effects, not by the success of their differentiated literal contents."[21] Interpreting the MacGuffin properly, then, entails a figurative interpretation in which we see the MacGuffin as informing a larger moral understanding of human relations. When we understand the MacGuffin as a role rather than as a thing, we are seeing it as Hitchcock intended when he sought to reduce the perfect MacGuffin to nothingness. By focusing on its functional status rather than its material nature we evade the facile criticism of the literal-minded critic who reads the paucity of the thing

19 Laclau, p. 40.

20 Another way to consider this point is in relation to the semiotic work of Roland Barthes. In this respect, we might say that the MacGuffin can be positioned as a second-order semiological system, a metalanguage that builds upon and exceeds the meaning of the first-order system. See Barthes, Roland. *Mythologies* [1957], translated by Richard Howard and Annette Lavers. New York: Hill and Wang, 2012.

21 Laclau, p. 33.

as fatal to the narrative. Such an argument has no meaningful force in the case of the MacGuffin. Because the particular meaning of an object in an equivalential arrangement is abolished in being constituted as an "absent fullness," the meaning of the MacGuffin operates at an entirely different plane. Along with Laclau, we can say that we measure Hitchcock's MacGuffins by their "equivalential mobilizing effects, not by the success of their differentiated literal contents."[22] What is consequential about the MacGuffin is precisely that it is inconsequential – insofar as its particular determination is irrelevant to its purpose.

Conclusion

> *The main thing I've learned over the years is that the MacGuffin is nothing. I'm convinced of this, but I find it very difficult to prove it to others.*
>
> – *Alfred Hitchcock*[23]

There is a wonderful moment in Hitchcock's *Shadow of a Doubt* (1943) that plays like a meta-commentary on the inconsequentiality of the MacGuffin and the principle of substitution. This is the scene where Uncle Charles follows his niece, Charlie Newton, into the kitchen where she has gone to get the dessert her mother prepared for a family dinner celebrating Charles' arrival at the Newton's home. A few moments earlier, the other members of the Newton family were happily treated to the various gifts Charles brought with him to show his appreciation for their hospitality. When it came to her gift, however, Charlie coyly demurred, refusing to accept her uncle's gift by explaining that his visit is more important to her than any present he might offer. Uncle Charles is insistent, however, and standing face to face in the kitchen he asks Charlie to extend her hand.

> *Charles:* Give me your hand, Charlie [He places a ring on her finger].
> *Charlie:* Thank you [turning away].
> *Charles:* You didn't even look at it!
> *Charlie:* I don't have to. No matter what you gave me, it'd be the same.

Charlie's comment is intended to deepen the spiritual bond she believes holds her and Charles together. But despite her tendency to see their relationship as defined in a mystical fashion – and despite her apparent blindness to

---

22 Laclau, p. 33.
23 Truffaut, p. xx.

the hints of illicit sexuality that haunt the scene – Charlie's words also illustrate neatly the importance of the substitutability of the MacGuffin. Charlie does not estimate the value of the ring as determined by the quality of the emerald to which her uncle subsequently draws her attention. Rather, she sees its importance as a gift, an object whose value is produced from the interests of the characters who cherish it – and who eventually chase it – because of what it symbolizes in terms of human relations. Later in the film, as Charlie comes to understand that the ring connects her uncle to a series of grisly murders, she becomes deeply concerned about its acquisition as do Charles and the police. But in the first moments of its introduction to the story the ring is merely a thing, arbitrarily chosen, and easily substituted for some other object Charles might have selected as a gift for his niece.[24] It doesn't matter whether it is a ring, a necklace, a pair of gloves, an ornament, or a book of poetry, the point is not the thing itself, but the way in which the characters will become attached to it, obsessive about its possession, concerned to realize the meaning of their relations through the meaning this object imposes upon those relations.

The MacGuffin is an object of indifference to the audience in respect of its particularity; however, it is important to note that it performs a necessary function in acting as a meeting point for the concerns, passions, and desires of the film's characters. Hence, we describe the MacGuffin more properly by designating it as a responsibility rather than a thing, and though it is represented onscreen as an object its significance is belied by its material appearance. We might say that in Hitchcock's world the MacGuffin shows that material things matter very little regarding their economic or cultural value, and that what really counts is the fact of human connection. Things are substitutable; people are not. The MacGuffin is a material embodiment of this principle despite its material being inconsequential.

---

24 I am not suggesting, of course, that the ring is without any specific meaning in relation to the hint of an incestuous relation between uncle and niece, only that this relation could have also been insinuated with other articles of jewellery or clothing. Certainly, the ring is a perfectly suitable MacGuffin for the film, but it is not indispensable in the context of the narrative.

Chapter 2

THE MYTH OF IDEAL FORM AND HITCHCOCK'S QUEST FOR *PURE CINEMA*

It is not permitted to the impure to attain the pure.

– Plato[1]

Teach me instead what purity is, how much value there is in it, whether it lies in the body or in the mind.

– Seneca[2]

Dialogue should simply be a sound among other sounds, just something that comes out of the mouths of people whose eyes tell the story in visual terms.

– Alfred Hitchcock[3]

Introduction

What did Alfred Hitchcock mean by the concept, *pure cinema*? The question is worth asking not only because Hitchcock frequently spoke about pure cinema, but also because his many references to the idea of cinematic purity were anything but consistent. Equivocation can be charming at times, of course, but it can also be confusing. That Hitchcock was equivocal as to how he framed his conception of pure cinema may be a bit of both, but however one regards his tendency for semantic slippage his lack of precision has not

1 Plato. *Phaedo*, 67 (a).

2 Seneca. *Letters from a Stoic*, translated by Robin Campbell. London: Penguin Books, 1969, p. 153.

3 Cited in Truffaut, François. *Hitchcock* (Revised edition). New York: Simon & Schuster, 1983, p. 222.

passed unnoticed among Hitchcock scholars. For instance, Thomas Leitch says that Hitchcock seems to have understood pure cinema in three different ways: as an *aesthetic* concern based on the principle of montage, as a *technical* matter rooted in a particular style of editing, and as an *empirical* issue best understood in relation to audience response. This list guides my analysis in this chapter, though I include a fourth item I refer to as the *primacy of the visual.* Of course, these categories are not completely isolated from one another as we will see shortly. Furthermore, my claim that Hitchcock was inconsistent is neither a slight nor an accusation. In fact, it may turn out that the different ways in which he developed his notions of cinematic purity are joined at deeper epistemological levels despite their surface differences.

The fact that Hitchcock offered different answers when questioned about his theory of pure cinema has prompted some critics to regard the concept with suspicion. For instance, the variation that is evident in Leitch's three formulations prompts him to conclude that Hitchcock's understanding of pure cinema was "dated, self-aggrandizing, and inconsistent."[4] Yet even as he acknowledges the slipperiness of pure cinema, Leitch concludes that the importance of the concept for "both Hitchcock and cinema in general can hardly be overstated."[5] For Leitch, then, Hitchcock's notion of pure cinema is beset by a range of problems, even as he admits that pure cinema is also one of Hitchcock's most important contributions to film theory. Hence, while we may not know for certain what actually constitutes pure cinema given Hitchcock's tendency for equivocation, we know nonetheless that it is an important aspect of Hitchcock's work. The leap required by this reasoning is obvious, but Leitch's position, as I hope to demonstrate, is not that uncommon. The equivocal nature of pure cinema is certainly cited as one of its flaws; it is also seen as one of its more persistent attributes. From the outset, therefore, we should take note that we are heading into paradoxical territory.

The value of an inquiry into the meaning of pure cinema gains further support from the fact that writers who rely on theories of pure cinema while analysing Hitchcock's films tend to range widely in the way the concept is understood. In other words, many writers believe that pure cinema is a guiding principle in Hitchcock's work, treating the notion almost reverentially as a vital if implicit presupposition regarding the essential nature of his films. But this attitude, though widespread, has been developed in the absence of any definitional consensus. Hitchcock's inconsistency may be something of a

4 Leitch, Thomas. *The Encyclopedia of Alfred Hitchcock.* New York: Checkmark Books, 2002, p. 263.

5 Leitch, p. 263.

blessing, then, in that it allows for such interpretive freedom. On the other hand, too much freedom can render the proposition that Hitchcock quested after pure cinema meaningless if none of us can say with precision what he was referring to.

This isn't to say that the idea of pure cinema is an academic free-for-all. Pure cinema *can* be defined if we are content with a definition produced at a relatively high level of theoretical abstraction and that cuts across some of the categories already noted. In that case we might follow Leitch and say that pure cinema is a series of interconnected historical, technical, and aesthetic notions where the ontological dimensions of visuality and montage are preeminent.[6] This account is satisfactory (if instrumental) insofar as it touches on the most common elements mentioned in the Hitchcock literature. However, if we are seeking a more comprehensive understanding of the concept and are also willing to entertain the variations and nuances found in the world of Hitchcock scholarship, we need to take a slightly broader view of the things Hitchcock and his various interpreters have actually written. This allows us to gain a clearer conception of both the practical and theoretical implications of pure cinema and further appreciate the value of the concept as it bears on matters of interpretation and critique.

The quest for pure cinema motivated Hitchcock's ambitions as a commercial filmmaker (he wanted to produce purely cinematic pictures) as well as his goal as an artist (he wanted his work to be pure in an aesthetic sense). Pure cinema, therefore, is both aesthetic and technical in nature, though the division between these concerns, as David Sterritt has observed, sometimes disappears in Hitchcock's ability to combine "high-art filmmaking [...] with enormous mass-audience popularity."[7] In fact, as Thomas Leitch hints, pure cinema may be precisely this ability to merge the artistic with the technical in order to achieve desired audience effects. Indeed, the way his films affected audiences was one of the principal measures Hitchcock applied in evaluating his work, and while it was terribly important to his commercial interests it certainly was not his sole concern, just as it was not the only way he thought

6 Richard Allen and Sam Ishii-Gonzalès write, "'Pure cinema' is a narrative told in purely visual terms: it is a distillation of the perceptual power particular to the experience of watching a movie [...] achieved through montage." This definition could also serve my purposes here, but it blends two notions of cinematic purity – visuality and montage – that I prefer to keep separate. See Allen, Richard and Ishii-Gonzalès, Sam, eds. "Introduction." In *Alfred Hitchcock: Centenary Essays*. London: BFI Publishing, 1999, p. vii.

7 Sterritt, David. *The Films of Alfred Hitchcock*. Cambridge: Cambridge University Press, 1993, p. 1.

about pure cinema. Cinematic purity could also be seen as an idealization of something that is practically unattainable, a goad to drive the artist onward despite the artist's awareness that there is no prospect of actual consummation. In this respect, pure cinema may have appealed to his Catholic sense of order; it may also have represented a commitment to an ideal condition connected metaphorically to the perfectibility of human nature. This would suggest that pure cinema is closer to Weber's ideal type in its abstraction than it is to a concern with technical proficiency.

At the same time, we should be cautious not to fashion pure cinema into something along the lines of a well-wrought film. It is not only that we need to put pure cinema into an appropriate context; we also need to acknowledge how the expression's apparent straightforwardness conceals an underlying ambiguity. *Pure cinema* is a somewhat pedestrian notion if we see it only as referring to visually driven and even minimalist filmmaking, a usage that risks draining the concept of significance.

That the phrase carries philosophical weight owes in some measure to the complex history surrounding the notion of purity. This history has its ancient foundations in traditions such as Platonic idealism, but contemporary formulations related to mediated representations are even more relevant.[8] For instance, Pierre Bourdieu debunks the ideal notions of a "pure gaze," "pure aesthetics," or "pure taste" as figments of a bourgeois imagination, saying that aesthetic purity is often a fiction promoted by class interests.[9] On the technical side, W. J. T. Mitchell (among others) observes that

> there are no "pure" media (for example, "pure" painting, sculpture, architecture, poetry, television), though the search for the essence of a medium [...] is a utopian gesture that seems inseparable from the artistic deployment of any medium.[10]

And John Belton makes a similar argument, going even further in his outright dismissal of the idea of pure cinema:

---

8 In the interests of space, I am not going to discuss the ancient antecedents nor the anthropological conceptions of purity in any detail. An engaging account of some of these matters with a focus on the relations among purity, social order, and authenticity can be found in Mullin, Amy. "Purity and Pollution Resisting the Rehabilitation of a Virtue." *Journal of the History of Ideas*, 57 (3), 1996, pp. 509–524.

9 Bourdieu, Pierre. *Distinctions: A Social Critique of the Judgment of Taste*, translated by Richard Nice. Cambridge, MA: Harvard University Press, 1984.

10 Mitchell, W. J. T. *What Do Pictures Want? The Lives and Loves of Images*. Chicago and London: University of Chicago Press, 2005, p. 215.

> any notion of "pure" cinema – of a mode of expression that is unique to the cinema and that has evolved autonomously out of the singular nature of the medium's raw materials – must be qualified by the essential impurity of the cinema's quasi-theatrical, quasi-novelistic mode of narration.[11]

On Mitchell's reading, all media are "impure," and any appeal to cinematic purity is faced from the outset with the countervailing fact of media hybridity. This is a subject of interest to scholars in the philosophy of technology, and I will pick up the idea that hybrid media are inherently impure media later in my discussion of Hitchcock's response to the introduction of sound to movies. It is important at this point only to note how notions of pure and impure objects and practices have deeply ingrained philosophical legacies.

If it is important to ask what Hitchcock meant by pure cinema, it might also be advisable to ask whether he ever actually achieved pure cinema, or whether, like *Vertigo*'s Scottie, he was seduced by a fantasy? Indeed, was pure cinema even a reasonable description of the films Hitchcock produced? And if one could argue that Hitchcock's striving after cinematic purity is an apt description of his practices, to which aspects of his films would we be referring? Their style? Their content? Their technique? Further, what role does the phrase "pure cinema" play in ongoing conversations about Hitchcock? Does it productively illuminate important aspects of his work, or does it wrap his films in a cloud of confusion?

In this chapter I offer provisional answers to these and related questions by examining the different meanings that have been ascribed to pure cinema. I begin with a consideration of Hitchcock's most common claims as to the meaning of pure cinema before moving on to discuss several of the interpretations that have been subsequently advanced by film scholars. It is not my purpose to offer a novel interpretation of the concept as might suggest a reformulation of our thinking about Hitchcock's intentions. My main goal is to inquire systematically into the history of the phrase as it has appeared and been applied in the field of Hitchcock studies. To this end, I largely avoid normative assessments, for given pure cinema's polysemic nature it would be unwise to suggest that whereas one film scholar has used the concept 'correctly' others have applied it 'incorrectly.' I simply want to sort through the

---

11 Whereas Mitchell's argument concerns the impossibility of so-called medium purity in a strictly technical way, Belton arrives at the concept of an "impure" medium via a historical argument. See Belton, John. "The Space of *Rear Window*." *MLN*, 103 (5), December 1988, pp. 1121–1138. p. 1121.

different ways in which the phrase has become a form of currency in the field of Hitchcock scholarship – a bit of cultural capital, as it were – in order to shed some light on the way in which Hitchcock is understood as an artist, and on the way his filmmaking was both historically located and technically developed. In the discourse of the academy, I want to problematize *pure cinema.*

The Purely Visual

Most of the critical commentary concerning *pure cinema* relates to Hitchcock's proclaimed interest in the visual dimension of film. A major reason for this interpretation is remarks Hitchcock made in his discussions with Donald Spoto where he said that his early exposure to German expressionism was so important in his formative years that his "models were forever after the German filmmakers of 1924 and 1925."[12] It is well known that during the time Hitchcock spent at UFA Studios in Berlin he was deeply impressed by the work of German filmmakers, especially director F. W. Murnau. In Murnau's films expressionism was both thematic and technical, with the real supplanted by realism through techniques such as forced perspective, point of view shooting, and the so-called unchained camera technique.[13] Hitchcock was intrigued in particular by the idea of using the camera to express the point of view of the film's characters rather than to limit it to the function of recording events such as would be the case in filming a stage play from a stationary location in the audience. Murnau showed Hitchcock how the mobile camera could enhance audience identification by placing the viewer in the position of the players in the narrative, showing us, for instance, what a character sees instead of showing us that same character in the act of seeing. This was a lesson Hitchcock applied with enthusiasm. To cite just one example, consider the moment in *Shadow of a Doubt* (1948), when Uncle Charles spots the ring on young Charlie's finger as she descends the stairs, deliberately trailing her hand along the balustrade to draw his attention to the fact that she is now in possession of the talismanic ring. The camera does not simply show us the ring; it shows us the ring as Charles sees the ring and then registers his reaction in a crucial close-up. Subjective tracking shots of this sort, which he

12 Spoto, Donald. *The Dark Side of Genius: The Life of Alfred Hitchcock.* New York: Ballantine Books, 1983, p. 75.

13 An excellent discussion of Murnau's influence on Hitchcock is Bade, James N. "Murnau's Last Laugh and Hitchcock's Subjective Camera." *Quarterly Review of Film and Video*, 23 (3), 2005, pp. 257–266.

learned from watching German filmmakers, became a standard technique in Hitchcock's repertoire.

Charles Barr has argued that Hitchcock was also influenced by Murnau's ability to dispense with authorial commentary and allow the camera to relate the narrative. At UFA studios, Hitchcock watched Murnau at work on one of his most famous films, *The Last Laugh* (1924), where only a single intertitle card is used (appearing near the film's end), and where "narrative, relationships, and emotions are conveyed lucidly by visual means."[14] Thus, when Hitchcock summarized his debt to German filmmakers in speaking with Spoto, he noted the influence of expressionist directors like Murnau who "were trying very hard to express ideas in purely visual terms."[15]

These comments certainly appear to show that Hitchcock's pure cinema could be understood as preeminently concerned with the visual aspect of film. More specifically, it was the visual aspect that derived not just from moving pictures in the broadest sense, but from the practices of silent film production where the story was told in images along with the judicious use of intertitle cards. Thus, "purely visual terms" is a phrase that must be set against the practice of anchoring the film narrative in text or sound. More significantly, Hitchcock's claims about silent film imply that a certain level of narrative sophistication must be included in our understanding of "purely visual terms." Pictures on their own, as Hitchcock was at pains to remind us, are only pictures, so in speaking of "purely visual terms" Hitchcock was not limiting himself to pictures. The experience of the purely visual is a dynamic experience, informed by specific cinematic techniques such as camera angles, editing, and shadows. Moreover, the idea of the purely visual played an important role in how Hitchcock thought about the relationship between filmmaker and viewer. With dialogue or intertitle cards, some form of discursive reasoning is required in the task of interpreting the film; that is, the viewer must read and decode the words on the screen. However, when the movie consists chiefly of images rather than discursive supplements, the viewer will enter the film in a different and more intimate fashion. The purely visual terms Hitchcock prized, then, are emotionally charged in ways that discourse can only – and rather poorly – imitate.

I call this approach the *visuality thesis of pure cinema*. Many film scholars have followed this thesis regarding the significance of "purely visual terms" in respect of the practices of silent films, finding this idea of linking

14 Barr, Charles. "Hitchcock and Early Filmmakers." In *A Companion to Alfred Hitchcock*, edited by Thomas Leitch and Leland Poague. Oxford: Wiley Blackwell, 2014, p. 57.

15 Spoto, p. 75.

cinematic purity with silent films crucial to their subsequent understanding of Hitchcock's movies. For instance, William Rothman embraces a version of the visuality thesis, telling us that "For Hitchcock, 'pure cinema' was born when Griffith's camera crossed the barrier of the proscenium."[16] Rothman's understanding of pure cinema as a product of early innovations in film technique is consistent with the interpretation of Hitchcock's ideas about "purely visual terms," and though Rothman focuses not on the German expressionists, but on D. W. Griffith, his point clearly connects pure cinema to the affordances of the unchained camera. Rothman regards pure cinema as a product of the way that the camera climbs onto the stage to bring the audience into the space occupied by the actors. On this reading, pure cinema is essentially the camera's ability to immerse the viewer in the fictional lifeworld of the performers through the appropriation of cinematic space. According to Rothman, then, pure cinema is achieved in large part as the consequence of a significant historical development: the mobility, or the unchaining, of the movie camera.

Of course, it is not simply that the camera enters the space of the players and thereby punctures the fourth wall. The camera's mobility also facilitates – indeed requires – the deployment of new practices in lighting and camera location. Crossing the proscenium encouraged the development of novel cinematic techniques of representation that further enhanced the viewer's sense of connectedness to the film's space. Though the viewer may sit in a fixed theatre seat, that is rarely her point of view. And this is because silent film developed alongside sensitivity to viewer positionality, subjectivity, and emotional and cognitive immersion. To engage the viewer meant the use of editing techniques, camera angles, close-ups, and lighting effects with silent film serving as the proving ground for these cinematic innovations.

Should we accept, then, that *pure cinema* designates the mode of visuality that characterizes the silent picture? As I have said, this is certainly a common claim, though we shouldn't lose sight of the fact that the visuality thesis also entails embracing the salience of silent film's particular style of exposition. This is an important consideration, for to tell a story either with or without sound (or dialogue) is to tell the story in quite different ways. Moreover, the way that the camera functions in relation to viewer subjectivity will also be greatly affected by the presence or absence of sound.

---

16 Rothman, William. "Virtue and Villainy in the Face of the Camera." In *The 'I' of the Camera: Essays in Film Criticism, History and Aesthetics.* New York and Cambridge: Cambridge University Press, 1988, p. 69.

To put that more plainly, if silent pictures were exemplary of pure cinema as Hitchcock appears to have suggested to Donald Spoto, then sound would be an intruder in the domain of visual purity, a contaminating influence in an otherwise unspoiled cinematic frame. This may seem an unusual proposition, but Hitchcock was surprisingly emphatic about the disruptive quality of sound recording in his interviews with François Truffaut. When cinema embraced sound, it became a hybrid technology, and it was this transformative moment about which Hitchcock could be unexpectedly dismissive.

The main discussion regarding sound's contaminating influence comes at the point in the Truffaut interviews when the two men are concluding their discussion of Hitchcock's silent film career. Truffaut asked Hitchcock for some final comments about his years making silent films before turning to talk about the director's entry into the world of sound productions. Hitchcock obliged with the following observation:

> *Hitchcock*: Well, the silent pictures were the purest form of cinema; the only thing they lacked was the sound of people talking and the noises. But this slight imperfection did not warrant the major changes that sound brought in. In other words, since all that was missing was simply natural sound, there was no need to go to the other extreme and completely abandon the technique of the pure motion picture, the way they did when sound came in.

Truffaut endorsed Hitchcock's critique of audio technology with some observations of his own, picking up in particular on the theme of cinematic perfection, and the part played by sound in the adulteration of film:

> *Truffaut*: I agree. In the final era of silent movies, the great film-makers – in fact, the whole of production – had reached something near perfection. The introduction of sound, in a way jeopardized that perfection. I mean that this was precisely the time when the high screen standards of so many brilliant directors showed up the woeful inadequacy of the others, and the lesser talents were gradually being eliminated from the field. In this sense one might say that mediocrity came back into its own with the advent of sound.

As this portion of the interview moved toward its conclusion, Hitchcock responded to Truffaut's points with a lengthier analysis of the changes that sound had brought to cinema, lamenting how the camera's mobility had failed to alter the tendency of many directors to shoot their film in a mainly theatrical fashion. This staged quality of contemporary films prompted Hitchcock to one of his best-known complaints about movies that consisted primarily of "photographs of people talking." After all, he suggested, "When we tell a story in cinema, we should resort to dialogue only when it's impossible to do otherwise."[17]

This exchange is important in framing the nature of the relationship among pure cinema, silence, and visuality. First, Hitchcock and Truffaut share a belief in asserting silent film's superiority to sound productions though they stop short of embracing completely an abstract idealism. That is, although they use terms in their discussion that suggest their clear preference for the silent film, they also hedge their comments with a series of qualifications. Hitchcock describes silent films as suffering "a *slight* imperfection" in being silent, and refers not to the actual attainment of purity, but to silent films being "the *purest* form of cinema." In other words, silent films come closer to the ideal of pure cinema than sound productions, though silent movies were neither perfect nor completely pure. For his part, Truffaut notes how silent films had "reached *something near* perfection," stopping short of an unqualified claim to faultlessness, though only moments later he seems willing to qualify his own qualified statement, arguing that "the introduction of sound [...] jeopardized that perfection." Hitchcock's final observation that dialogue should only ever be the filmmaker's "final resort" indicates that he is speaking of something more properly regarded as better cinema, if not actual pure cinema.[18]

I realize this is parsing both filmmakers rather closely, and that the nuances in this exchange may therefore seem overemphasized. However, I think that the key issue has less to do with the absoluteness of a purely cinematic achievement than it does with the necessity of contextualizing the theory of pure cinema in reference to actually existing forms of film practice. And when Hitchcock and Truffaut set out to provide such context, it is interesting that they end up claiming that cinematic purity is tied historically to silent film and to the problem that arises when sound not merely alters, but ultimately adulterates the silent picture. Hence, while pure cinema, as Rothman says, may be discerned at that moment when the camera crossed the proscenium, this technological innovation – the mobile or unchained camera – differs in important respects from the subsequent innovation of bringing sound into

---

17 Truffaut. All quotations cited here are from page 61.

18 It is interesting to add here Walter Benjamin's countervailing claim that "the sound film did not change anything essential" in distinguishing stage from cinematic performances. See The Work of Art in the Age of Mechanical Reproduction (orig. 1936). *Illuminations*, translated by Harry Zohn. New York: Schocken Books, 1968, p. 229.

film production. The mobile camera and sound recording were both important developments in film history. However, *while the former (camera mobility) helped to purify the cinema, the latter (sound) contaminated it.* Hence the purity of silent films as Hitchcock and Truffaut understood it was based partly on the assumption that the fusion of different media produced degraded modes of representation. The visuality thesis of pure cinema emphasizes silence as much as it advocates for images, although it does so by taking a normative view of these technological changes. Hybrid media, the conclusion runs, are impure media.

The relationship of sound to the concept of pure cinema can also be traced by following a more literal understanding of purity as a form of cleanliness. In this respect, we can cite the ideas of anthropologist Mary Douglas, who designates dirt (or pollution) as "matter out of place."[19] According to Douglas, cultural forces define things, people, or practices as defiled or impure by reference to custom rather than essence. In her view, things that are said to be pure only become impure when something disorders the initial (pure) condition. The pure thing becomes unclean owing to the presence of a contaminating element – even when the contamination is created by something which, in a different context, we would regard as pure. Sand tracked across a clean floor makes the floor "dirty" because the sand is matter out of place, not because sand can be defined unequivocally as dirty. Sand adulterates a clean floor by being in the wrong place: on the floor, not on the beach. We might think of pure cinema in these terms, then, as a form of unadulterated cinema.

Thinking of purity as the condition of being uncontaminated focuses on how orderliness is enforced by keeping foreign things outside the frame of reference. Thus, a film could be described as *pure* on the condition of being uncontaminated by things that would undermine or pollute its otherwise pristine state. In relation to film this notion of purity may seem a strange conception, but Hitchcock seems to have included a version of this argument in lamenting the introduction of sound as an intrusive element that upset a previously silent, pristine order. Sound, in this anthropological reading of purity, is a form of matter out of place.[20] Sound was a contaminant.

Understanding pure cinema according to the visuality thesis, then, refers us to the expressionistic tendency in early German film to reduce the use of intertitle cards to a minimum to express the narrative in the silent images on the screen. The use of the unchained or mobile camera is also important in the

19 Douglas, Mary. *Purity and Danger: An Analysis of the Concepts of Pollution and Taboo.* London: Ark Paperbacks, 1966, p. 35.

20 One might think of the intrusive voice-over as being "matter out of place."

visuality thesis insofar as it indicates the centrality of the viewer's immersion in the action, an immersion that is chiefly affective in the form of audience response. The introduction of sound thus changed filmmaking in substantial ways that Hitchcock was inclined to regard as a kind of degradation. That dialogue was, as Hitchcock said, a last resort, suggests its supplementary character, and Hitchcock (and Truffaut) lamented the tendency of filmmakers in the years following the silent era to highlight dialogue at the expense of the visual, a reordering that could be regarded as a switch from revelation to explanation. We might say, then, that the engaging qualities of the purely visual techniques for emplotment were sacrificed to the preciseness entailed in discursive or expositional narratives. This could even be read as a form of linguistic turn that has undermined the aesthetic beauty of film though it has made possible more complex narratives than could be achieved in the silent era. In terms of the visuality thesis, therefore, we could say that the aesthetic quality of films was forever lost when the explanatory function of language came to the fore. With the arrival of sound, cinema was disenchanted.

Pure Cinema as Montage

The visuality thesis in its various formulations captures many of the dominant issues Hitchcock often focused on when describing the idea of pure cinema. But it is not the only approach to pure cinema Hitchcock favoured, nor the only view that Hitchcock scholars have entertained. There is another view of pure cinema that is more technical than aesthetic, more concerned with technique than with visual wholeness. This approach can be designated the *montage thesis of pure cinema.*

One of the first and more enthusiastic proponents of this view is Robin Wood who suggested that when examined closely, Hitchcock's pure cinema "invariably turns out to be based on the possibilities of montage."[21] For Wood, the emphasis Hitchcock placed on the primacy of visuality can be understood as a subset of the cinematic practice of editing according to a montage principle. In other words, one can argue that the process of montage constitutes the method by which the images are arranged; montage is the technique that lies back of the artistry. I find this claim compelling, but I also believe that there are reasons to treat montage separately as a way of approaching the meaning of pure cinema.

21 Wood, Robin. *Hitchcock's Films Revisited.* New York: Columbia University Press, 1989, p. 215.

An essential principle of montage is that it replaces the linear causality of determination with an associative logic of relationships, for montage dispenses with the strictly temporal by focusing instead on thematic processes of association. The "possibilities of montage" that Wood describes, therefore, point to an awareness of that which is otherwise; that is, if things are possible rather than determined, then they may have turned out differently, or otherwise, from how they are represented. Montage thus demands a good deal of decision-making in post-production where the identification and assembly of the relevant portions of the film takes place. Thus, Hitchcock said that combining different images and sequences in post-production was the essential aspect of creating a cinematic narrative, and that in assembling the images according to the dictates of the story, the filmmaker was able to provoke certain reactions and elicit necessary emotions from the filmgoer. Emphasizing montage, then, often involves a concerted focus on audience reaction.

The idea of an associative logic as indispensable to montage has been advanced by the philosopher Slavoj Žižek, another advocate of this formulation of the montage thesis. Montage, he argues, permits the "horizontal coexistence of two lines of action," a process that Hitchcock deployed frequently, as in the famous tennis match/lighter retrieval scene in *Strangers on a Train* (1951).[22] This form of montage – which is more conventionally described as parallel editing – fashions a version of the real from specific spatial and temporal distortions, an important consideration that once again harkens to the influence of German expressionism. Žižek argues that montage establishes a metaphorical relation that both divides and links specific sequences in a film. In the case of the sequence just mentioned from *Strangers on a Train*, Bruno's attempts to retrieve the lighter from the sewer inform the tennis match Guy is playing. And, of course, every shot in that match mirrors Bruno's increasing anxiety as he tries to regain possession of the all-important lighter. Uniting the two men across the many miles that separate them is the setting sun, its indifference mocking their respective struggles. The two sets of events, as Žižek claims, are thus divided (spatially) yet linked (thematically). We can therefore say that the structure of montage is the dialectic of disparate sequences united through an editing process sensitive to their thematic parallels.

Montage splinters the scenes and reconstitutes the significance of the objects and subjects within the scenes according to a metaphoric and horizontal relation. Combination is the key issue at work here, a point that finds its most obvious line of connection with Hitchcock in his several references

22 Zizek, Slavoj. "The Hitchcockian Blot." In *Alfred Hitchcock: Centenary Essays*, edited by Richard Allen and S. Ishii Gonzalès. London: BFI Publishing, 1999, p. 124.

to the Kuleshov effect.[23] One illustration of this connection can be noted in a 1963 interview with the journal *Cinema*, where Hitchcock is explicit in his belief that montage was the key to pure cinema. As he told the interviewer,

> pure cinema is pieces of film assembled. Any individual piece is nothing. But a combination of them creates an idea.[24]

In this interview, Hitchcock states clearly that pure cinema is about achieving a desired effect via juxtaposition, that it entails the creation of wholeness from disparate and otherwise unconnected images. According to Hitchcock, assembly (or combination) dispensed with the restraints of everyday temporal/spatial relations, not so that reality would be effaced, but in order that *the sense of reality* would be enhanced. Pure cinema might well be, as Hitchcock claimed, "pieces of film assembled," but it is the intelligibility of the assembly that is required for effective emplotment.

In his interviews with François Truffaut, Hitchcock said several things about pure cinema as it relates to montage, too, but he often pointed to audience manipulation as the goal of editing, intercutting, and arrangement, suggesting that affect was his principal driving interest. "It is essential to separate clearly the dialogue from the visual elements," he told Truffaut, and "whenever possible, to rely more on the visual than on the dialogue." But "whichever way you choose to stage the action," he went on, "your main concern is to hold the audience's fullest attention. [...] The screen rectangle must be charged with emotion."[25] Similarly, to the interviewer of *Cinema*, he claimed:

> I put first and foremost cinematic style before content. Most people, reviewers, you know, they review pictures purely in terms of content. I don't care what the film is about. I don't even know who was in that airplane attacking Cary Grant. I don't care. So long as that audience goes through that emotion! Content is quite secondary to me.[26]

---

23 An interesting account of Hitchcock's interest in Lev Kuleshov's famous experiment appears in Fletcher Markle's 1964 documentary, *A Talk with Hitchcock*, broadcast originally on the CBC and available online.

24 On Style. Interview with *Cinema*. In *Hitchcock on Hitchcock: Selected Writings and Interviews*, edited by Sidney Gottlieb. Berkeley: University of California Press, 1995, p. 288.

25 Truffaut, p. 61.

26 On Style. Interview with *Cinema*. In *Hitchcock on Hitchcock: Selected Writings and Interviews*, edited by Sidney Gottlieb. Berkeley: University of California Press, 1995, p. 292.

Hitchcock's focus on the viewer's emotions, coupled with the idea that emotional manipulation was the endpoint of pure cinema, supports a processual theory of cinematic purity rather than a strictly aesthetic or even technical one. For example, Hitchcock said that he believed *Psycho* succeeded as "pure film" precisely because the picture's impact on audiences was independent of its message, its subject matter, and its actors' performances. As the citation above suggests, *Psycho*'s content was secondary to its style. It was "tremendously satisfying," he elaborated, "to be able to use the cinematic art to achieve something of a mass emotion."[27] When mass emotion is your goal, and cinematic purity comes from the achievement of that goal through the practice of montage, the veridical must inevitably be secondary to style.

Hitchcock told Truffaut that "the placing of the images on the screen, in terms of what you're expressing, should never be dealt with in a factual manner. [...] You can get anything you want through the proper use of cinematic techniques, which enable you to work out any image you need."[28] In the present context, Hitchcock's devaluation of the "factual" in service to the cinematic raises some interesting questions. For instance, if Hitchcock subverted specific features of everyday vision to give the image a convincing appearance, in what respects must the image be convincing? Given that our unaided sight tends toward a correspondence theory of truth, how would cinematic truth differ from factual truth? The answer Hitchcock appears to endorse is that the merely factual is essentially denotative, and that when attention is diverted from the image as strictly objective to a conception of the image as bound to constructivist properties of human perception, then we gain a greater and more affective experience. We could say, therefore, that the image is convincing to the extent that its cinematic arrangement (the assembly of individual pieces of film) evokes an emotional response that is itself believable. And montage is a powerful perceptual process because it dispenses with criticality in favour of an emotional immediacy. Hitchcock used montage to establish emotional facticity rather than naked factuality.

Montage and visuality are united in their focus on the silence of images. And as I suggested earlier, one could argue that montage is the technique by which the art is realized, that the assembly of Hitchcock's "pieces of film" entails guidance from specific narratological principles to make the assembly meaningful. But while elements of the visuality thesis are discernible in the montage thesis, the montage process of assembly points not to an essential form of visual denotation, but to the direction of an overarching human

27 Truffaut, pp. 282–283.
28 Truffaut, p. 265.

intentionality – the auteur's vision. The visuality thesis rests in part on the idea of the purity of the image without reference to its constructed essence, but once we entertain montage as constituting a contending version of pure cinema, that form of purity disappears and is replaced by the cognitive imprint of the director as designed in the associative logic of thematic combination. Despite similarities between the two theses, then, placing visuality and montage side-by-side helps to underscore a fundamental inconsistency in how Hitchcock expressed his concept of pure cinema.

Pure Cinema in the Ontology of the Poetic

Although the dominant approaches to understanding pure cinema have centred on visuality and montage, not every Hitchcock scholar is beholden to visuality or montage as the sole explanations of Hitchcock's conception of pure cinema. Several other accounts of pure cinema have been offered in the pages of Hitchcock scholarship, two of which I want to consider here as especially significant in the way that they bear upon ideas of purity and ideas about the cinematic.

The first position is George Toles's argument which I designate the *poetic view of pure cinema*. Borrowing directly from Archibald MacLeish's famous poem, *Ars Poetica*, Toles says that pure cinema belongs to a world "where images, like poems, should not mean but be."[29] This assertion suggests an approach to cinema steeped in the principle of autonomous art; it also incorporates aspects of the visuality thesis insofar as it contains traces of the idea of denotative purity. But Toles also challenges conventional ideas about the relation between symbols and reference, and it is this separation that I believe makes his argument novel.

Toles says that pure cinema is an anti-discursive form of representation, and that its true character is found in its aesthetic autonomy rather than its being solely referential. In other words, by distinguishing between *being* and *meaning*, Toles seeks to abandon the distant referent and embrace the immediately present. As the image on the screen is the essence of cinematic presence, its being is a form of purity untouched by the adulterating influences of culture. Moreover, by linking his conception of pure cinema to MacLeish's poem, Toles further suggests that the purity in *pure cinema* is not merely understood

29 Toles, George. "'If Thine Eye Offend Thee …': *Psycho* and the Art of Infection." In *Alfred Hitchcock: Centenary Essays*, edited by Richard Allen and S. Ishii Gonzalès. London: British Film Institute, 1999, p. 164. The final stanza of Archibald MacLeish's poem, *Ars Poetica*, reads, "A Poem Should Not Mean/But Be."

as innocence, but as an aesthetic principle opposing the idea that meaning is immanent. Meaning is produced by judgement, truth-seeking, and verification, and in rejecting these principles poetry manages to be meaningful in a moral and aesthetic sense without seeking the approval of truth as the arbiter of value. Hence Toles says images are like poems in that they should be free of the domination of those principles and conventions that see truth as correspondence with some external power, a power that invokes its authority to produce reasons and compliance. Imagistic purity would therefore be an emancipation from the tyranny of discourse.

A similar argument is found in Roland Barthes's analysis of photographic images. According to Barthes, there is a weakness in photographs in respect of their meaning, and in order to decide how images come to mean at all we must distinguish between the literal image (the uncoded iconic image) and the connotations suggested by that image (the coded iconic image).[30] However, the uncoded iconic image – the pure or literal image – is rather difficult to conceptualize as it functions as a kind of hyperbolic ideal; indeed, Barthes ultimately refers to it as "Edenic denotation" so as to acknowledge that it is materially unrealizable, an Edenic paradise. We can imagine, if only hypothetically, that it is possible to point the camera and capture a "pure" image, an image unaffected by any preexisting conceptions embraced by, or embodied in the photographer. Aside from the act of dropping your camera accidentally and activating the shutter, it is hard to see how such a thing might exist. Nonetheless, as his use of "Edenic" makes plain, Barthes is dealing here with an ideal condition, so we can proceed on that basis.

As a theoretical concept Edenic denotation is useful in thinking through the way in which purity, in being assigned to either photographic or cinematic representations, helps to indicate through a comparative analysis the status of the coded image. In other words, the impure or coded iconic image is a repository of cultural meanings, and this is essential to the condition of its interpretability (this is why, according to Toles, the image should *be* but not *mean* if it is to remain pure). The possibility that an image can mean is therefore related to its coded or impure condition, for meaning is a product of the discourses of critique, discourses that do not discover but impose meaning upon the image. To say that an image is impure simply because it means, is to say that meaning, which is attributed rather than discovered, undoes the purity of the image as it exists prior to interpretation.

30 Barthes, Roland. Rhetoric of the image (originally published 1966), *Image-Music-Text*, translated by Stephen Heath. New York: Hill and Wang, 1977, pp. 32–51.

The idea of a literal image bereft of a code constitutes a form of aesthetic minimalism, especially as the pure image could only lose its claim to purity to the extent that other factors or substances are introduced into the previously pristine order. Thus, Barthes claims that Edenic denotation is achieved via a process he calls *eviction*; that is, we evict the cultural elements from our interpretation of the image to the point that we are left with a pure image, one that is utterly denotative and culturally uncoded. To take this argument as a genuinely methodological practice we might say that by imagining a purer image than the one we have, and by actively cleansing the image of its various ideological "impurities," we learn something about the social constructedness of that image even as the goal we pursue – itself a state of Edenic denotation, or a state of pure cinema – is recognizably futile in the way that any quest for an Edenic perfection will never reach its destination. However, in the act of eviction we will identify those aspects that must be evicted if we are to reach Barthes' Edenic state, and in doing so we identify the coded elements of the cultural order. So, we seek out the pure image not because we believe we will find it, but because during the search we come to understand in the end how and why no image can really be pure. It is interesting to note that Hitchcock's conception of pure cinema runs from past to present (from silent to sound films), whereas Barthes' approach travels in the opposite order (from impure to pure).[31]

What I take Toles to mean, then, is that images themselves have meaning insofar as we ascribe meaning to them, and that in doing so we adulterate their initial state of purity. In a state of being, the images stand free of intervention in the form of meaning-ascription, and thus pure cinema could indeed be something close to the perfection of the silent film era so lovingly described by Hitchcock and Truffaut. One might also think here of René Descartes, seeking a first philosophy by "evicting" the major philosophical traditions as he seeks to discover the bedrock truth – a pure truth – on which all knowledge is based. So too, Toles invokes the ideal of the pure image as a foundational object upon which interpretations are added to the point that the purity of the initial state is lost. Like Barthes, we can seek to evict these interpretations in search of the original state of being to which meaning remains external. The pure image – the image that will only be and not mean

31 Here we might think of the Catholic sacrament of confession during which the penitent "evicts" her sins in reciting them for the priest in order to gain absolution. Confession is a form of eviction in which a purer condition is achieved than was the case prior to entering the confessional.

– is produced in a moment of aesthetic inspiration rather than knowledgeable intention.

This idea has profound difficulties. It is hard to maintain that the pure image or the un-interpreted poem would be recognizable as either an image or a poem without any meaning being ascribed to either. Hitchcock's pure cinema, too, would seem to resist absorption into the sort of purity being described here, for his films could never be sufficiently free of interpretive activity as to be Edenic to the point of having no referential qualities. Toles's point is an interesting one, then, but it is unclear to me that he is really getting at the idea of purity in the sense Hitchcock meant in speaking of pure cinema. To be blunt, no image can just be rather than mean, except in the sort of ideal fashion Barthes suggests, where the concept is used strictly in a comparative way to make a larger theoretical point. It may be, of course, that Toles's claim is salvageable by bringing the montage thesis into play and contending that the ontological essence of the single image must, at some point, yield to the meaning-giving power produced by combination with other images. But this may stretch Toles's intentions beyond the literary effort he is making. Moreover, it is a strategy that only works by adding meaning to the purity of his initial argument.

It is also difficult to overlook the fact that in being divested of cultural coding, as Barthes describes, the image might also be depoliticized, and thus the cinematic representation may be regarded as pure insofar as it appears without any ideological interests. Of course, this suggests yet another way we can understand pure cinema, where the purity to which Hitchcock alludes is taken as a reference to political naiveté. In fact, this is an argument that has been advanced by James Morrison in his study of Hitchcock's two Irish films, *Juno and the Paycock* (1930) and *Under Capricorn* (1949). Morrison cites Hitchcock's theory of pure cinema by advising readers that "given Hitchcock's avowals of allegiance to 'pure cinema,' it has always been easier for critics to view his work in the context of formalist-aestheticism than to examine the political ramifications his work may substantiate, even despite those avowals."[32] According to Morrison, the formalist implications of pure cinema militate against political interpretations, an observation that suggests that style trumps text in how the work is evaluated. By Morrison's account, then, pure cinema can be framed as an apolitical practice; that is, cinematic purity, interpreted as a quest to raise style over substance, makes it difficult for

32 Morrison, James. "Hitchcock's Ireland: The performance of Irish identity in *Juno and the Paycock* and *Under Capricorn*." In *Hitchcock: Past and Future*, edited by Richard Allen and Sam Ishii-Gonzáles. London and New York: Routledge Books, 2004, p. 193.

the viewer to see any of Hitchcock's films as informed by a political subtext. If pure cinema is all about surfaces, in other words, then it has little to say about the subtleties of the narrative that might lead to overtly political – or, indeed, sociological, cultural, or even religious – interpretations. Thus, Toles's argument could be supported by an appeal to the notion that the purely ontological is meant precisely as a counter to the prospect of a political reading of the film, and that Barthes's ideal of Edenic denotation is somehow a product of a claim to interpretive neutrality.[33] As Hitchcock professed never to care what his films were about, perhaps Toles is correct, and Hitchcock's works might be, but not mean. If so, cinematic purity could then also be conceptualized as the repudiation of intellectualism and cultural analysis.

The Unfamiliar Close-Up

The final approach to pure cinema that I consider appears in Joe McElhaney's (2004) analysis of Hitchcock's film, *Notorious* (1946). McElhaney relates the idea of pure cinema to the practices of the camera though his argument is only minimally concerned with the concept of montage. Looking at *Notorious* as a formal structure, McElhaney explains that almost no Hitchcock film uses the close-up "as frequently and systematically." Indeed, by McElhaney's count, *Notorious* has "119 close-ups and 72 extreme close-ups, a combined total of 191 shots in a 101-minute film."[34] These are impressive numbers, and critics have long noted the film's claustrophobic intimacy, especially in several of its most celebrated scenes in which Cary Grant and Ingrid Bergman are featured. This extensive use of the close-up is not entirely surprising, of course, as Hitchcock once wrote that "everything begins with the actor's face."[35] In *Notorious*, however, it does seem that Hitchcock was intent on creating a particular kind of intimate cinema in which facial close-ups played a preeminent role.

McElhaney's analysis turns on a syllogistic argument that connects the close-up to the idea of pure cinema. He begins by saying that "central [to

33 Barthes's ideas about zero-degree writing could be understood as another way of trying to explain theories of photographic or literary purity.

34 McElhaney, Joe. "The Object and the Face: *Notorious*, Bergman and the Close-up." In *Hitchcock: Past and Future*, edited by Richard Allen and Sam Ishii-Gonzáles. London and New York: Routledge, 2004, p. 66. I might add that I have not checked McElhaney's calculations.

35 Hitchcock, Alfred. "Film Production." In *Hitchcock on Hitchcock: Selected Writings and Interviews*, edited by Sidney Gottlieb. Berkeley: University of California Press, 1995, p. 218.

Hitchcock's intentions] was the close-up's role in filming objects and the camera's power to 'mystically' bestow life upon them."[36] This mystical power is especially important in considering the affective quality of the close-up in representing the face, for in the physiognomy of the human face – and, in particular, the face of Ingrid Bergman – McElhaney sees a transcendent power that moves the narrative forward while deepening the affective dimensions of that image.[37] In other words, the story is told in the display of changing emotions as seen in the expressions of its actors. Furthermore, McElhaney argues, the close-up is connected to an "essentialist discourse on film" that dates from the 1920s, and which, he claims, is captured neatly in Hitchcock's invocation of "pure cinema."[38] Therefore the close-up, McElhaney argues, is emblematic of pure cinema and the debt that modern films owe to the emotional power that was conveyed in silent film's traditional stylistics.

McElhaney's argument is clearly rooted in a specific understanding of silent film, and what he calls the iconic status of the face in films of that era. "It is obvious from the beginning of [Hitchcock's] career," he writes, "that the close-up is being asked not simply to serve as a classical narrative tool and fluidly insinuate itself into a causal chain but to signify in an extreme manner."[39] This belief in the structural significance of the silent film's presentation of faces and objects in close-up puts McElhaney in agreement with Hitchcock and Truffaut in regarding sound as an adulterating influence in film, though McElhaney acknowledges that Hitchcock "adapted quickly and easily to the introduction of sound, transposing the formal concerns of his silent films with a minimal amount of struggle."[40] Nonetheless, sound changed the representational force of the image such that a close-up of the face in the sound film lost much of the "iconographic boldness that it [had] during the silent era."[41] As he describes it, the close-up has a fundamental power that is evident in the silent era, the power to transform the face (and other objects) into a fetish. This helps explain McElhaney's claim that the close-up is an aspect of the "essentialist discourse on film," for it is the nature of the close-up to recapture the central role of the immersive power of the image. The fact that *Notorious*

36 McElhaney, p. 68.

37 A similar observation has been made by Peter Ackroyd who writes that in *Notorious*, Ingrid Bergman's face "is frequently seen in close-up as if it were a form of pure cinema, intimate and pre-verbal." Ackroyd, Peter. *Alfred Hitchcock*. London: Chatto & Windus, 2015, p. 121.

38 McElhaney, p. 69.

39 McElhaney, p. 68.

40 McElhaney, p. 69.

41 McElhaney, p. 72.

uses so many close-ups enables the film to reassert the "iconographic boldness" of the face despite the adulterating presence of sound.[42]

McElhaney's argument is familiar in its references to silent film as foundational in constituting Hitchcock's ideas about pure cinema. What sets his argument apart from this more conventional account of silent film is the view that the close-up, as a classic example of the mode of representation customary in the silent film era, engages the viewer in a deeply affective manner that is mystical in its effects. To overcome the limitations consequent upon an absence of sound, the silent filmmaker uses the close-up to round out the emotional contours of the narrative, using the face and other objects as vehicles of signification whose import goes beyond mere referentiality. In *Notorious*, objects "are situated in such a way that they assume wide-ranging implications within the film as a whole, revealing their 'signifying and emotional aspects.'"[43] Thus, Alicia's coffee cup, whose contents have been poisoned, is filmed in extreme close-up, making it appear much larger than it really is and greatly exaggerating its lethality.

This appeal to emotionality is something I touched upon earlier. However, in McElhaney's approach to cinematic purity, the emotional dimension of the closely filmed object or face serves as a narrative device with corresponding denotative and connotative aspects. The silent film has a plot, of course, but somehow emplotment is best realized in the affective appraisals of the unfolding story as these are registered on faces and revealed in the technique of the close-up.

I am drawn to several aspects of McElhaney's argument. However, I think that some of the key theoretical concepts he uses are presented in an attenuated manner, making his overall argument problematic. Moreover, because he relies on several unstated principles related to art criticism, McElhaney covers over gaps in his presentation with ideas that are (perhaps deliberately) vague and potentially confusing. For instance, the idea that the close-up "bestows life" on the objects it frames and the claim that the close-up signifies

42 In an essay that echoes elements of McElhaney's argument, Sam Ishii-Gonzáles argues that pure cinema "can convey not only acts or emotions but also the mechanisms of thought" (136). Ishii-Gonzáles is not referring to clairvoyance with these comments, but to a form of transcendence that configures the purity of cinema to forge an intimacy between viewer and screen such that subjectivity is positioned along the interstices of this relationship. See Sam Ishii-Gonzáles. Hitchcock with Deleuze. In *Hitchcock: Past and Future*, edited by Richard Allen and Sam Ishii-Gonzáles. London and New York: Routledge, 2004, p. 136.

43 McElhaney, p. 70. The phrase "signifying and emotional aspect" in this passage comes from Sergei Eisenstein whom McElhaney is referencing.

in "an extreme manner" are both sufficiently nebulous as to call out for additional explanation beyond what McElhaney provides. The act of signification rarely admits of degrees, and to say that something signifies in "an extreme manner," though it may itself be an example of that practice, is to risk both hyperbole and confusion. Hence, the way McElhaney links the close-up to the idea of pure cinema could benefit from the presentation of further context.

Rather than dismiss McElhaney's analysis, however, it might be possible to find this missing context in literary formalism. Given that McElhaney analyses *Notorious* from a formalist point of view, this approach has much to recommend it. Hence, I believe we can apply the theory of estrangement or defamiliarization (Russian, *ostranenie*) as a means of clarifying some of the central points that McElhaney develops in seeking to show how the close-up is evidence of pure cinema. If pure cinema is art, maybe it is art produced from the process of defamiliarization.

An extreme close-up can render the otherwise commonplace object (including the face) unfamiliar owing to the way that shadows fall across the object, how it draws our attention to otherwise overlooked qualities, or how it appears in comparison with other objects in the frame. Consider how close-up photographs of tiny objects like insects, water droplets, or electronic circuit boards make otherwise quotidian things appear unnatural, distorted, or alien. Because the close-up shows the familiar object as unfamiliar, it can arrest both perception and interpretation by compelling the viewer to a reconsideration of his or her customary habits of understanding. We may know the object is such-and-such, but we see it in a way that is completely unfamiliar.

The formalists' theories regarding *ostranenie*, or defamiliarization, took this idea a further step in claiming that defamiliarization, in addition to checking our normal practices of interpretation, was a principal technique of art. This position is particularly associated with the Russian formalist, Viktor Shklovsky (1893–1984).[44] Shklovsky argued that art derives from the process of turning the familiar into the unfamiliar – not to render interpretation impossible, but in order to enrich our understanding of the depicted object by showing it in a new and unexpected light, much as McElhaney talks of the close-up as signifying in "an extreme manner." According to Shklovsky, defamiliarization allows us to see the aesthetic potentiality of the object rather than to see only the object itself. This leads him to suggest that the object is fundamentally incidental, and that what *is* important is that our perception of that object will be transformed in the process of its defamiliarization.

44 A popular account of defamiliarization can also be found in Lodge, David. *The Art of Fiction*. New York and London: Penguin Books, 1992. See especially pp. 52–55.

Shklovsky's theories were predicated on his claim that as we become increasingly familiar with the people and objects around us, we begin to adopt an unreflective form of perception. Multiple viewings initially allow us to recognize objects clearly, but repeated viewings change everyday recognition into perceptual automatism. "The object is in front of us and we know about it," he says, "but we do not see it – hence we cannot say anything significant about it."[45] But if that same object is made unfamiliar, it is rediscovered, for we become aware of it in novel and surprising ways, for "art removes objects from the automatism of perception."[46] Therefore, Shklovsky sees the process of defamiliarization as essential to the production of art, distinguishing between the purpose and the technique of art as follows:

> The purpose of art is to impart the sensation of things as they are perceived and not as they are known. The technique of art is to make objects 'unfamiliar,' to make forms difficult, to increase the difficulty and length of perception because the process of perception is an aesthetic end in itself and must be prolonged. Art is a way of experiencing the artfulness of an object; the object is not important.[47]

In the cinema, a face appears on screen – it is right in front of us, as Shklovsky would say – but perceptual automatism prevents us from truly seeing it or from being able to comment about its significance. But in close-up, and especially in prolonged exposure on the screen, the face assumes an unfamiliar quality. Indeed, the close-up can be disorienting, providing a point of view that Shklovsky says is "obviously created to remove the automatism of perception."[48] In the act of being defamiliarized the object is presented artistically so that its "perception is impeded." Hence, we perceive it with heightened sensitivity, seeing it not only as an object filmed in close-up, but as an object which, in being defamiliarized, evokes a deeply affective response. Therefore, we could say that the close-up defamiliarizes the object so as to elevate the sensation of perception above the automatism of everyday familiarity. The close-up reinforces an impressionistic mode of seeing in which the object serves as conduit rather than as reference. If the face or object filmed in close-up is pure cinema, then this might be owing to its being an image

45 Shklovsky, *Viktor. Art as Technique* (1917). Translated by Lee T. Lemon and Marion Reis. In David Lodge ed., *Modern Criticism and Theory: A Reader.* London: Longmans, 1988, pp. 16-30, p. 18.

46 Shklovsky, p. 18.

47 Shklovsky, p. 18.

48 Shklovsky, p. 18.

that is poetic, a "vision" rather than a discursive description. By this account, pure cinema is art, and it is art produced from cinematic technique. The diachronic aspect of montage – the assembly of pieces of film – is therefore less important than the synchronic exposure of the single image in close-up. Hence McElhaney enters the world of silent film practices in search of pure cinema, but returns with a different explanation from those we have already considered, an explanation that downplays the principle of montage and elevates the principle of the close-up and its tendency to defamiliarize the object and transform it into art. For McElhaney, pure cinema is art insofar as it demands a perceptual strategy that sees artfulness in the objects being represented on the screen.

Conclusion

Although I have not exhausted the different ways in which pure cinema has been theorized and described, I have touched on several of the most important conceptions of cinematic purity as it was understood by Hitchcock and several of his well-known interpreters. Most of the accounts discussed here – especially the visuality and montage theses – are in keeping with Peter Ackroyd's description of Hitchcock as a "poet of cinematic imagery."[49] Nonetheless, reviewing these different approaches doesn't answer the question whether pure cinema was preeminently a visual aesthetic or the product of technical manipulation. I suspect that some would say that this distinction is moot, and that it is more appropriate to say that the two main theses are linked insofar as montage is the principal technique for producing the purely visual aesthetic Hitchcock prized. I have separated the aesthetic from the technical not because I doubt the importance of that relation, but because I believe that in discussing them separately, we are able to avoid falling into a trap of cinematic determinism. In other words, montage may not always produce pure cinema; nor is it necessarily the case that pure cinema can only arise from the technique of montage. Furthermore, Hitchcock frequently related pure cinema to the emotional responses of his audience, and such responses, as we have seen, cannot easily be put down to a single technical practice, the whole of the film experience being essential to shaping the way viewers engage in the activity of viewing. Owing to Hitchcock's interest in audience response, it would be at least understandable if one were to claim that pure cinema could be reduced to a technique that succeeds when viewers respond as the filmmaker intended. But while this interest in the audience's

49 Ackroyd, p. 61.

collective affectivity – and Hitchcock's unabashed enthusiasm for manipulating the filmgoer's emotions – is well known, any attempt to place pure cinema under such psychological constraints hardly seems fair considering the extensive literature on the subject. Moreover, we must keep in mind a point raised at the outset concerning the divide between Hitchcock's commercial ambitions and his aesthetic aspirations. I am not entirely sure if a definition of pure cinema that would gain universal assent would bring these two Hitchcocks together, although tying the businessman to the artist more tightly might help reconcile his internal *doppelgänger.*

I began this chapter with several questions about the meaning of pure cinema, and I will end by referring to those questions with a few observations. In the first instance, I think it is fair to say that the theory of pure cinema appropriately describes Hitchcock's films in respect of their technique. I believe this to be the case in the sense that the idea of pure cinema is really an acknowledgement of the foundational quality of the silent film tradition, especially its stylistic forms of representation such as close-ups. The montage thesis of pure cinema neatly captures this aspect of pure cinema with its focus on the range of editing techniques that developed in the years before the introduction of sound. Hence cinema was pure, according to Hitchcock, so long as it remained faithful to the conventions that arose during film's formative history. How far we are willing to extend that history forward or backward in time is a matter of debate. However, as a filmmaker who was schooled in his craft during the silent film era, it is understandable that Hitchcock's own sensibilities were unalterably formed in that period. He was, throughout his entire working career, a silent film director, albeit a silent film director who was comfortable working in sound.

However, pure cinema remains a chimera in other respects. If it is taken in the attenuated ontological analysis offered by George Toles, the notion of purity is suspect. We cannot escape the need to interpret photographs and films, and if in the practice of hermeneutic investigation, we adulterate the objects we examine in the very act of interpretation, then we are really left with an impoverished and unhelpful conception of purity. For Hitchcock, pure cinema was revelation, not exposition, and in its revelatory practice it forged alliances with spectators at a deeply emotional level. Yet nothing Hitchcock sought – an emotionally engaged audience, technical proficiency, visually appealing images, cleverly assembled pieces of film – is foreign to contemporary filmmakers. If we push pure cinema too hard in trying to get it to conform to some larger artistic principles, we encounter resistance from Hitchcock himself who regularly denied that his films could be considered art. But if we turn around and head in the opposite direction, we run into a countervailing force resisting the effort to make Hitchcock into a commercial showman, the Hitchcock who prided himself as an admired auteur.

Whereas Leitch describes Hitchcock's interest in pure cinema as "dated," it might be more appropriate to see it as nostalgic. Indeed, the most important question may not whether Hitchcock ever achieved pure cinema, but whether it provided him with useful inspiration for his work. Here, I think, the answer is an unqualified yes. Pure cinema is an ideal rather than a technical accomplishment, and it is precisely its ideal condition that renders it of lasting importance in Hitchcock scholarship.

Chapter 3

AMBIGUITY AND COMPLEXITY IN *THE BIRDS*

While causalist explanations may be appropriate for events, they do not work for the domain of meanings.

– Roy J. Howard[1]

The blackbird whirled in the autumn winds.
It was a small part of the pantomime.

– Wallace Stevens[2]

All you can say about *The Birds* is nature can be awful rough on you.

– Alfred Hitchcock[3]

Introduction

One of the lessons my students have taught me over the course of many Hitchcock seminars is that *The Birds* (1961) can be a difficult film to interpret. There are several reasons for this opinion, of course, some focused on the surrealistic atmosphere Hitchcock achieves in the film, others concentrated on the way the narrative casually brings the quotidian world into contact with the fantastic. Naturally, my students recognize these issues and regularly bring them forward for discussion, but this is rarely their main concern.

---

1 Howard, Roy. *Three Faces of Hermeneutics: An Introduction to Current Theories of Understanding.* Berkeley and London: University of California Press, 1982, p. 92.

2 Stevens, Wallace. "Thirteen Way of Looking at a Blackbird." In *The Collected Poems of Wallace Stevens*, edited by John Serio and Chris Beyers. New York: Vintage Books, 2015, p. 99.

3 Hitchcock, Alfred. "On Style." In *Hitchcock on Hitchcock: Selected Writings and Interviews*, edited by Sidney Gottlieb. Berkeley and London: University of California Press, 1995, p. 294.

Indeed, their principal complaint regarding *The Birds* is that the film fails to conclude with the traditional offer of a unifying resolution.

This argument is not easily refuted, for there is no disputing that the film concludes on a bleak note, just as there is no disputing that the nature of the narrative's problematic all but guarantees no easy escape from the birds – figuratively, of course, and perhaps in a more literal sense as well. But then, Hitchcock's tendency was often to leave his viewers suspended between apprehension and frustration, at times preferring uneasiness to contentment as a concluding sentiment.[4] *The Birds* follows this pattern closely, leaving its audience suspended over an abyss of terrifying uncertainty, with Hitchcock refusing the call for the satisfaction of release. Owing to the discomfort produced by being held in a state of suspension, it is hardly surprising that this feeling of deferment is experienced by many as a disappointment.

My students' protest rarely includes displeasure that the film closes unhappily because the expected romantic liaison has potentially been frustrated, or because a beloved character has been sacrificed to the mayhem. Instead, they object to the fact that *The Birds* doesn't actually end – at least not in the conventional sense. And it is on this point that they frequently raise an interesting argument that focuses not on the conventions of the Hollywood film, but on the empirical problem of causation. The essential argument they present is that Hitchcock doesn't provide adequate information in the film to make sense of the narrative's dominant events: the fact that the birds launch deadly and systematic attacks on people. Indeed, my students often go on to say that Hitchcock could have made a better effort to explain (rather than lampoon) the underlying cause for the birds' behaviour, as though his decision to ridicule the value of explanation constitutes an attack on the viewer. I believe that this can be an important consideration in terms of how some filmgoers might approach *The Birds* as a work of art, even though linking Hitchcock's alleged failure (or outright refusal) to provide an explanation for the birds to the broader issue of an aesthetic judgement of the film can certainly be regarded as contentious. Nonetheless, the fundamental issue raised in this argument is important: How do we get from the birds to *The Birds*?

For a time, I tended to think that the main elements of this criticism were rooted in a poorly conceptualized understanding of the aims of the film, and in an effort to defend Hitchcock against these complaints I found myself telling students that the course of the human drama developed in *The Birds* is one of the more psychologically interesting of his films. My students, however, saw

4 On the idea of suspension and hanging in Hitchcock's films, see Morris, Christopher. *The Hanging Figure: On suspense and the Films of Alfred Hitchcock*. Westport: Praeger, 2002.

this observation as an act of interpretive desperation – possibly even distraction. The central concern of their argument has little to do with such matters as the psychological dispositions of the characters, or whether their romantic interests are depicted realistically. Their argument is that the entire narrative turns on a sequence of events for which no obvious account is discernible, that the film is bereft of a sustainable argument or a logically plausible explanation. In short, the problem is the film's *causal inexplicability*, a problem that for some viewers makes the effort at suspending disbelief untenable. With many seminars discussing Hitchcock's films behind me, I have come to realize that to inquire about the meaning of *The Birds* is, in many cases, to wrestle with the reasons underlying the actions of the birds.

In what follows I consider these issues in more detail by discussing *The Birds* in the context of what I will simply call a problem of meaning. My discussion of the film – perhaps ironically – will have rather little to do with explaining what the film means, however. In fact, I make no claim to knowing better than anyone else what *The Birds* means, though there is certainly no shortage of work on that score. To be sure, the film has amassed an impressive legacy of interpretive labour over the years, encouraging approaches that range from oedipal drama to structural semiotics, from feminist critique to literary romanticism. However, by raising issues framed by interpretive practice rather than cinematic content, I want to carry out a slightly different kind of analysis. Although I do not rely on a strictly structural approach, I will focus on the way meaning is constituted from specific modes of interpretive activity. In this sense, the chapter is informed by a concern with ideas related to sense-making, and not necessarily with the sense that is made in various interpretations of the film.

This does not mean that I am not entirely without an interpretive strategy, however, for if we are to talk about the problem of meaning in *The Birds* some modest gestures toward the problem of interpretation are inevitable. Still, my approach is not beholden to advancing one particular interpretation of the film or discounting the value of specific readings. Instead, I want to approach the problem of meaning by considering the movie in relation to a problem more commonly raised in philosophical hermeneutics. In the context of Hitchcock's film this problem translates into the following question: How can we understand *The Birds* if we struggle to explain the birds? I suggest that my students' frustration with the film shows that in trying to understand *The Birds*, some viewers find themselves unable to move past the birds; that is, viewers may be so intent on finding a plausible explanation for the story's primary action that they abandon the film as an aesthetic achievement altogether. This is an intriguing hermeneutical problem that shows how interpretive strategies might lead to disappointment rather than pleasure if we are convinced that making sense of specific aspects of a narrative is a prelude to a more holistic conception of the overall project. If we stay in the field of explanation – and especially if we regard explanation as essential in making sense of the narrative – the ways in which we understand the entire text will certainly be affected. Hence, my goal is to inquire after the problem of how important it is to explain the birds if we are to understand *The Birds*.

Complexity and Ambiguity in *The Birds*

The Birds is a cipher, a film that provokes a range of meaning-making strategies that at times may seem more forced than derived. "All sorts of suppositions have been imposed upon it," writes Peter Ackroyd. "The birds represent female aggression, the male will to power, or a universal attack on the 'meaning system'."[5] Ackroyd's idea that interpretations of the film are frequently imposed is partly a result of the challenges the film presents in respect of more traditional analytic schemes, but it also follows from a strategy the director pursues throughout the film: debunking explanations for the birds' behaviour before those explanations can gain traction. At different points in the film, in other words, characters attempt to decode the birds' actions only to encounter a sentiment of dismissive hostility – from other characters, certainly, but at times from Hitchcock himself.[6] In a sense, then, *The Birds* proclaims its events as interpretable only to subsequently indicate why attempts at explanation are flawed and unworkable. It is no wonder that viewers sometimes try to impose a meaning on the text when the most obvious entry points are continually thwarted. Let me offer two examples of this practice where both the viewer's and the characters' efforts at decoding the film's meaning by way of attempting to account for the birds are denied.

---

5 Ackroyd, Peter. *Alfred Hitchcock*. London: Chatto & Windus, 2015, p. 217.

6 At several points in the film, interpretive strategies that seem at first to be potentially helpful in understanding the film are brought forward only to suffer the ignominy of peremptory dismissal. For instance, when Annie tells Melanie that from the outset Mitch's mother, Lydia, disapproved of her relationship with Mitch, Melanie wonders what Annie might have done to warrant Lydia's dislike.

> *Melanie:* Well, what had you done?
> *Annie:* Nothing. I simply existed. So, what's the answer? A jealous woman, right? A clinging possessive mother? Wrong. With all due respect to Oedipus, I don't think that was the case.

Although psychoanalytic readings of Lydia and Mitch's relationship are common in the Hitchcock literature, in this short passage Hitchcock anticipates and then dismisses psychoanalytic interpretations outright. Naturally, his dismissal hardly prevents the viewer from presenting a Freudian account of Mitch and Lydia, but Hitchcock appears eager to draw attention to that particular interpretive strategy only so that he might render it useless. (See also note 8.)

The most famous scene in which characters debate the prospect of a feasible explanation occurs in the diner, where a group of people argue over a range of possible reasons for the bird attacks. This conference immediately follows the attack on the children at the school. The ornithologist is especially glib, as she denies that such attacks could even be taking place since, among other reasons such as the biological fact of their small brains, birds of different species would never join forces. The doomsday prophet (who is seriously intoxicated) proclaims the marauding birds are evidence of biblical end times, while a distraught woman (who shelters her children like a mother hen) declares that Melanie is a supernatural incarnation of evil who must, somehow, be the cause of the avian terror. Hitchcock demonstrates that these three explanations, which come from scientific, religious, and supernatural points of view, are all unacceptable. The ornithologist's scientific account is undermined by her haughty indifference to the facts to which viewers are already privy: we have witnessed the attacks ourselves, and for her to say it could not happen registers as scientific hubris. The religious explanation is poisoned by the drunken incoherence of its spokesman, for his scriptural enthusiasm is easily explained as a case where the liquor is doing the talking. And the superstitious view is motivated solely by the fearful despair of a panicked mother. It is not an explanation so much as it is an instance of impassioned desperation. Each explanation is dashed the moment it is spoken, its impossibility demonstrated mainly as a product of questionable ethos. Explanations for the birds, this scene seems to tell us, will ultimately turn out to be pointless.

Whereas the diner scene is the film's most famous indication of Hitchcock's scorn for plausibility, there is another less celebrated moment in the film where Hitchcock's strategy is developed with greater subtlety, a scene where explanations for the birds are again discounted and ridiculed. This involves the police visit to the Brenner home following the bird attack on Melanie, the children, and the Brenner house. Deputy Al Malone, the sole representative of officialdom in the picture, is a slightly awkward character who advises that the birds might have been drawn to dive down the Brenner's chimney because they were attracted to the light.[7] A moment's reflection makes clear that this explanation is nonsensical as the attack occurred in daylight; more importantly, it reveals how the authorities are determined to identify an objective, clearly defined cause, that they are led by a passion for reason. In other words, Deputy Malone's wisdom is attenuated by blind obedience to

7 That the town's constabulary are practically invisible throughout the narrative, and incompetent when they do appear, is hardly surprising given Hitchcock's tendency to mock the pomposity of authority and expertise. *The Birds* is no different in terms of the director's desire to deflate the self-importance of authority figures. See Chapter four on *The Wrong Man* for more on this theme.

a narrow form of rationality. Standing in the middle of the Brenner living room following the bird attack that has left the house in shambles, Malone appears a strangely nonchalant sceptic, unwilling to consider the accuracy of the accounts that Mitch, Melanie, and Lydia provide. Evidence lies all around him in the chaos left by the swarming birds, but he sees none of it. When Mitch points out that the birds had earlier attacked some children at Cathy's birthday party, Malone suggests that the children must somehow have been at fault. This response angers a distraught Lydia, who tries to overcome Malone's single-mindedness – and some might say dull wittedness – by trying to provide further details of that attack.

> *Lydia:* The children were playing a game, Al. Those gulls attacked without […]
> *Malone:* Now, Lydia, "attack" is a pretty strong word, don't you think? I mean, birds just don't go around attacking people without no reason, you know what I mean? The kids just probably scared them, that's all.[8]

In one sense, Malone is perfectly correct: birds do not ordinarily attack people for no reason, and in pointing this out to both Lydia and the viewers, he calls into question the very story Hitchcock has been presenting. We know that what we are witnessing cannot realistically happen, yet to have a character from within the story decry the absurdity of those same events challenges the possibility of even a figurative account of the narrative. Malone's focus on the absence of a good reason for what has just been described leads him to deny that those events could have taken place, and this has implications for the viewer whose identification with both the Brenners and Melanie can only be sustained by taking side against Malone's logic. The fact that Mitch is a lawyer trained in the use of logical argumentation adds an additional layer of irony to the scene.

In his application of Occam's razor, Malone is quick to challenge Lydia's imputation of motive. For birds to *attack* is the sort of thing that falls outside our conventional worldview – the sphere of reason – and thus it must be doubted or denied. The impetus for Malone's immediate response to Lydia's use of the word *attack* – he does, after all, interrupt her – is his worry that to say "attack" grants the birds more agency than he is prepared to accept. When a raptor

8 Something interesting in Malone's speech pattern can be discerned in his tendency to use the tag-on construction: "don't you know"; "You know what I mean"; "That's all." Even the sentence ending in "you know what I mean" begins with Malone saying, "I mean." There is a good deal of certainty about what things mean in Malone's discourse, and a great deal of finality, too ("That's all"). But his failure to fully understand or believe proves to be his undoing.

attacks its prey, agency is subordinate to instinct, no matter how intelligently the predator carries out its hunt. To attack people, then, requires more than instinct – or something terribly different from instinct – and this would mean that the birds are acting on motives that exceed their behavioural repertoire. Deputy Malone's search for *reasons* to explain the conduct of the gulls, crows, and chimney sweeps is thus pointless insofar as he already has good reasons for doubting the legitimacy of whatever reasons he might conceive or that the Brenners might offer. For Malone, reasons are acceptable to the extent that they can legitimately be considered causally relevant, and thus he suggests light from a chimney, or the annoying behaviour of children, as determinately antecedent to the events the Brenners relate. The key to understanding Malone's point of view is recognizing how he frames the accounts that Mitch and the others provide, and that framework, while perfectly appropriate to his usual investigative procedures, becomes an intractable obstacle in the context of the events at hand. Barring unsubstantiated expressions of agency, Malone is able to maintain a strictly scientific approach to resolving the problem of the birds. His by-the-book response to Lydia's frustration is simply to reiterate that neither she, Melanie, nor Mitch has provided him with a believable reason. On this point Malone is correct, and without reasons on which he might base an investigation the event would be not only unimaginable but clearly impossible.

That Malone refuses to entertain the possibility that the birds attack for a reason – for Malone is committed to rational thinking – means that the verdict pronounced by the authorities is that there can be no explanation for the birds. This is significant, for if the birds' behaviour is literally unexplainable, then an effective course of action for dealing with the attacks is impossible from the position of official rationality. Hence the terror of *The Birds* is produced in part from what I referred to earlier as the problem of the causal inexplicability embedded in the film's narrative. With no acceptable explanation at hand, any move toward resolution is thwarted. The matter of explanation is linked, therefore – though in some uncertain way – to the issue of understanding. To make that connection clearer, however, we need to return to the problem of meaning. Based on what we have said to this point, is the meaning of *The Birds* to be found in the inexplicable nature of the birds?

The Meaning System and the Aesthetic Divide

With the very notion of a reasonable account for the birds' behaviour blocked each time the issue of a rational explanation is sought from within the film, one can see why, as Peter Ackroyd suggests, interpretations of the film are sometimes imposed awkwardly on the narrative. However, Ackroyd's final point, which sees *The Birds* as an attack on the essential question of the "meaning system," is also relevant here. Indeed, this suggestion has received a good deal of attention from critics over the years. If *The Birds* aims to make a problem of the practice of meaning-making – to essentially challenge the possibility of meaning as discoverable within the particular historical and cultural coordinates of the cinema – then one might sensibly conclude that some form of aesthetic ambiguity is being substituted for more traditional ideas about interpretability. Of course, this is still interpretation of a sort, though its point, insofar as it denies the validity entailed by what Ackroyd calls the "meaning system," may be to indicate the arbitrary nature of a form of cinematic hegemony that encloses the film within the embrace of genres, studios, the star system, and even the contours of the conventional narrative format. The meaning of the film, on this account, is found in its abstruseness, indecipherability, and opaqueness. It would stand to reason, then, that the best we can do is impose meaning on a film that adamantly refuses to yield to the usual methods of interpretation.

This idea that *The Birds* is intended to defy understanding and frustrate viewers has led some to consider the production as making sense only in the way that abstract art makes sense – which is to say that *The Birds* is non-representational. Critics who fall into this group tend to approach the film in search of a philosophical meaning which allows us to pass over the tricky questions raised by the instrumentalism of a black-and-white concern with explanation. For example, Robin Wood puts the non-representational quality of *The Birds* in terms that are similar if not identical to those indicated by Ackroyd with his suggestion that "uncertainty is the keynote of the film."[9] No doubt this is true; however, *The Birds* is not unique in this respect as many films play with the motif of uncertainty, though few have been so widely viewed outside the art-house theatre. More significantly, even fewer have enjoyed the legacy of exasperated responses that has been the fate of *The Birds*, a legacy that has seen audiences divided on the very subject of its putative uncertainty. Furthermore, denunciations of the film have ultimately formed an important part of the way that the film's uncertainty has been received, and it is a matter of both curiosity and importance that the detractors of the film be taken seriously. In some ways, the history of the contradictory readings offered by devotees and critics sheds some light on how the film is assessed in terms of its aesthetic qualities.

David Sterritt, for instance, has commented on the film in precisely these terms regarding the matter of audience response, noting that the legacy of the film includes its tendency to divide viewers into two factions: those who

9 Wood, Robin. *Hitchcock's Films Revisited.* New York: Columbia University Press, 1989, p. 172.

applaud the film as complex and those who denounce it as ambiguous. As Sterritt puts it, "*The Birds* is the most loudly debated" of Hitchcock's films,

> dividing critics and audiences into rival camps: those who call it one of his most complex and rewarding achievements, and those who assail not only its performances and allegedly unconvincing character relations, but, more important, its unyielding ambiguity and its insistence on mixing the stuff of everyday life (and movies) with elements of unbridled fantasy.[10]

Note that while Sterritt places ambiguity in opposition to complexity without directly suggesting a normative judgement, I believe that this is exactly the assessment he intends. Those who see the film as complex, he says, find *The Birds* deeply satisfying, while those who read the film as ambiguous, regard it as disappointing, uneven, and fantastic. On Sterritt's account, then, complexity and ambiguity are metrics that allow us to sift viewers into "camps" according to how they value the overarching concept of cinematic "difficulty."

I take Sterritt's point to be useful insofar as we are probably far less neutral with our description of *The Birds* as difficult, or challenging, than we might want to believe. At the same time, Sterritt's scheme can be a risky manoeuvre, for not every film that is regarded as ambiguous is complex, any more than the opposite connection obtains. However, Sterritt doesn't simply chastise those who decry the film for being ambiguous, for he goes on to note that owing to its "unyielding ambiguity," *The Birds* is also criticized for theatrical failings: weak performances by some of the cast, uneven and possibly incomplete character development, and a tendency toward slippage between genres. Indeed, the "unconvincing character relations" to which Sterritt refers are curious for the way they seem intended to force viewers to view as problematic matters that Hitchcock could have treated far more conventionally. They are, in other words, further illustrations of the defiance of the meaning system and a celebration of the ambiguous.[11]

---

10 Sterritt, David. *The Films of Alfred Hitchcock*. Cambridge: Cambridge University Press, 1993, p. 120.

11 One of the commonly discussed of these problems is the nature of the relationship between Mitch Brenner and his mother, Lydia, a relationship that has occasioned considerable appeals to psychoanalytic (and other psychological) models for insight. But while this relation may be unconvincing, in relation to Sterritt's suggestion, it is useful to Hitchcock in advancing the uneasiness of the narrative. Moreover, Mitch and Lydia's relationship also serves as a frame for an additional mystery, namely the

As a way of handling the dialectic of the ambiguous and the complex, Sterritt's separation of the film's viewers into admirers and detractors can also be used to address theories of taste as bound to class or, perhaps, cognitive sophistication. This point does not necessarily devolve to the conclusion that people who admire the film's complexity understand it in ways that are impossible for those who decry its ambiguity, though this may turn out to be true in some cases. What it does suggest is that matters of decipherability have both positive and negative valences; in addition, these evaluative registers may well be more emotional than cognitive. In other words, what we are talking about is an aesthetic impulse, not a logical proposition. Some viewers may prefer challenges that produce dissociated and non-linear modes of thinking, texts that are complex, challenging, and multi-levelled. Such texts have been described by Roland Barthes as *writerly*, and this concept would appear to apply to *The Birds* when its complexity (as opposed to its ambiguity) is emphasized. Thus, *The Birds*, as Sterritt says, is satisfying in a way that is wholly irreducible to practices of sense-making for those who value its complexity. One or more aspects of the narrative manage to evade assimilation in the folds of a grand, interpretive gesture, and it is this part of the story, this remainder that can't be readily digested, that makes the experience rewarding.

For other viewers, Sterritt suggests, this denial of interpretive wholeness is to be condemned for denying viewers the satisfaction (and the pleasure) of logical determination, for the film appears to this group of viewers as mystifyingly ambiguous. (This is, of course, the essential argument raised by my students.) Thus, the distinction Sterritt draws suggests an appeal to the high art/low art distinction, though he avoids those terms. The key point I want to emphasize here, then, is that in speaking of *The Birds* as difficult, one needs to be mindful of the fact that what makes the film difficult – difficult to interpret, difficult to appreciate – can also be the very thing that makes the film a rewarding experience. Complexity and ambiguity can be taken to represent the interpretive strategies of different communities of viewers, and these strategies produce rewarding or disappointing viewing experiences. Neither group of viewers necessarily makes 'more' or 'better' sense of the film, for both must deal with the problem Hitchcock refuses to answer: the fundamental inexplicability of the birds.

---

curious age gap between Mitch and his younger sister, Cathy. Separated by approximately twenty years, it is understandable that Mitch displays an affection for Cathy more paternal than brotherly, but the reason for the difference in their ages is never discussed – or even acknowledged. The peculiarity of this familial pattern is made even more apparent as Cathy comes to play the part of a surrogate daughter to Melanie and Mitch who become her symbolic parents.

But where Sterritt stops short of making an overt appeal to the high art/low art duality, other writers have been more willing to accept this division as central to how audiences have approached *The Birds.* Consider Donald Spoto's analysis. Spoto begins with an observation reminiscent of Sterritt by proclaiming that *The Birds* is "Hitchcock's least accessible motion picture."[12] Spoto then goes on to argue that *The Birds,* in addition to enjoying its reputation as a classically inaccessible film, "reveals its richness like a demanding art novel or a complex symphony, only after considerable effort." The idea of interpretive effort is significant – as is Spoto's reference to complexity – and echoes Sterritt's notion of *The Birds* as a "rewarding achievement." It also follows the venerable argument made famous by Clement Greenberg that real art is difficult art, and even Robin Woods's point that what makes Hitchcock's films worth studying is that they constitute a kind of art.[13] Viewers must be prepared to work for their pleasure, and the reward for their labours will itself constitute an aesthetic achievement. However, having drawn the high art/low art distinction, Spoto then suggests a slightly paradoxical twist, acknowledging that "even ardent Hitchcockians are among those mystified and disappointed by this picture." However, lest this seem too condemnatory, Spoto abruptly rescues the film from the taint of disappointment by claiming that "*The Birds* is certainly among his half-dozen masterpieces and one of the purest, most darkly lyrical films ever created."[14]

In saying that even devoted viewers of Hitchcock's films may be mystified and disappointed by a film that is nevertheless prized for its cinematic purity and dark lyricism, Spoto highlights the importance of the film's paradoxical qualities.[15] Moreover, he sees this mix of impenetrability and artistic merit as coterminous and possibly inter-reliant. But while we might debate whether the difficulties of the film are essential in the construction of its aesthetic quality, or its status as a masterpiece as reasons for its interpretive density, Spoto is certainly correct in assessing the film as mystifying to some and disappointing to others even as these emotions are contained in larger constellations of feelings related to the work as aesthetically appealing. Based on Spoto's description, we might say that the film's inaccessibility and complexity are essential to its greatness, and that in noting the relation between inaccessibility and

12 Spoto, Donald. *The Art of Alfred Hitchcock: Fifty Years of His Motion Pictures* (2nd edition). New York: Anchor Books, 1992, p. 329.

13 Greenberg, Clement. *Art and Culture: Critical Essays.* Boston: Beacon Press, 1971.

14 Spoto, pp. 329–330.

15 This notion echoes the views of Cleanth Brooks regarding poetry. See Brooks, Cleanth. *The Well-Wrought Urn: Studies in the Structure of Poetry.* New York and London: Harcourt, Inc., 1970.

merit, Spoto positions himself in the camp of the enlightened viewer. Indeed, Spoto clearly embraces the high cultural properties of *The Birds* in regarding it as a text that evinces the properties of "a demanding art novel or a complex symphony," a view at odds with the common assessment of Hitchcock as a merely popular filmmaker, but a claim that reveals Spoto's allegiance to the view that *The Birds* is indeed high art. In addition, by placing both audience mystification and audience disappointment side-by-side with these high art qualities, Spoto further proclaims the film's paradoxical structure. Hence, we might argue that to have the rewarding experience David Sterritt celebrates, or to appreciate the visual symphony Donald Spoto describes, is to take seriously rather than literally the causal basis for the birds' behaviour, whereas to be mystified and disappointed is to take literally rather than seriously the same events.

The Nature of *The Birds*/the Birds as Nature

It is fair at this point to pause and to ask how this sequence of distinctions illuminates *The Birds*. As I have already said, explaining the birds and understanding *The Birds* are two distinct interpretive exercises. Thinking about the birds means dealing with problems of causal determination; thinking about *The Birds* raises questions of aesthetic appreciation. Thus, we can say that when we discuss the birds, we are talking about the problem of how to account for, or how to explain, their behaviour, and this means treating the birds as natural objects perhaps best described in the discourse of natural science. On the other hand, when we discuss *The Birds*, we are not dealing with explanation but with understanding, and therefore our focus shifts from the determination of causality to the figurative domain of aesthetics.

In addition, as I have noted above, these two interpretive modalities can produce rather opposed readings. In the first case, it is possible that viewers who are preoccupied by Hitchcock's decision not to explain the birds' behaviour may find the film ambiguous and aesthetically weak; their response will be shaped by a concern with the narrative gap between the birds and their conduct, a gap that for many constitutes a significant impasse. On the other side, those viewers who feel no obligation to explain the birds seem more likely to appreciate the film for its complexity, and to regard the work overall as aesthetically successful. When we focus on the problems raised by the birds then, we are returning to my students' concern with how best to explain them; and when we focus on *The Birds* as a cultural object, we are directing our attention to the work in respect of its artistic dimensions. A simple schematic of these points, outlined in the following table, may be useful.

The Birds	High art	Complexity	Human nature
The birds	Low art	Ambiguity	Nature

As already indicated, some viewers find *The Birds* to be a complex work with high artistic ambitions which can best be understood by acknowledging its refusal to accede to the causal laws of the natural sciences. In this respect, such viewers are untroubled by the lack of conventional explanation for the behaviour of the birds. On the other hand, there are other viewers who regard *The Birds* as an ambiguous film precisely because the birds defy causal or rational explanation. These viewers remain unconvinced of the film's artistic merits owing to its failure to rationally account for its principal dramatic action. According to this view the film is simply ambiguous, not complex. The issue seems to come down to whether one demands an explanation for the birds as necessary to an appreciation of *The Birds*.

Many readers will recognize the outlines of this argument as deriving from the philosopher, Wilhelm Dilthey. Dilthey argued that it is because we can interpret nature as an impersonal object or assemblage of essential forces that we can focus on the invariable laws of nature without being concerned by the absence of intention in our explanations of natural phenomena. I can explain the motions of the planets without worrying about the intentions behind their movements, for there is none. Indeed, for Dilthey, explanations of nature inevitably entail a repudiation of agency, as the certitude of unvarying laws is required to render natural phenomena objective, and not as part of some grand plan or teleology. Thus, nature can be explained because we can use mathematical principles and an ahistorical standpoint to produce provable predictions.

By contrast, Dilthey argues, human nature is approached not via an ahistorical and strictly empirical mode of interpretation, but according to the principle of understanding, or *verstehen*.[16] Whereas the main procedure of the natural sciences is to search for a causal explanation, the central procedure of the human sciences is to understand in respect of our common lived experience. As Dilthey says:

> The human sciences are distinguished from the natural sciences in that the latter take as their object features which appear to consciousness as

16 The difference between understanding and explanation I am using here is commonly located in the works of Dilthey and Max Weber, the concepts – *erklären* (to explain) and *verstehen* (to understand) – were first introduced in academic circles by the German historiographer, J. G. Droysen.

> coming from outside, as phenomena, and as given in particulars; for the former, in contrast, the object appears as coming from within, as a reality, and as a vivid original whole. It follows therefore that for the natural sciences an ordering of nature is achieved only through a succession of conclusions by means of linking of hypotheses. For the human sciences, on the contrary, it follows that the connectedness of psychic life is given as an original and general foundation. Nature we explain, the life of the soul we understand.[17]

Dilthey's claim that we *explain* nature but *understand* human nature is well known in hermeneutics. As Richard Palmer says, Dilthey demonstrated that "understanding is the mental process by which we comprehend living human experience," for whereas "scientific explanations are seldom valued in themselves but for the sake of something else," understanding – in Dilthey's sense – is "that special moment when life understands life."[18] In fact, Dilthey's influence has been extensive, and his work has found a home in a number of social sciences.[19] Along with the obvious contributions his work made to philosophical biology, Dilthey's investigations were also important in the development of phenomenology and show up especially in the work of Hans-Georg Gadamer.[20] Echoes of Dilthey's thinking are also apparent in the work of British philosopher Peter Winch who claims that while "our understanding of natural phenomena is in terms of the notion of cause," an "understanding of social phenomena involves the categories of motives and reasons."[21] Dilthey's

---

17 In Howard, Roy J. *Three Faces of Hermeneutics: An Introduction to Current Theories of Understanding.* Los Angeles and London: University of California Press, 1982, pp. 15–16.

18 Palmer, Richard. *Hermeneutics: Interpretation Theory in Schleiermacher, Dilthey, Heidegger, and Gadamer.* Evanston: Northwestern University Press, 1969, p. 115.

19 See, for example, Giddens, Anthony. *New Rules of Sociological Method: A Positive Critique of Interpretive Sociologies.* New York: Basic Books, 1976.

20 The reference to Gadamer is, of course, to Gadamer, Han-Georg. *Truth and Method* (Second, Revised edition). Translated by Joel Weinsheimer and Donald G. Marshall. London and New York: Continuum. On the matter of philosophical biology, several sources might be mentioned, including the work of Erazim Kohak whose nature philosophy is plainly indebted to Dilthey's thinking: "For, in understanding as in sense perception, it is when we stop speaking that we begin to hear; when we stop staring, things emerge before our eyes; when we stop insisting on our explanations, we can begin to understand" (Kohak, Erazim. *The Embers and the Stars: A Philosophical Inquiry into the Moral Sense of Nature.* Chicago and London: University of Chicago Press, 1984, p. 40).

21 Winch, Peter. *The Idea of a Social Sciences and its Relation to Philosophy* (orig. 1958). New York and London: Routledge Books, 2008, p. xi. A similar point is drawn by Roy

influence has spread widely, and although his investigations failed to achieve a completely systematic unity, the problems that preoccupied Dilthey remain central to current historical and hermeneutical investigations. To this day, in diverse areas such as continental ethics, or philosophical humanism, the distinction between explanation (nature) and understanding (human nature) remains important.[22]

The Question of Genre

Doing justice to the impact Dilthey has had on current philosophy and interpretation theory would take me well beyond the point I want to make in bringing his distinction between explanation and understanding to bear on Hitchcock's work. Therefore, I will put aside a more detailed discussion of Dilthey's philosophical legacy and refocus my attention on film analysis so that I might circle back to *The Birds*. I will do this by way of concentrating on the matter of cinematic genre.

Keeping Dilthey in view, let us consider *The Birds* as it expresses the dichotomy between explanation and understanding in relation to the structural properties that define it as belonging to a specific genre. This is a bit of a challenge, however, because *The Birds* has been described over the years as falling into a range of genres, including mystery, horror, drama, and even science fiction. However, it is the film's designation as belonging to the disaster movie genre which, in my view, has the greatest claim on the movie's generic affiliation. Although many film scholars have pointed out that *The Birds* is somewhat unstable in terms of genre, a strong case has been made for seeing

---

Howard mentioned above, who distinguishes between the worlds of "happening" and "acting." As he writes, "birds building nests belong" to the world of happening, while "people convening to write a constitution, to put on a play, or possibility to build houses belong to the latter [the world of acting]" (Howard, p. 40).

22 I should add that in some circles the distinction that I am drawing from Dilthey goes by different terms. In some philosophical circles, the difference is sometimes described as being between *naturalistic* and *intentional* explanations, though the word *explanation* is used in both instances here (a "naturalistic explanation," and an "intentional explanation") and thus some confusion might arise. But the point is essentially the same. When our ability to explain things naturalistically fails us, it is sometimes easy to fall back on an intentional account, and hence the invocation of deities, spirits, and supernaturalistic powers when a naturalistic explanation is not possible. In the case of *The Birds*, we might say that viewers might be tempted to switch from naturalistic explanations of the birds to intentional accounts of their motives to bridge the gap I have been describing.

the film as most closely fitting the disaster category, and this is the argument I will follow.[23]

An elementary but significant feature of the disaster genre is found in the work of film scholar Howard Suber.[24] Suber says that the principal theme in the disaster film – that is, the disaster itself – is generally insufficient to carry the entire narrative of the film, for disasters lack the agentic malevolence that makes for a persuasive nemesis. Hence, he says that disaster films need a secondary story (or second narrative level) to keep the film from sliding into banality. This second narrative level is not simply a different version of the prevailing disaster, however, and is usually developed in the context of a love story or by way of focusing on the main character's efforts to reunite with a lover, lost friends, or family members. Viewers might try to explain the disaster, but the second narrative level demands understanding. In Suber's view, the disaster film requires a corresponding and complementary subplot focused on the interplay of human emotions. Indeed, we often refer to this secondary plot as the human-interest element, a parallel storyline that provides the viewer with a personalized entry point into the narrative's events. For the disaster film to be successful, the audience must care about certain of the characters, and this is the task assigned to the human-interest story. A volcanic eruption is visually arresting and awe-inspiring, but without a rag-tag group of intrepid explorers trying desperately to escape the sun-hot lava sliding toward the unprotected hamlet there is no genuine narrative to captivate the viewer. Vampires are unnatural and malevolent; natural disasters like volcanoes are merely natural. The audience needs that secondary storyline to feel the tug of emotional engagement.

Most viewers are aware of this arrangement, and probably understand the intrinsic value of the secondary plot as it shows the impact of the disaster on the safety and security of a particular (and sometimes privileged) group of people. However, Suber goes further than merely asserting the narrative value of centring the disaster film on the emotional lives of characters playing the role of protagonists. To be sure, the lure of identification is important, but the principal difficulty the disaster film must confront is the facelessness of the film's adversarial force. Audiences cannot easily muster animosity against the impersonal powers of nature – floods, hurricanes, earthquakes, fires – for

23 See, for example, Humbert, David. "Desire and Monstrosity in the Disaster Film: Alfred Hitchcock's *The Birds*." *Contagion: Journal of Violence, Mimesis, and Culture*, 17, 2010, pp. 87–103.

24 Suber, Howard. *The Power of Film*. Studio City, California: Michael Wiese Productions, 2006.

these powers represent fate, not intent. Hence the argument favouring the disaster film's traditional structural form, Suber maintains, is simple: "Nature, by itself, is an inadequate dramatic antagonist."[25]

Suber's point is significant for suggesting that villainy is most effective when constituted from the sphere of intentionality. The impersonality of the natural disaster militates against the assignment of intention, and thus to generate dramatic tension the narrative conventionally includes a portrayal of the struggles of a select community or individual. In *The Birds*, therefore, it follows from Suber's analysis that the birds are inadequate as dramatic antagonists because they are a part of nature, and thus a secondary story is formed around the human emotions at work in a series of familial and romantic relationships at the secondary narrative level. Rather than focus on the entire population of Bodega Bay where every resident is under attack from the birds, Hitchcock trains his story on the Brenner family and Mitch Brenner's new love interest, Melanie Daniels. This concentration on a subset of the town's residents is a necessary part of the storytelling process.

What is particularly compelling in Suber's argument is that the structural form that he identifies helps to further our appreciation of the dichotomy Dilthey draws between explanation and understanding. If our attention is directed to the problem of the causal inexplicability of the birds, we lose sight of the secondary narrative level where a different interpretive practice, that of understanding, is at least possible. This isn't to say that the birds are unimportant to *The Birds*. However, an explanation for their behaviour certainly distracts us from trying to understand the lived experience of the principal characters. If we are to enjoy the complex and rewarding film as described by Sterritt and Spoto, we need to understand the inherent problem that arises if we become overly concerned with mere explanation.

By placing Suber alongside Dilthey we can connect the issue of cinematic structure with the hermeneutical problem of separating explanation from understanding. This is because Suber's point concerning nature's insufficiency as dramatic antagonist can be partly accounted for by the corresponding claim that nature is something for which we seek explanations. In other words, explanations are provable accounts, not lived experiences, and there is technically nothing about nature that is antagonistic from a narrative viewpoint. Volcanoes do not erupt because they are evil; they erupt because they are volcanoes. Hence, nature's inadequacy for the part of antagonist is connected to the fact that not only do we explain rather than understand natural events, but natural events can *only* be explained and never understood in the

25 Suber, p. xx.

way that understanding happens in our encounters with human nature. The consequences that natural events hold for humans (earthquakes as well as murderous birds) are precisely the sorts of things that we can know, things that are true independently of whether an acceptable explanation is discovered. So, we can understand the Brenner's fear and anxiety because we can imagine the potency of their emotional and physical reactions to their situation. This is true even though it is impossible for us to find an explanation for the birds of *The Birds* that would be universally agreed upon. Explanation, one might say, can be a distraction from the human business of making sense of the lived experiences of people.

The Birds: Sounding Off

There is one other aspect to *The Birds* that further illustrates this argument concerning explanation, understanding, and intention, and this is the soundscape Hitchcock and his audio technicians developed for the production. In an analysis of the elaboration of Hitchcock's aural style, Elisabeth Weis famously observed that *The Birds* "deals abstractly with fear" rather than with concrete objects perceived as inherently frightening. Sound, rather than sight, in other words, was the primary mode by which the terror of the birds was conveyed, and in a clever and rhetorically sophisticated argument, Weis turns the idea of fear of the unseen into a form of fright greater than that which is generated by the object that stands before you.

What made Weis' position unusual is the fact of the birds themselves – their actual appearance in the film – for they are clearly represented as a manifestation of the traditional object of fear. But as Weis sees it, the birds lack what we might call the affective gravity to serve as classical objects of fear, for they are neither abject nor grotesque; neither uncanny nor surreal; neither conventionally revolting nor classically frightening. The birds are not monsters; they are only birds. Hence Weis suggests that the birds "are less important for what they are than for the reactions they elicit."[26] And such reactions as the viewer experiences, she goes on, are not produced by the film's images of massing and dive-bombing birds, but by the electronically produced bird shrieks on the soundtrack, the emotional centre of the film. For Weis, the dissociative quality of sound in *The Birds* is its most horrifying feature.

26 Weis, Elisabeth. "The Evolution of Hitchcock's Aural Style and Sound in *The Birds*." In *Film Sound: Theory and Practice*, edited by Elisabeth Weis and John Belton. New York: Columbia University Press, 1985, p. 303.

Many other writers, some clearly influenced by Weis, have remarked upon the sound design of *The Birds* as significant in the way the film develops tension, with its discordant and at time disquieting properties. Not all of these commentators view the central role played by the film's sound production in as favourable a light as Weis, but there is general agreement nonetheless that the film's acoustic design is a powerful and unsettling experience.[27] Moreover, given that the film has no musical score, a number of writers have noted the film's many scenes marked by a disconcerting silence, seeking to enclose these sequences within their investigations of the soundtrack. For her part, Weis sees these noiseless moments as an equally significant part of the film's acoustic design, arguing that Hitchcock's mastery of the overall aural production is so precise "that the birds can convey terror even when they are silent or just making an occasional caw or flutter."[28] That the innocent wing flap conveys terror owes to the fact that throughout *The Birds*, silence operates as an anticipatory feature, in the way that shadows or facial close-ups serve as foreshadowing devices in the visual domain. William Rothman makes a similar point, arguing that "the eerie stillness" of the birds prefigures in its ominous quietude the anticipation of "a sonic beating of wings" that is more frightening than any of the film's visual effects.[29] Because we are viewers focused on the screen directly in front of us, we cannot turn our heads to locate the

27 One example of a negative assessment of the soundscape used in *The Birds* appears in Penelope Huston's critique of Hitchcock and the *auteur* approach to film studies more generally. Huston claims that in *The Birds* "most of the menace [comes] from the electronic soundtrack, to cover the fact that the birds are not really doing their stuff." Huston's complaint that the birds are not "doing their stuff," that is, not up to the task of terrifying the audience, rests on an unstated principle: namely, that the menace (or perhaps the suspense) in *The Birds* is illegitimate for being derived from the film's sound and not from its images. Of course, this is a somewhat dubious proposition as there is no particular reason why Hitchcock should have been beholden to cinema's visual element that he would forswear an interest in the emotive power of sound. What is significant about Huston's comment, however, is that it indicates a tendency among film critics – less common today – to disparage sound as inferior to the visual. Perhaps this hierarchical ordering has something to do with the fact that sound is important insofar as it disappears whereas images must be stabilized in our field of vision to be interpreted – we do, after all, experience after images but not after sounds. As filmmakers have come to appreciate the way that sound has the capacity to contextualize images, we can readily observe cinema's increasing attention to sound design. See Huston, Penelope. "The Figure in the Carpet." *Sight and Sound*, Fall (4), 1963, p. 164.

28 Weis, p. 305.

29 Rothman, William. "The Universal Hitchcock." In *A Companion to Alfred Hitchcock*, edited by Thomas Leitch and Leland Pogue. Oxford: Wiley Blackwell, 2014, p. 347.

source of the birds in advance of their attack; they arrive on the scene after the sound of their approach, and it is this sound that conjures up the image in advance of its on-screen appearance. Thus, fear comes from the expectation of the image, not from the image itself.

Conclusion

At several points in *The Birds* characters ask 'why.' At first, the question is focused on things that are merely unusual: Why are there so many birds in the sky? Are they gathering because they have been blown inland by a storm? Has a stray gull been distracted by light? Was an accident at sea simply a result of the birds' voracious appetites as they set upon some fishing nets? Later the characters are shown asking far more serious kinds of questions: Why are the birds attacking? Is there something intentional in their behaviour that has previously been unrecognized? Can we find a pattern to their behaviour that can be decoded to explain what is happening? Why now, and why here?

Dilthey restricted motive (as well as reason) to the realm of understanding and thus to the domain of the human sciences and human behaviour. Nonetheless, in asking why the birds attack, many viewers appear concerned with uncovering a motive that resists reduction to a strictly naturalistic cause such as would be the case in arguing that the birds are merely acting on instinct or are suffering from disease. This concern with motive is problematic in the context of the conventional disaster film which, by definition, is entirely unconcerned with motive – at least at the primary narrative level, for to ask why the volcano has erupted is to ask an uninteresting question in the realm of the disaster film. For as Suber indicates, the traditional disaster movie deals with environmental and other sorts of catastrophes, such as fires, tsunamis, and earthquakes, and to ask about motive with such events as these is to ask an unanswerable and ultimately foolish question. However, in making the antagonistic element in *The Birds* biological creatures, Hitchcock has stretched the notion of the traditional disaster film in an interesting direction. Hitchcock's birds are not like earthquakes, cyclones, or floods, despite being firmly located in nature in everyday, conventional descriptions. And yet their conduct is beyond any reasonable notion of normal avian behaviour and therefore falls outside the laws of nature. On the other hand, animal behaviour cannot always be easily ascribed to the clockwork regularity of natural law, for behaviour is by definition driven by a range of factors that will often include motive, even among animals. That the birds wreak havoc on Bodega Bay is certainly very much a disaster, and that birds are a part of the natural order is undoubted. However, their behaviour is so aberrant that one might reasonably wonder just how firmly they are rooted in nature given their unpredictability. *The Birds*, we might say, are as unpredictable as they are inexplicable. Still, the question "why do they attack?" continues to be posed as relevant to the hermeneutical practice of Hitchcock scholarship.

This movement from mainly observational questions, about things for which explanations are possible to questions for which no explanations will be found, parallels the film's narrative movement, as well. *The Birds* intensifies the call for explanation as it develops, building toward a climax of anxious anticipation only to end with its main characters setting off on a journey as hopeless as it is reckless. The frustration produced by this strategy prompted Jean-André Fieschi to say that in *The Birds* "the tension isn't aimed at solving a mystery, but at elaborating and developing it."[30] That *The Birds* does not solve the mystery it develops is down to its overt refusal to explain the birds. This is a failure to some and a triumph to others. In either case, however, it clearly suggests that the brilliance and the failing of *The Birds* is fundamentally the same: a proclamation of the victory of mystery.

---

30 Cited in McElhaney, Joe. "Touching the Surface: Marnie, Melodrama, Modernism." *Alfred Hitchcock Centenary Essays*, p. 88.

Chapter 4

TELLING THE TRUTH AND *THE WRONG/ED MAN*

I have now undertaken, in my eighty-third year, to tell you my personal myth. I can only make direct statements, only "tell stories." Whether or not the stories are 'true' is not the problem. The only question is whether what I tell is *my* fable, *my* truth.

– Carl Jung[1]

A life story does not consist simply of a collection of facts or incidents. It also requires sequence, since from sequence causality can be inferred; and notions like causality, accident, and reasons are crucial in shaping the meaning of a life story.

– Charlotte Linde[2]

Looking back is sometimes amusing – and sometimes humiliating. It is not a thing I care to do as a rule.

– Alfred Hitchcock[3]

A Childish Prisoner

Throughout the course of his life, Alfred Hitchcock enjoyed telling interviewers about the time he was locked in a jail cell at the behest of his father.

The incident was prompted by an act of misbehaviour that itself is a subject of speculation, but from most accounts it was of so trifling a nature that

1 Jung, C. G. *Memories, Dreams, Reflections* (orig. 1957), edited by Aniela Jaffe, translated by Clara Winston and Richard Winston. New York: Vintage Books, 1989, p. 3.

2 Linde, Charlotte. *Life Stories: The Creation of Coherence.* Oxford: Oxford University Press, 1993, p. 8.

3 Hitchcock, Alfred. "My Screen Memories." In *Hitchcock on Hitchcock: Selected Writings and Interviews,* edited by Sidney Gottlieb. Berkeley and London: University of California Press, 1995, p. 7.

in later years Hitchcock said that he could not recall with certainty what he had done to upset his parents. Whether the offense was grave or not was of little concern to Alfred's father, however, for William Hitchcock's idea of discipline was tinged with Edwardian notions of strict parental duty and in consequence of Alfred's misconduct he resolved to teach his young son a lesson. Having composed a message for the on-duty officer, William sent young Alfred off to the local police station with instructions to hand the note to the officer. The policeman read the memo, and then escorted Alfred to the cellblock where he locked the boy in for several minutes before releasing him with an ominous warning: "This is what we do to naughty boys." Hitchcock said the trauma of that moment of sham incarceration accounted for many of his lifelong anxieties, especially those regarding the police.

The story has the earmarks of a typical Hitchcock narrative with its unflattering portrayal of the police, its depiction of the innocent subject caught in the grip of heartless institutional forces, and its representation of justice as unfeeling in its instrumentality. It is no surprise, then, that the story appears in virtually every biographical account of Hitchcock where it is usually presented as illustrating that decisive moment at which his fears and phobias concerning authority figures were crystallized. For his part, Hitchcock was aware that the story, which intimated that he was a victim of paternal cruelty hard to imagine today, had a darkly comic side as well, and thus in his adult life he tended to relate the tale in a light-hearted style, pausing with calculated practice at anticipated laugh lines. That the story finds a place in the standard profile of Hitchcock's upbringing indicates its value for those wanting to understand the reasons behind the director's critique of authority, for the narrative appears tailor made for the task. Nonetheless, there are a few things about the story that are worth exploring when considering the narrative as a potentially determinative event in young Alfred's life.

Consider first that the police officer is a willing accomplice of Alfred's father, and that he plays the part of surrogate parent and the role of state official with disturbing keenness. This is significant insofar as the tale represents the police as an extension of the family, a fact that suggests that the law expands (and to a degree usurps) the rights and obligations of familial authority. More important, erasing the boundary between public and private spheres suggests the prospect of an endless encroachment of bureaucratic power into one's personal world. Hence, this blurring of the legal and the ethical became an important theme in Hitchcock's work, and in this anecdote, we can see the basic structure behind this merger. In the tale of Hitchcock's faux incarceration, both moral precepts and common folktales ("this is how little boys should behave") come into direct contact with the established authority of the law, an authority ordinarily external to the sphere of the family whose foundations rest on the ethical precedents of the community. Moreover, in being warned by the policeman that "this is what *we* do to little boys," the indistinct reference for the pronoun is both interesting and fearsome. Was this the voice of his father, the police as an institution, or authority writ large? For young Alfred, this confusion would also have been compounded by the union of folk wisdom and legal doctrine, for the claim that little boys should avoid misbehaving is a maxim, not a law; a form of proverbial wisdom steeped in nostalgia, not an instrument of legal practice. Consequently, to be threatened with jail for a harmless moment of childish disobedience would be horrible not only for the separation anxiety it might inflame, but also for violating the border separating the judicial from the moral. The resulting ontological insecurity, the persistent fear that no enclave was safe from the reach of carceral forces, effectively describes Hitchcock's description of his lifelong anxieties.

Along with the conflation of family and precinct, the anecdote also shows the police displacing justice with terror, ousting reason with fear. Even as the incarceration story collapses distinctions between the private and the public and erases the boundary between the ethical and the forensic, it preaches the ameliorative power of anxiety. Although Alfred had broken no laws, the penalty meted out for his conduct was determined beyond the safety of the family in a context formally set aside for criminal activities. This fusion of domestic and public spaces points to the permeability of the metaphysical boundaries within which the innocent might feel safely enclosed, a persistent theme in Hitchcock's films. And for a terrified child, it might also signal the panoptic quality and disciplinary power of the state. In private or in public places, young Alfred learned, naughtiness will be detected and punished severely. Fear of the police thus ran parallel to an equally pervasive fear of the panoptic society where disciplinary power, diffused across every level of social life, had also invaded the family home.

The Truth of the Matter

In addition to adding some context to the detention incident, these observations help to clarify a possible reason for Hitchcock's tendency to represent social and cultural authority as forces more to be feared than admired. Hitchcock's apprehensions concerning authority, therefore, might be a product of early childhood trauma. This would seem to be the point behind Hitchcock's intentions when relating the tale. "This is why I have turned out as I have," he seemed to be saying.

Yet, the story also has certain problems that have provoked a substantive question that continues to concern some Hitchcock scholars. This question focuses not on the theme of traumatic memories and their impact in later life, but on the narrative details Hitchcock provided in telling the story. The question biographers sometimes raise is short and direct: Did it really happen?

As I have already mentioned, this story is featured in virtually every account of Hitchcock's childhood, yet many of his biographers – the very people who report the story – regard the tale as suspect. Some have argued that the story is simply too incredible to be taken seriously, and that it represents the sort of playful nonsense one would expect from a consummate storyteller – Hitchcock was, after all, a first-rate prankster. However, film historians are not swayed to the argument that the story is false simply because Hitchcock was a renowned joker. They are also suspicious of the story because the narrative itself is an unreliable document, a tale for which there is no definitive text. Many of the story's details varied over the years depending on when and to whom Hitchcock was speaking. In some accounts Hitchcock says he was as young as five or six; in others he suggests he may have been closer to eleven. Other aspects of the narrative change as well, including the nature of his misbehaviour, and the possibility of a previous friendship between his father and the police officer who supposedly agreed to William's request. Though many of these inconsistencies are minor, they have fortified the scepticism of writers who are doubtful that the narrative recalls an actual event. Even as his biographers want to preserve the story as containing something of value in relating Hitchcock's life, they simultaneously appear reluctant to attest to its truth.

Among the many biographers who tell the story while simultaneously expressing doubt about the imprisonment anecdote is Patrick McGilligan. McGilligan complains that

> when Hitchcock told the story to interviewers, as he did relentlessly over the years, the story grew and mutated. The infraction changed. His age changed. [...] Hitchcock's maternal grandfather was a constable [...] and in at least one version the policeman in the boyhood's [*sic*] story was a family friend, in on the joke.[4]

All of this is true. Hitchcock enjoyed telling the story to interviewers down the years (many of whom would have known about it from previous interviews) even as he was unconcerned about keeping the details perfectly aligned from one account to the next. However, owing to the possibility that Hitchcock was a young boy when the imprisonment is alleged to have taken place, it

---

4 McGilligan, Patrick. *Alfred Hitchcock: A Life in Darkness and Light.* New York: HarperCollins Publishers, 2003, p. 8.

could be argued that it is unfair to hold Alfred to so high a standard as to appear to expect something close to perfect recollection. Naturally, there are reasons some writers want to hold Hitchcock to this standard. The two most obvious reasons are the frequency with which Hitchcock related the story, and the importance he appears to have attached to its explanatory power. These motives have combined to make the narrative an enduring element in accounts of Alfred's formative years while also serving as foundational to the sensibility underlying his art. Hitchcock kept the story alive by recounting it in the course of numerous interviews. On television programmes and in public speeches, he related the event not merely as an amusing story (though that dimension was usually present), but as an actual recollection he was certain his audience would find both entertaining and instructive.[5]

Whereas these inconsistencies have led McGilligan (and others) to doubt the tale's veracity, it is curious that despite their scepticism, these doubters continue to include Hitchcock's incarceration story in their biographies. This observation is not meant as a criticism of the biographer's craft or as a recommendation that their books would be better off without the story. Rather, I am simply observing that whereas Hitchcock historians remain committed to keeping the incarceration narrative going, they have sometimes found themselves forced to retreat factuality when assessing the story's value. That is, the story may not be factual, but it is a useful and valuable tale, nonetheless. It is not truth that makes the story valued, but some other quality.

Indeed, some writers seem willing to take the imprisonment tale not as an actual recounting, but as a demonstration of the power of narrative in the process of sense-making. Many biographers regard the story of Hitchcock's detention as a fictional depiction of the sort of thing that *could* have happened rather than as a factual account of what *did* happen. The incarceration anecdote remains important to Hitchcock scholars – even those who assume that it is false – because they believe that even though it is likely untrue it nonetheless constitutes a valuable contribution to our understanding of the director's life story.

The challenge I want to take up in this chapter, then, is to investigate this childhood story more closely before connecting the results of this inquiry to my reading of Hitchcock's film, *The Wrong Man* (1956). First, I want to discuss the incarceration anecdote in order to uncover the reasons why a story, which

5 A notable illustration of his fondness for the tale appears in his acceptance speech for his Lifetime Achievement Award from the American Film Institute in 1979. In this account, Hitchcock describes himself as being "no more than six years of age." https://www.youtube.com/watch?v=pb5VdGCQFOM&t=339s.

many writers believe to be untrue, is told by those same writers as an important contribution to our understanding of Hitchcock's life. What especially intrigues me is the conflict that arises when one accepts that a story can be biographically relevant when it can also be shown that the story is not causally determinative. This disjuncture raises several interesting questions. How can you relate a tale admired for its subsequent influence on your subject's life when you also believe that tale is inauthentic? What categories aside from true or false can be applied in the case of a biographical reminiscence? To be more specific, if the story is empirically false, does it possess explanatory value in the context of Hitchcock's life, nonetheless? If so, how do we define this value? These questions are presented in the context of a discussion of the various authors who have attempted to deal with the problem of a false narrative to which they nevertheless appear in other respects to remain committed. The imprisonment narrative would seem to be important owing to its value as a sense-making device in the context of Hitchcock's life story. That it is probably false means seeking out some category other than truth by which its biographical significance can be preserved.

Second, following my analysis of the ways that various writers have presented the incarceration narrative, I turn to Hitchcock's film, *The Wrong Man* (1956). Hitchcock's childhood anecdote and his 1956 film are tangentially related insofar as they share a mutual concern with questions of truth and falsity in the context of judicial reasoning. These common interests include the problem of how best to prioritize our interpretations of events in respect of the opposition between empirical and figurative readings. And, in both instances, the matter of the law is uppermost as an interpretive procedure that colours both narratives in the stark hues of inhuman bureaucratic proceduralism. Alfred Hitchcock's and Manny Balestrero's situations are representative of a cultural predicament in which the innocent person, in being interpellated by the law, is given shelter in a newly constituted criminal identity as a way of escaping the trauma of accusation and the dissolution of familial relations. Although there are obvious differences in their situations, there are interesting points of resonance between Balestrero and Hitchcock that become apparent once we consider how, in both narratives, truth is ultimately rendered irrelevant to the proceedings of the legal machinery. While the truth of Hitchcock's story remains a point of debate, and Balestrero's harrowing ordeal is a matter of public record, in both accounts there are points of contact which, if provisionally regarded as authentic in respect of their meanings, allow us to read *The Wrong Man* as a meditation on the sorts of concerns Hitchcock's tale – true or false – reveals in its symbolic, mythical formulation. Both men are defined as having violated the dictates of the law – defined rather informally in Hitchcock's case – and both suffer the consequent application of legal procedures. Incarceration strips Manny and Alfred temporarily of their freedom and renders them acutely conscious of their vulnerability to bureaucratic powers. In suggesting the autonomy of administrative forces, I am following a line of critical analysis that will be filled in more completely in the latter part of the chapter. In anticipation of that argument, let me state here that it is important to my reading that truth is understood as an incidental consideration in both circumstances, for with no guarantee that the truth of the matter is provable we are encouraged to accede to the sense-making measures of an anonymous bureaucratic apparatus. In that sense, the two narratives can be understood as existential meditations on the nightmare of randomness.

The Truth of a False Story and the Falsity of a True Story

What would follow if we considered Hitchcock's incarceration story as symbolic, or figurative, and not as the recollection of an actual event? This approach certainly has its advantages. For one thing, the interpretive freedom we are allowed in putting the question of factuality to the side is appealing in the context of both literary and psychological approaches to the story's significance in Hitchcock's life. Keeping in mind that the event would have occurred over a century ago – Hitchcock was born in 1899 – and that it would therefore be impossible to find definitive proof of the tale's veracity, a symbolic reading removes the need to uncover such proof. And because it releases us from the obligation to find irrefutable proof, different interpretations are allowed to flourish unconstrained by the domination of empiricism.

Figurative readings have certain disadvantages, however, the most obvious being that in leaving unsettled the question of whether the incident actually happened, we lose the conventional value a personal story serves in underpinning a process of causal determination. If the story is an allegorical or symbolic anecdote told without regard to sequence or chronology, then it could not have influenced Hitchcock in the way he traditionally related. By turning to a symbolic strategy of interpretation we forfeit the determinative force of causality, and this loss makes the story's claim to influence difficult to establish.

In recognition of this difficulty, one of the strategies pursued in several allegorical readings is to argue for the plausibility of the story while remaining non-committal as to its veracity. In other words, one common approach favoured by those in what might be called the allegory camp is to argue that the story could certainly have occurred given that certain contextual factors make the story plausible, even while commitment to the matter of truth or falsity must be held at arm's length. For instance, Donald Spoto says that given

Hitchcock's "Cockney family background in a society that hated policemen," there is every possibility that the story was fabricated, for in a cultural milieu defined by suspicions and fears about authority figures, the local police were very high on that list.[6] Put simply, there are sociological reasons relating to class and geography that could explain why we might be sceptical of the story. Spoto provides us with these reasons by offering some contextual information about Hitchcock, his family's socio-economic background, and a generalization about prevailing societal attitudes. In making these observations Spoto provides motives for an obvious conclusion: Hitchcock's father never did the dastardly deed. However, Spoto himself stops short of explicitly advocating this conclusion. He is prepared to call the story's veracity indeterminate and leave it at that.

There are problems with indeterminacy when trying to relate a life. For one, it can leave the biographer in an awkward situation in the effort to balance antithetical positions. Writers are keen to tell the story despite the abovementioned reasons for being sceptical – after all, it is an especially vivid and useful story – but they are equally concerned to establish their credentials as serious-minded investigators. Hence various forms of equivocation have been practised by Hitchcock scholars trying to determine how best to relate a story they suspect might be false – including Donald Spoto. They want to continue to tell the story of young Alfred's time in the cells because biographical reminiscences are helpful in revealing character, motivation, and meaning. At the same time, they want to avoid appearing committed to a story whose veracity is questionable. Hence the rhetorical manoeuvring ensues, for if the tale cannot be proven to be authentic just how should it be presented?

Donald Spoto deals with this concern by straddling the divide between truth and falsity, stationing one foot firmly in each province, and leaving the question of truth open to the reader. A different strategy is to challenge the significance of these provinces altogether and to argue that there is a false dichotomy at play in seeking to determine between the true and the false. With this strategy, the story of Alfred's traumatization at the hands of the British police does not require definitive adjudication because the truth or falseness of the narrative is irrelevant. Adopting this approach, one takes the question of the story's truth or falsity as a distraction rather than an imperative. And once we leave the issue of authenticity behind, the issue that emerges is how to separate doubt from belief while continuing to hold onto both. That

6 See Spoto, Donald. *The Dark Side of Genius: The Life of Alfred Hitchcock.* New York: Ballantine Books, 1983, p. 15.

is, the biographer's challenge is how to doubt the truth of the story while having faith in the story's value.

The ingenuity of writers managing this juggling act is notable. For instance, consider how a sympathetic biographer like John Russell Taylor tries to find the appropriate balance between belief and doubt. In his account of the incident, Taylor tells the essential details of the prison narrative in the course of relating the story of Hitchcock's childhood before saying, with no apparent sense of irony, that "Hitchcock himself has told the story so often he is not sure himself any more if it is true."[7] Now, while Taylor is probably aiming here for humour, there are also serious issues at play in his suggestion. For example, by referencing Hitchcock's failing memory, Taylor releases himself from any obligation he might have as a biographer to settle the question of the story's truth or falsity. If Hitchcock's memory is the culprit for our state of indeterminacy, can Taylor – or anyone else – really be expected to know the truth? Hitchcock's uncertainty regarding the certainty of his incarceration story makes third party accounts of that tale entirely uncertain.

However, if we accept Taylor's speculation that the question of the prison story's validity is lost in the mists of Hitchcock's fading memory (if it was, in fact, a genuine memory at all), the story's value would now consist in providing a context for understanding specific themes in Hitchcock's work even though it describes no actual event around which this context was formed. The story is valuable as a symbolic narrative, then, and not as an empirically verifiable event. The narrative is not a faithful memory but a moral lesson concerning the legacy of a painful ordeal – even an account of how childhood trauma can persist to the point of providing a crucial touchstone for the adult artist – though in the case of this particular artist the story would appear to be a fanciful one.

Taylor goes further than promoting sheer indeterminacy in the way that Donald Spoto favours, perhaps because he is aware that the bugbear of factuality has not been dispensed with entirely even with his appeal to humour and uncertainty. Some other element is required to further advance his claim that truth and falsity are equivalent – or, more properly, irrelevant. Taylor's addition to his argument concerning the incarceration tale is to recast it not as a strictly humorous, indeterminate tale, but as an example of an apocryphal story. He writes:

7 Taylor, John Russell. *Hitch: The Life and Times of Alfred Hitchcock* (orig. 1978). New York: De Capo Press, 1996, p. 28. For a similar view, see Sloan, Jane E. *Alfred Hitchcock: A Filmography and Bibliography*. Berkeley: University of California Press, 1993, pp. 1–2.

> The story is so convenient, accounting as it does for Hitchcock's renowned fear of the police, the angst connected with arrest and confinement in his films, that one might suspect it of being in the *ben trovato* category.[8]

A ben trovato tale, a "well invented story," is one that should be true, but which may well be false. Its principal function is to not to recollect but to illuminate. Such stories have appeared in a variety of cultural forms, though their empirical falseness is usually recognized from the start. The main reason we tell (and retell) them, therefore, has little (or really nothing) to do with their truth status, but with their value as illustrative fables – in this case, a fable that helps explain Hitchcock's views of authority.

Or so it would seem. The problem with Taylor's suggestion is rather basic, for if the incarceration story is understood as a ben trovato tale, it falls plainly on the side of falsity, and once again, the causal force of the story as an explanatory anecdote vanishes. So, even if we take Taylor's suggestion as a serious rather than a humorous attempt to make the tale figurative in this way, it is still hard to remove all interest in the question of the saga's truth. Taylor's strategy does not entirely dispense with the problem of verisimilitude because the narrative's potency is not easily separated from the prospect of it being true. To put that differently, this is not just any story; neither is it a retelling of a well-known myth dressed up in contemporary costume. This is a story that people continue to believe is true in part because, as McGilligan points out, Hitchcock told it relentlessly down the years, and he told it as though it was the recounting of an actual memory. If people knew for certain that Hitchcock was fabricating the story, then interest in the tale would by now have vanished. Thus, the narrative draws some of its power from the prospect of its being factual. Indeed, Hitchcock's story continues to provoke debate precisely because that possibility forms the basis for why many readers are interested in the story at all. But were we to know for certain that young Alfred was never placed in a prison cell, would we continue to treat that story as possessing any useful or explanatory power? I am not sure. In any event, it does seem that Taylor is unable to resolve all doubts about the anecdote by turning it into a ben trovato story.

---

8 Taylor, p. 28. Ben trovato can be translated as "if it is not true it is very well invented." A ben trovato, story, then, would be a story that is apt but untrue. In English, though it may not fit perfectly, we might describe such a tale as apocryphal.

A Myth of Origin or a Personal Myth?

John Taylor is not alone in seeking to convert the incarceration narrative into something that can be freed from the constraint of having to decide between its truth and falsity. Other writers have tried to convert the story from an actual reminiscence into something more figurative, more allegorical, more symbolic. And in doing so they have frequently invoked the concept of myth. I want to consider two specific examples of this strategy.

The first is Michael Wood's argument that the tale's "symbolic import far outweighs any documentary effect." There is a whiff of confident dismissal here, and the brevity of the declaration enhances the certainty of the assessment. Regardless, it is an argument worth dissecting.

Notice how Wood's claim applies a metric of semanticity to the problem of Hitchcock's alleged incarceration by basing the notion of value on a consequentialist argument. That is, the value of the story is removed from the realm of the true/false dichotomy and located in a different domain: results. Wood makes the effect (or consequence) of the story more important than knowledge of its truth or falsity by asserting the presence of a value that is irreducible to experiential truth. Whether it happened – what he calls its "documentary effect" – just isn't all that important, for its "symbolic import" is all we need attend to. Thus, the story has symbolic significance first and foremost, and Wood understands this symbolic import as containing the explanatory power the tale possesses in accounting for Hitchcock's views of authority.

This is elaborated in greater detail in Wood's book. The key question is how we are meant to understand the nature of the symbolic power to which he refers. Wood's answer is to invoke the idea of myth:

> This is a myth of origin for a distrust of authority, and in Hitchcock's films this distrust takes a very particular form: the inability to believe that policemen, or any other figures of institutional command, know how to do anything except take orders or collude with father figures (or fathers). This means that they will, in one way or another and almost infallibly, get things wrong. They are not to blame if they can't think for themselves, or if reality is too difficult or elusive for them; but they are not to be relied on either.[9]

9 Wood, Michael. *Alfred Hitchcock: The Man Who Knew Too Much.* Boston and New York: Houghton Mifflin Harcourt, 2015, p. 2.

I am unconvinced that all the ideas presented in this particular citation hold together in the way that Wood suggests, but for the moment those objections can be put to the side. My interest is with Wood's claim that the story should be taken as a myth of origin with no ironclad claim to being empirically verifiable, an idea that dispenses with those difficult-to-prove claims to authenticity, but which brings the notion of mythic thought into the discussion. Because Wood values the story for its "symbolic import" and overlooks its "documentary" deficiencies, he interprets the narrative not as an event with causal properties, but as a tale whose importance arises non-deterministively. This mode of interpretation has a good deal going for it. As Karen Armstrong writes, "A myth is true because it is effective, not because it gives us factual information." This is an especially apt observation in the case of creation myths, for as Armstrong writes, "creation stories have never been regarded as historically accurate; their purpose was therapeutic."[10] What this means is that if the story of the ersatz incarceration did not actually happen and consequently shape Hitchcock's penchant for mistrusting authority, it nonetheless retains symbolic value of a therapeutic variety. Wood's idea of symbolic import is thereby valued in the same way myths are told and respected.

In suggesting that the story is an origin myth, Wood effectively neutralizes the problem of causation by negating the significance of chronology. Chronology is a central part of the causal power of narratives, so revising our ideas about chronology also entails revising our tendency to privilege causation in the context of the biographical narrative. Thus, by calling the incarceration narrative a 'myth of origin' Wood prioritizes the symbolic above matters of time and causation and is thereby led to define a theory of value independent of empirical truth. This is because origin myths, as Mircea Eliade says, "devaluate time."[11] That is, they dissolve time in making claims regarding the symbolic importance of the tales of creation that form our societies, for such tales refer to events outside of human history. In the present context, mythic narratives can be biographically important, according to Wood, because they represent rather than shape, and they represent because they annul time and focus not on the documentary record of events – which is a chronicle of time – but on the significance of the tale as a way of shaping or making sense from a holistic perspective. The myth of origin is created after the creation.

---

10 Armstrong, Karen. *A Short History of Myth*. Toronto: Vintage Books, 2005, pp. 10, 131.

11 Eliade, Mircea. *The Myth of the Eternal Return* (orig. 1954), translated by Willard R. Trask. Princeton and Oxford: Princeton University Press, 1971, p. 85.

In designating the incarceration narrative as a myth of origin, Wood makes the truth of the narrative irrelevant. His account also enables us to tell the story as though it were true because in whatever way we understand the truth of the tale, this will lie in its symbolic import and not in its fidelity to actual events. Yet here again, problems crop up when the genre is taken from the study of classical mythology and applied to real lives where the idea of truth is far more mundane. The main difficulty, as I see it, is that converting a biographical anecdote into myth means that we are prepared to abandon cause-and-effect forces of influence. Thus, if we insist that this story has value in the context of Hitchcock's work because it was a defining moment in his life, this is ordinarily because of an elementary logic that underlies our thinking: the event was causal in the sense of having occurred, and in having occurred it thereby shaped Hitchcock's attitudes toward authority. But if it never actually happened, if it is a myth of origin, then it has no claim to being part of a causal chain of influence. Wood's "symbolic import" is thus a reading which relies on a negation of the reality of the events in question. Simply put, if Hitchcock was never put in a jail cell as a child, then there is no causal influence to uncover, no significance to the story other than its interest to us as a narrative that symbolizes in colourful detail what a reasonable explanation for Hitchcock's attitudes might look like. Given the opportunity to offer a fictional account of how Hitchcock came to mistrust authority when he turned to filmmaking, this is precisely the sort of story one might concoct.

Thus, we might look for another way we can make the truth or falsity of the story irrelevant that allows us nevertheless to escape the problems that arise when the chain of causal determination is broken. Could we say that the story may not have happened while simultaneously proclaiming its significance as a formative event in Hitchcock's life? These questions take me to the second of the approaches I want to discuss in which the author discounts the empirical truth of the story while holding fast to its biographical significance in the context of a form of mythic interpretation. The author in this case is film scholar, Patricia Ferrara.

Ferrara follows the approach we have seen taken by other biographers by listing several reasons why we should regard a literal understanding of Hitchcock's jail story as preposterous. Following this inventory of reasons explaining why the narrative is unbelievable, Ferrara then suggests a way of maintaining interest in the story regardless of its dubious claim to being true:

> He [Hitchcock] told Truffaut that he couldn't think of anything he'd done to deserve it; he was his father's "little lamb without a spot," and never did anything wrong. He told Knight he was locked up for an unspecified minor offense, for simply being "bad." Rohmer and

> Chabrol report that the offense was specifically riding the London busses. Although the incident may or may not be true, it falls into the category of personal myth which, true or false, people use to structure their life experiences into some sort of pattern. It is in this way divorced from the "real" facts of his life, and enters into the grey area of an artist's own explanation of his work.[12]

Ferrara says that the story of his childhood incarceration helped Hitchcock to organize his "life experiences into some sort of pattern" that was ultimately "divorced from the 'real' facts of his life." And her proclamation that the category of true or false is irrelevant (or unimportant) leads her to offer us instead "the category of personal myth." As with Spoto, Taylor, and Wood (among others) Ferrara locates the narrative outside the class of things that are true or false by placing the story in a "grey area" of artistic self-definition. And she identifies this grey area as the field of the *personal myth.*

The theory of the personal myth derives from the work of the psychoanalyst, Ernst Kris.[13] As a way of reading Hitchcock's narrative, Kris's theory of the personal myth addresses many of the issues raised to this point as they would be seen from a Freudian perspective. In particular, Kris is concerned with issues of memory and meaning. I am not going to offer a detailed critique of Kris's therapeutic interpretations, nor spend time putting his psychoanalytic theories in historical context. Rather, I will offer only a brief account of his arguments sufficient to indicate why Ferrara says Hitchcock's story is understandable if conceptualized in terms of the theory of personal mythology.

Kris says that during therapy patients occasionally relate autobiographical stories in which periods of their lives, or individual episodes, are distorted or "reworked" to allow the patient to present a cohesive and meaningful personal history. As a practising analyst, Kris says one part of his therapeutic work consists in "piercing" these personal myths to discover the underlying truth being hidden or screened by such memories. For instance, in one case study Kris describes his sessions with a financially successful man who for years had been relating a personal story concerning the age he first attended college. As it turns out, this patient's story was factually incorrect in terms

---

12 Ferrara, Patricia. "The Discontented Bourgeois: Bourgeois Morality and the Interplay of Light and Dark Strains in Hitchcock's Films." *New Orleans Review*, 14 (4), 1987, pp. 79–80.

13 Ernst, Kris. "The Personal Myth: A Problem in Psychoanalytic Technique." *Journal of the American Psychoanalytic Association*, 4, 1956, pp. 653–681. I might add that Ferrara makes no mention of Kris in the article cited here.

of his personal chronology. Without his being aware of having done so, Kris says, the patient had essentially deleted two years from his life story (he told people he began college at the age of 14 when he really started attending at age 16) and substituted two different years from an earlier period in his life for the missing time. In making this substitution, the patient "remembers" his life in a way that shields him from certain sexual anxieties, and thus the narrative that has grown from this act of misremembering is an illustration of what Freud referred to as a screen memory. The patient has an autobiographical story – a personal myth – which nicely explains his current situation but does so only because it is wrong. In terms of the patient's perception of himself, the incorrect version works better than the correct version because the former tale is more in keeping with his wishes. For this particular patient, the unconscious misrepresentation of his age supports an interpretation he has of himself as a kind of "superman," and owing to his subsequent success in college and his financial accomplishments following graduation, the story he has embraced, despite its mistaken features, makes sense of how his adult life has turned out. During therapy, the patient learns that the empirical details he associates with his memories are wrong, and in being made aware of the mythic nature of the story, he makes psychological progress in other parts of his troubled life.[14]

As with the story of Hitchcock's prison detention, one might want to know the truth status of these personal myths. This is a question psychoanalysis treats as largely unimportant owing to the way in which Freudian analysis understands how our memories are formed and recollected. In our early years, Kris says, memories merge "imperceptibly with the pleasure in fantasy life, since in fantasy the lost is always near and the wish always fulfilled." When we reflect on memories from our childhood, in other words, it is sometimes difficult to know for certain which parts are genuine, which parts are fiction, and which parts have been borrowed from other stories. There may be no single event upon which an individual memory is anchored, but a series of unconsciously interposed episodes from which we derive a coherent life narrative. We do not "inherit" our memories so much as we create them. According to Kris, this is because

14 "He had not gone to college at fourteen but at sixteen and thus the superman fantasy was considerably curtailed. This fantasy had gained new vividness and great importance for him when he left home at eighteen, went far away [and] into the 'great' world." Ernst, p. 664.

> the dynamics of memory function suggest that our autobiographical memory is in constant flux, is constantly being reorganized, and is constantly subject to changes which the tensions of the present tend to impose.

Sometimes, Kris says, we add events to our childhood recollections in later life, especially "when the need for a past becomes particularly pressing."[15] This need arises when a traumatic memory can be effectively screened by the "recollection" of a past event that shields the individual from the pain of that remembrance by substituting a separate memory – a personal myth – that alleviates the discomfort and makes present circumstances cohesive with that mythic story. Kris's patient mentioned above persistently told a story – that is, he had a personal myth – that explained his scholarly and financial successes via an account of his intellectual precociousness, a gift that allowed him early entry into university. In treating this memory as "real" he was able to push aside thoughts he preferred to avoid while constructing a self-image that was an effective explanation of the pattern by which his life experiences were interconnected. In psychoanalytic terms, the personal myth serves the economic function of repression.

If we were to carry this analysis further while remaining faithful to Kris's psychoanalytic model it would be necessary to revisit biographical particulars of Hitchcock's childhood in greater detail than is available. Of course, surmises can be made about the primary psychoanalytic material required for this work but as these would be based on secondary accounts from many decades ago, it is difficult to see how they could be distinguished from clever guesswork. Did Hitchcock's Oedipal desires lead him to fantasize about his father as the agent behind this terrible act of incarceration? Did Hitchcock come to believe the narrative was true because it served his unconscious desires so successfully? Is it possible that the story is a screen memory that Hitchcock was able to use as a way of blocking a more traumatic memory he wished to ignore? I have no way to answer these questions. Although psychoanalytic approaches to the study of Alfred Hitchcock's films are common, my aim is not to construct a Freudian account of Hitchcock's childhood. Rather, I simply want to ask whether it is possible to apply Kris's model of the personal myth – and Patricia Ferrara suggests we can – to make sense of this one incident involving his father, the police officer, and the jail cell.

To that end I think that the theory of the personal myth, which makes Hitchcock's story valuable independent of its claim to being true, establishes

---

15 Ernst, pp. 678, 679.

a potentially useful psychological foundation for the narrative's enduring appeal in explaining Hitchcock's life. It might also exonerate the biographers who continue to treat its symbolic meaning as an important explanation of the director's worldview even as they remain sceptical about its truth. Further, we can invoke the idea of the personal myth without accepting that its primary function was to shield Alfred from the emotional pain of a psychosexual ordeal; in other words, the theory of a personal myth need not be useful only as a way of explaining specifically psychosexual traumas. To follow this approach and jettison the sexual element is not an especially unusual step, I should add, for many analysts have rejected the notion that the aetiology of childhood trauma invariably includes the psychosexual dimensions that Freud invoked. Many analysts prefer to see the notion of the personal myth as a product of the child's normal tendency to mix fantasy and reality – as when they think their stuffed animals are conscious. Jung, for instance, felt that Freud was too keen to see a sexual aetiology as the basis for every screen memory, arguing that traumatic events in childhood often lack the sexual charge that Freud said was the foundation of all repressions. Hence, we can follow Ferrara's suggestion without necessarily also agreeing that the theory necessarily entails acceptance of the sexual bases that Freud favoured.

The question, then, would be what we gain with the theory of the personal myth. The dividends are modest, I concede, but I believe that the theory of the personal myth can explain the Hitchcock prison narrative as a story that provided its narrator with a meaningful pattern to account for aspects of his artistic output by suggesting a coherent, plausible, foundational tale. In addition, the theory of a personal myth presents the story as one whose truth or falsity is not its most significant metric given that it is potentially a synthesis of disparate episodes. The personal myth is a construction, in other words, and not strictly a reminiscence. In the present case, Hitchcock may have derived portions of this story from real events and then, without the intention of consciously deceiving his listeners, embroidered that tale with more elaborate details, some equally true but borrowed from other occasions and possibly from other people. Some of the details may also have been fantasized or occurred in dreams. This intertextual account would help explain the narrative's shifting details and the tenacity with which Hitchcock held to the kernel of the story. With the theory of the personal myth, we could say that the incarceration narrative is important though it was not causally relevant in the ways that Hitchcock offered. Its significance lies in how it evades the suppositions of chronology even as it renders the question of its truth value immaterial. It is emblematic more than it is determinative. Even though it may largely be fantasy, then, it might still have causal significance, for if Hitchcock believed it was true, he might well have shaped his filmic narratives in accordance with the biographical consistency the incarceration myth would have defined. Moreover, the myth would be embraced only to the extent that it could provide the meaningful pattern to which Ferrara refers; that is, its value can be located partly in the meta-communicative function it serves.

The foregoing discussion of narrative truth and causal determination thus leads to the view that the significance of Hitchcock's story of childhood imprisonment might best be found in some form of mythic consciousness. Ernst Cassirer argues that mythical thought dispenses with traditional ideas about causality and thereby enables the thinker to imagine his life in holistic terms unfettered by the demands of linear time.[16] Therefore, whether Hitchcock's recollections were true to the facts is less important than what the story meant as a source to which he could appeal in seeking to make sense of his phobias and anxieties, particularly as these manifested in his films. The prison tale became a way of accounting for his fear of authority despite the difficulties of establishing it as actually true, difficulties which mainly disappear if one adopts a mythical viewpoint. Whereas it was not causally determinative in a chronological sense, it could at least offer an attenuated form of justification for both his personal fears and the cinematic representations of authority figures as the coldly inhuman apparatchiks he often ridiculed.

The Wrong/ed Man

> You better think of another story.
> Something plausible.
>
> - *The Wrong Man* (Lt. Bowers)

Although it is easy to find illustrations of Hitchcock's fear of authority brought to life in his films, it is more challenging to see in his movies a scene, an image, or even a character whose representation reflects the frightened

16 Cassirer's theories on mythical thought are more complex than this brief mention suggests, but one passage that clarifies my main point is the following: "Whereas empirical thinking is essentially directed towards establishing an unequivocal relation between *specific* 'causes' and *specific* 'effects,' mythical thinking, even where it raises the question of origins as such, has a free selection of causes at its disposal. Anything can *come from* anything, because anything can stand in temporal or spatial contact with anything." The specific event(s) is/are less important, then, than the interpretations subsequently offered. (Cassirer, Ernst. *The Philosophy of Symbolic Forms, Volume II: Mythical Thought*, translated by Ralph Manheim. New Haven: Yale University Press, 1953, p. 46).

little boy, the imposing jail cell, or the blind cruelty of the jailor. Challenging but not impossible, for I believe that *The Wrong Man* (1956) comes close to referencing the origin myth of Alfred's fateful day in jail. Considered in its barest details as the story of a person wrongly imprisoned, the film speaks directly to the anxiety and the depersonalization that Alfred Hitchcock's story of his childhood incarceration brings vividly to life. As with Hitchcock's own story, *The Wrong Man* concerns itself principally with the trials and tribulations of a wronged man.

The film raises several key questions we have already discussed concerning the truth or falseness of particular narratives. In *The Wrong Man*, some of these questions appear within a story that shifts from a predominantly realistic mise en scène to an attenuated form of magic realism as when Manny Balestrero, the film's protagonist, is found innocent in direct consequence of a petitional prayer. At one level, then, the issue of truth and falsity is inscribed in the storyline itself and is thereby moved into the background where it functions as an element of the plot. At other times the question of truth – as in the truth of what we are seeing – is placed very much in the foreground. For instance, the film's claim to be biographically faithful is probably its most cited truth-claim, and the fact that the film was shot in a black-and-white documentary style indicates Hitchcock's effort to sway audiences to accept the film as faithful to reality. At the same time, the film's assertion to be a documentary has been described as a misnomer, for with the casting of well-known Hollywood actors (Henry Fonda and Vera Miles) the film's genre is more docudrama than documentary. This criticism does not warrant a lengthy discussion given that the question of documentary realism does not apply in the case of a film drawn from actual events, especially when those events were reinterpreted and represented in specifically cinematic ways. Moreover, the critique has also been blunted by the intervening decades to the point that I doubt that modern viewers take seriously Hitchcock's introduction that the film is "a true story […] every word of it."[17] Viewers need only to look at the original account of Balestrero's predicament as it appeared in *Life* magazine to realize that Hitchcock had altered the story to fit the demands of the Hollywood narrative, and that while the story was based on real events it certainly was not a completely accurate rendition of Manny Balestrero's plight. Still, the film is precise in its purpose of tying innocence to the question of truth – that is, truth as it is defined by the police and the justice system, institutions for which the truth turns out to be a quality of narrative and appearance.

17 These lines are from Hitchcock's opening prologue which substitutes for his usual cameo. The prologue's austerity highlights his desire to present the film as true-to-life.

Of course, I am not suggesting that *The Wrong Man* replicates the narrative of Hitchcock's childhood stint in that jail cell. I am saying that there are thematic parallels that might well have encouraged Hitchcock to adapt the *Life* magazine article of Manny Balestrero's arrest and trial for film. Some of these parallels are obvious while certainly others are more subtle. For instance, the theme of the wrongly accused man (or child) is an obvious commonality, whereas the reframing of identity, which I will describe shortly, is less apparent. What is particularly significant in both instances, I feel, is the impotence of innocence as a defence against accusation, something that is hinted at in Hitchcock's story of temporary imprisonment, but which is treated extensively in *The Wrong Man.* So, while it should be clear that I am not suggesting a one-to-one mapping as though Hitchcock adapted his own experience for the film, I do argue that there are several motifs that draw the two narratives into union.

The Film

In his opening prologue, Hitchcock informs us that *The Wrong Man* (1956) is based on actual events. In being centred on a true story, the film was a departure for Hitchcock who usually found source material in works of literature rather than popular magazines. On the other hand, Hitchcock was generally willing to experiment, and *The Wrong Man* allowed him to complete something quite different from the other film he made in 1956, a remake of *The Man Who Knew Too Much* (originally made in 1934), and the surreal *Vertigo* which he would complete two years later. *The Wrong Man* is a departure from Hitchcock's traditional style of film.

The plot concerns a case of mistaken identity. A nightclub musician named Manny Balestrero is erroneously identified by several female employees from a local insurance office as the man who robbed them at gunpoint some weeks earlier. Manny is picked up and questioned by police in an efficient, non-threatening, and business-like manner. He responds to their questions with courtesy and forthrightness – though he is clearly confused by their suspicions. Following this interview, Manny willingly accompanies two police detectives to several locations in his neighbourhood where armed robberies have recently been committed and, at the detectives' directions, Manny walks into and out of the establishments in front of staff employees for identification purposes. Once he has completed several of these visits Manny is returned to the police station for additional questioning.

During this second round of interrogation Manny is asked to reproduce the hold-up note used by the robber. The note's text is dictated by Lieutenant

Bowers, who asks Manny to complete this task three separate times.[18] The police then compare one of Manny's drafts to the real hold-up note. As both Manny's note and the original message were written in block capitals there is nothing significant to distinguish between them. However, when he is informed that he has made the same spelling error in one of his notes as was made by the robber, Manny's nervousness begins to shift into denial and anger. The three women from the insurance agency he visited the previous day are then brought in and each identifies Manny as the robber. With the spelling mistake, the eyewitness identifications, and Manny's acknowledgement that his family's present financial picture is challenging, the police charge Manny with armed robbery and he is processed and led to a cell. The following morning, he is driven to court to be formally charged and enter a plea. Because the 5,000-dollar bond is greater than his family can cover on short notice he is forced to endure another night in jail before being released the following morning.

Manny's wife, Rose, grows increasingly despondent as the trial approaches. She becomes convinced that her unexpected dental bills are responsible for having landed Manny in his difficulties, as Manny had only gone to the insurance offices in the first place to inquire about the cash value of their current life insurance policy. Rose's mental and emotional anguish grows, and she eventually withdraws into a catatonic and uncommunicative state, forcing Manny to have her committed to an asylum.

On the third day of Manny's trial, a juror suddenly stands up during the cross-examination of a prosecution witness and asks, "Judge, do we have to listen to all this?" The question clearly suggests that the juror is biased against Manny and thus his lawyer, Frank O'Connor, requests and is granted a mistrial. A date for the retrial is set, but before the second trial begins the real criminal is caught during an attempted robbery of a neighbouring delicatessen. Manny rushes to the sanatorium to tell Rose the good news, but she is unresponsive. A coda tagged on to the film explains that Rose eventually recovered her health following Manny's acquittal. The final scene frames Manny, Rose, and their two children happily relocated to Florida where they enjoy their lives away from the public spotlight.

In fact, Rose Balestrero never fully recovered. The real-life Manny Balestrero sued the city and the insurance agency for 500,000 dollars for false arrest but settled for 7,000 dollars. The 22,000 dollars Balestrero was paid

18 In reality Balestrero completed six drafts.

by Warner Brothers for the film rights went mainly to pay for Rose's medical expenses. There was, in truth, no happy ending for the Balestrero family.[19]

The Shaping of an Identity

Manny's story may have been appealing to Hitchcock owing to his well-publicized fear of authority and his interest in the endemic uncertainty of social life. It may also have been tempting for its indictment of the single-mindedness by which the justice system sometimes operates. Indeed, *The Wrong Man* can be seen as a study in the fictions we call justice and truth, suggesting that police investigations and judicial proceedings sometimes operate as self-enclosed systems driven by presuppositions that are difficult (if not impossible) to challenge. Hitchcock does not oppose justice to some other system in his film, for that would be far more revolutionary a political position for him to assume. But he does show that when carried out with a sort of inhuman efficiency, even the most objective of judicial procedures can result in serious injustice.[20]

To represent the instrumental logic of the justice system, Hitchcock's canvas is bleached of colour and framed with cinematic minimalism. These stylistic decisions produce a bleak and haunting quality that heightens the viewer's anxiety while deepening the claustrophobic isolation to which Manny is delivered. The starkness of the sets also combines with the modulated emotions of the bureaucrats (the police) who perform their tasks with mechanical precision. The exactness of the detectives' diction portends the regimented orderliness of the judicial system which functions with a singularity of purpose that is routine in systems divested of compassion. From the moment he is photographed and fingerprinted, Manny is made coextensive with the surrogate markers of his identity; he becomes his mug shot and his fingerprints.

19 On 15 January 1957, Manny Balestrero appeared on the CBS game show, *To Tell the Truth*. The premise of this long-running network programme was simple: three contestants, two imposters, and the real subject were asked questions for approximately ten minutes by a celebrity panel whose task was to determine which of the three was the real subject, in this case, the real Manny Balestrero. Prize money was awarded in amounts of 250 dollars for each incorrect vote, meaning more prize money would be earned if the contestants could successfully fool the celebrity panellists. Two of the panellists chose the wrong man on Balestrero's appearance, earning the three contestants 500 dollars to divide among them.

20 On this way of conceptualizing efficiency, see Stein, Janice Gross. *The Cult of Efficiency*. Toronto: House of Anansi Press, 2002.

The Wrong Man also ingeniously invokes Hitchcock's definition of suspense as contingent on the audience being in possession of knowledge denied to certain characters in the movie. As viewers, we know that Manny has committed no crime because Hitchcock's opening prologue has informed us that the story is a recounting of actual events, so we know in advance of the opening scenes that the police and witnesses are wrong. However, the real clues to Manny's innocence are more referential than demonstrated. A standard day for Manny is shown in the film's opening sequence, much of it run behind the credits to reinforce its quotidian routine. Through its representation of Manny's typical bourgeois life, this sequence establishes the impossibility of Manny deviating from his predictable patterns, and as criminal behaviour would be an enormous deviation from that everyday routine, there is little doubt of his innocence. Viewers are given a privileged position regarding Manny's integrity from the moment at which he is first introduced.

However, we learn quickly that innocence is a poor weapon for fending off accusations. And as the accusations against Manny multiply, they become more definitional than material. In other words, Manny sees his identity as a respectable husband and conscientious father slowly but systematically stripped away as the police investigation runs its course. He is concerned that his sense of personhood is being violated, and that in being addressed as a suspect – and in being named as someone whose very appearance makes him a suspect – Manny struggles to find the words that will convince the police that he is not the man they are after. His identity is methodically recast by those in a position of power who assume the right to name Manny according to their interests.

This power to rename, to reframe, and to remake identity is made evident in Manny's first interaction with the police. Having determined from their interviews with the insurance office staff that the man they are looking for is Manny Balestrero, the detectives drive to his home and mill around their cars, smoking casually while watching for his return. When Manny starts up the walk to his front door, one of the detectives calls to him using a shortened version of his first name: *Chris*. As Manny goes by a diminutive form of his second name, Emanuel, he is unsure whom the police are addressing. The result is a short but poignant first encounter.

Detective: Hey, Chris. Your name Chris?
Manny: You calling me?
Detective: Is your name [...] Christopher Emanuel Balestrero?
Manny: Yes, it is.
Detective: We wanna talk. We're police officers.
Manny: What about?

Detective: Come to the precinct and help us out.
Manny: I'm just getting home. I'd like to tell my wife where I'm going.
Detective: Oh, you'd better come along and tell her later.

It is not terribly surprising that the police are unsure how to address Manny. Although many people go by a shortened or familiar version of their first name, far fewer go by a short version of their second name. For this reason, the detective's failure to greet Manny correctly would therefore seem to be a small and incidental mistake. However, the fact that the police hail him incorrectly – that they misidentify him – initiates a process by which Manny's identity is meticulously reshaped by bureaucratic interests. From the moment the police call Manny by the wrong name, they begin to systematically undermine his selfhood with a gesture of untoward intimacy. And as with all gestures of unearned familiarity, this wrong appellation also suggests they have it in their power to control him. Manny does not recognize himself in the name by which the police address him, just as he is unable to recognize himself in the characterization that unfolds during interrogation. As his engagement with the police and the justice system progresses, Manny is slowly estranged from himself.[21]

Manny's loss of personal identity is one of the more disturbing aspects of the film. He is interpellated as a criminal by the police and his subsequent actions and comments are interpreted with remarkable ease as support for that new identity. When he agrees that he has been in the offices of the Prudential Insurance Company that was recently robbed, he is unable to explain his actions in a way that forestalls the increasing solidification of his newly acquired criminal identity. Telling the detectives that he went to the insurance office to find out how much money he could borrow against his wife's policy to pay for her emergency dental work, the detectives turn this statement into an admission that Manny had the necessary motive to commit robbery.

Det.: Today, you went to ask about a loan?
Manny: Yeah.
Det.: You need money, then?

21 A quick note on Balestrero's name. *Christopher* comes from the Greek for "Christ bearer" owing to the legend that St. Christopher ferried Jesus across a river while the latter was a child. *Emmanuel,* of course, comes from Hebrew, "God is with us."

Manny: Yes, I told you, for the dentist.
Det.: What do you make a week at the Stork Club?
Manny: Eighty-five.
Det.: That's the take-home pay?
Manny: Yes.
Det.: You play the horses?

The suddenness of the shift from Manny's salary to the subject of gambling is less than subtle, and Manny notes the implication of that shift immediately. His countenance changes to the look of guilty man, though this change reflects his guilt about playing the horses rather than guilt over his ever having committed a crime. And whereas he is only able to offer answers that address specific questions, the detectives are free to roam more broadly and to suggest alternative concerns to which Manny feels obliged to respond. His replies, however, grow increasingly defensive as he tries to shield himself from both innuendo and direct accusation by appealing to the mundane facts of his life. Manny *becomes* a criminal because the authorities possess the power to enforce that identification.

Manufacturing Guilt

This power to enforce a specific identification is crucial to the theme of misidentification as it is developed in the film. *The Wrong Man* focuses on the dilemma the innocent man faces when his behaviour is redefined by authorities empowered to transform conjectures into probabilities, and probabilities into allegations of fact. This is made possible because of the willingness of various police and justice agents to diffuse their responsibility throughout the system and thereby accept their roles as largely performative and unreflective. The presence of a cynical and efficient bureaucracy in charge of legal procedures results in an impersonal and highly professional organization. It is therefore unsurprising that many commentators have pointed to the parallels between Hitchcock's narrative and Kafka's *The Trial.* For example, the film historian, Joseph McBride, says that

> of all filmmakers, Alfred Hitchcock is the closest to Kafka. His style has the same lucidity and syntactical logic, the same orderliness and simplicity mocking the chaos of the world situation, though with an accompanying tragic sense perhaps attributable to his skeptical Catholicism. *The Wrong Man*, the admirable rough draft for *North by Northwest* drawn

> from an actual incident of an arrest similar to that in *The Trial*, lacks the giddy humor of Hitchcock's later film but could well serve as a step-by-step illustration of how to film the nightmarish aspect of Kafka's world.[22]

Several other Hitchcock scholars have drawn a similar connection. Taylor refers to *The Wrong Man* as a "Kafkaesque nightmare," and Spoto calls the film "Hitchcock's ultimate excursion into the twilight world of Kafka."[23] David Sterritt suggests that "parallels with Franz Kafka's *The Trial* are easy to find,"[24] echoing a similar observation made by Eric Rohmer and Claude Chabrol.[25]

François Truffaut goes further in developing the comparison between Kafka and Hitchcock. In the introductory remarks that preface his interviews with Hitchcock, he says that if "one accepts the premise that cinema is an art form, on a par with literature," then Hitchcock should be placed "among such artists of anxiety as Kafka, Dostoyevsky, and Poe."[26] This is certainly heady company, and one might wonder how Hitchcock would have reacted to such accolades. Nonetheless, it is apparent that for many writers the case of Manny Balestrero resonates strongly with Kafka's chilling 1914 story, the principal thematic link usually identified as the intransigence of mindless bureaucracy. Lesley Brill, for instance, puts this point well:

> Justice in *The Wrong Man* looks like that in Kafka's *The Trial*: an arbitrary, incomprehensible exercise in bureaucratic brute force. The combination of power and rigidity in the institutions of the law looks as if it will be fatal for its innocent victims.[27]

Of course, there are also several ways in which the two texts differ. For instance, one important difference between Hitchcock and Kafka concerns

---

22 McBride, Joseph. *Orson Welles*. New York: De Capo Press, 1996, pp. 157–158.

23 Taylor, p. 237.
Spoto, Donald. *The Art of Alfred Hitchcock*. New York: Anchor Books, p. 256.

24 Sterritt, David. *The Films of Alfred Hitchcock*. Cambridge: Cambridge University Press, 1993, p. 67.

25 Rohmer, Eric and Chabrol, Claude. *Hitchcock: The First Forty-Four Films*, translated by Stanley Hochman. New York: Frederick Ungar Publishing, Co. 1979, p. 148.

26 Truffaut, François. *Hitchcock* (Revised edition). New York: Simon & Schuster, 1983. Hitchcock, p. 20.

27 Brill, Lesley. *The Hitchcock Romance: Love and Irony in Hitchcock's Films*. Princeton: Princeton University Press, 1988, p. 120.

the nature of the state. Unlike *The Trial*, *The Wrong Man* suggests that one does not find cases of unjust arrests only in totalitarian countries. Manny lives in the world's preeminent democracy and hence his difficulties have nothing to do with specific curtailments of his political liberties; rather, he is a victim of the inexorable movement of the law and its self-sufficient procedures as these are guaranteed by that law. Indeed, Manny's political freedom is never challenged, and his reverence for its privileged status is conveyed in the folksy wisdom he dispels to his two sons concerning equality and mutual respect. Reverence for the wisdom of the law is common sense to Manny who naïvely regards his innocence as an inescapable conclusion the police will eventuality realize. Manny assumes the position of a virtue theorist who believes that his moral character – and his innocence – will decide events in his favour.

However, it is precisely at this juncture between common sense and innocence that Manny's guilt is constructed. At several points in their interrogation, Bowers and Matthew tell Manny that their procedures will be entirely transparent, and that all the information relevant to his situation will be communicated to him as immediately as possible. In addition, they assure him that innocence will constitute a complete defence against the charges they are investigating: "An innocent man has nothing to fear," Lt. Bowers tells Manny, "Remember that." Such high valuation of innocence, it turns out, is an empty phrase used by the police to fulfill the requirements of their performance. Moreover, the claim that the innocent man, unlike the guilty person, has nothing to fear is actually a way of rendering the suspect suspicious. For though he is innocent, Manny *is* fearful, and a good deal of his anxiety comes from not knowing details of his situation despite assurances from the detectives that nothing pertaining to his detainment will be withheld. His anxiety produces feelings and expressions of guilt which serve as important bases for the detectives' presumption that they have the right man.

On the matter of guiltlessness, Manny's innocence turns out to be simply an alternative narrative to the story the police and prosecutors decide upon. This is made evident when Lt. Bowers tells Manny, "You better think of another story. Something plausible." To this demand Manny responds with the only defence he has: "But it's the truth." This counterclaim is somewhat ridiculous in the context of the situation in which Manny has landed, and the hollowness of his claim to be innocent is more desperate than assertive. Yet desperation is virtually all that Manny has left. He slowly comes to realize that the truth is insufficient as a defence, that it fails as a means of persuading the detectives to consider his character, his moral rectitude, his cooperative behaviour, his family obligations, his responsible work life, and his willing capitulation to his socio-economic station. Manny's so-called truth is simply the proclamation of his innocence, and to proclaim his innocence is merely to proffer a tautological protestation that he is speaking the truth. To continue asserting the truth of his innocence is an argument the detectives dismiss as just another (implausible) story.

Corruption and the Banal

It is important to note that it would be unfair to say that Lt. Bowers and detective Matthew are operating outside of legal procedures, or that they are gaining an illicit advantage over Manny by fabricating evidence, for the police behaviour we see in *The Wrong Man* is free of overt corruption.[28] A degree of manipulation is present in the interrogations, of course, and there would certainly be ethical problems today in having an uncharged suspect ferried to crime scenes on the possibility that he might be identified by the robbery victims. However, the intent behind Hitchcock's mode of representing the police is clearly to highlight their administrative scrupulousness and the banality of their workaday lives. He is not out to cast aspersions on their moral character. He may have disliked and feared the police, but he doesn't suggest that they are acting from felonious motives.

On the other hand, it is clear that what Hitchcock shows us in *The Wrong Man* is meant to reveal how efficiency is converted into inhumanity when the goal is to produce the guilty subject. This is one of the privileges of authority, and it is represented throughout the film in a way that plainly resonates with a concept first described by Stanley Milgram in 1974 as the *agentic state*.[29] According to Milgram, an individual is said to be in an agentic state, or an agentic condition, when his or her actions are not autonomous (self-directed), but heteronomous (other-directed). In an agentic state, in other words, one individual acts as an agent for another. In *The Wrong Man*, the police exercise their agency continually while Manny finds his agency thwarted. From the moment Manny is hailed by the wrong name, to the request that he walk through the establishments he is suspected of robbing, Manny performs according to specific rules of conduct laid out by the police without pausing to give thought to whether those rules accurately map his own beliefs and

28 There is one exception to this claim. In his opening statement to the jury the prosecutor claims that during police questioning Manny admitted that he owed money to organized crime because of unpaid gambling debts. This is completely untrue and could suggest corruption in the police detachment, at the prosecutor's office, or both. Its inclusion in the film, however, is anomalous and strikes me as an error on Hitchcock's part.

29 Milgram, Stanley. *Obedience to Authority: An Experimental View* (orig. 1974). New York: Harper Perennial Modern Classics, 2009.

desires. For their part, in acting out their roles as agents of the state, the police are relieved of the responsibility of having to deal with Manny at a personal level. He is a body to be shunted about from precinct to courtroom, from courtroom to jail, and from jail back to his home. He is "in the system," and having been processed by that system his identity is configured by the presuppositions of the agents who oversee that system's procedures. Communication in the agentic state is institutionalized, and people become objects within a larger social structure. All of this makes for an efficient means for handling people without the contamination of emotional engagement. In the beginning, Manny gives himself over to the police so that he can, in his words, do whatever he can to help. However, the police take this offer as an admission, and Manny must deal with the consequences of his cooperation as it systematically is redefined as collusion. Manny exercises just enough agency to assist in his own re-identification as guilty.

Hitchcock's suggestion is that when the law doesn't offer the security we expect, it is not so much that the law has failed, but that it has worked too well. The law is less concerned with uncovering guilt than it is with assigning guilt; less concerned with discovering truth than it is with manufacturing the truth. This suggestion comes rather close to ideas developed in the critical legal studies movement which challenges the notion that justice is dispassionate, free of political bias, and absent of any personal prejudices.[30] For critical legal theorists, none of these assumptions holds true. Instead, critical legal theorists argue that justice is a concept designed to serve class interests, and that the judicial system treats certain factors as essential when they are really socially constructed values. These arguments are on prominent display in *The Wrong Man* where the inexorable nature of the legal system, the deceptive benignity of the agents that serve that system, the social construction of the criminal through agentic reframing, and the disavowal of the truth as just "another story" indicate that Hitchcock's is a far more systemic critique than might first be gleaned from a superficial viewing. Though Manny is the wrong man insofar as he is actually innocent, as far as the police are concerned, he is the right man insisting on the wrong story.

---

30 The key article that started this movement is by Unger, Roberto. "The Critical Legal Studies Movement." *Harvard Law Review*, 96 (3), 1983, pp. 563–675. Other important contributions include Hunt, Alan. "The Theory of Critical Legal Studies." *Oxford Journal of Legal Studies*, 6 (Spring), 1986, pp. 1–45, and Finnis, John. "On The Critical Legal Studies Movement." *The American Journal of Jurisprudence*, 30 (21), 1985, pp. 21–42.

Conclusion

Whereas Manny is innocent of the charges for which he is arrested, he is guilty in a different, very Hitchcockian way: moral culpability. He explains to the police that he occasionally bets on the horses, yet he tells his wife that he only pretends to play, calculating how his imaginary bets would have turned out had he really wagered. Hence, he is guilty of gambling and then concealing this fact from Rose. He is also guilty of being less than a perfect husband. When Rose explains that she will need expensive dental work, Manny visibly winces at the thought of another unexpected expense. And though he tries to conceal his displeasure at this bad financial news Rose can read Manny's nonverbal expression of annoyance. Manny's sense of his guilt, then, is mainly tied up with questions of virtue, and not with matters of law, and in blending these two realms he experiences pangs of conscience that come to the fore during his police interrogation. He is, as was young Alfred, the "naughty boy," innocent of serious wrongdoing, but guilty of irrelevant moral failings. As with many Hitchcock characters, Manny's moral weaknesses are emblems of the normal inadequacies that beset all of us. These imperfections are then subsequently converted into stories of social failure for which punishment is rightfully due. The severity of the punishment – incarceration – is entirely out of keeping with the nature of the wrongdoing. In both Alfred's childhood reminiscence – that personal myth of improper incarceration – and the story of Manny Balestrero, the illusion of criminal conduct becomes the basis for the exercise of legal force. Moreover, both Manny and Alfred, illegitimately subjected to harsh treatment, remain scarred in different ways by their respective ordeals. Alfred Hitchcock claims to have suffered lifelong consequences because of his five minutes of incarceration – however improbable the event. And although Hitchcock subsequently attempted to sanitize Manny's ordeal with the unconvincing dénouement to *The Wrong Man*, the material facts point in the opposite direction. Manny's financial losses because of his arrest were significant, and his relationship with Rose was irreparably damaged as she never recovered from the ordeal.

In both narratives the inhumanity of bureaucratic machinery constitutes the main agent of traumatization. The unfeeling and relentless movement of the judicial system was, in Manny's case, the primary agency by which he was stripped of his personhood and reframed as a criminal. From the moment the police interpellated Manny with a wrong name, to the procedures by which he was systematically reduced to being identified with the surrogate markers of fingerprints and mug shot, Manny's subjectivity was ultimately turned over to the control of the authorities. The prerogative of ascribing him a name, a number, and an identity was made a matter for the police and the justice system. Manny lost all sense of personal autonomy.

Hitchcock's childhood story suggested that he, too, was made conterminous with the abstraction of a "naughty boy," and thus removed from the social networks of family and friends en route to this re-designation. While his situation, real or imagined, differs in important ways from Manny's, the similarities are striking. In being redefined as "naughty" or guilty, the subject loses agency and assumes the identity (or social role) which is provided by the vested powers. Moreover, both Alfred and Manny were cut adrift from their respective families, from the foundations by which they could claim their place in the social order. Denied the privilege of an autonomous identity, the Kafkaesque nightmare of stolen selfhood becomes the basis for a lifelong distrust of those anonymous authorities who reserve for themselves the right to control – and to name – all others.

Chapter 5

ALFRED HITCHCOCK'S *BLACKMAIL* AND THE PROBLEM OF MORAL AGENCY

I'd prefer to build a film around a situation rather than a plot.

– Alfred Hitchcock[1]

It is half the art of storytelling to keep a story free from explanation.

– Walter Benjamin[2]

Introduction

In this chapter I examine the problem of moral agency in the work of Alfred Hitchcock by focusing on a representative moment in one of his early British films, *Blackmail* (1929), his first sound production. Approaching Hitchcock's work in this way enables me to present a view of his films that is consistent with some of the literature extolling his continuing relevance to film studies, feminism, the field of communication, and even philosophy.[3] It further allows me

1 Truffaut, François. *Hitchcock* (Revised edition). New York: Simon & Schuster, 1983, p. 203.

2 Benjamin, Walter. "The Storyteller: Reflections on the Works of Nikolai Leskov." In *Illuminations*, translated by Harry Zohn. New York: Schocken Books, 1968, p. 89.

3 See Steven Sanders as one illustration of this tendency. Sanders, Steve. "Why be Moral? Amorality and Psychopathy in 'Strangers on a Train'." In *Hitchcock and Philosophy: Dial M for Metaphysics*, edited by David Baggett and William Drumin. Chicago: Carus Publishing, 2007, pp. 175–185. Also, Tom Cohen's two-volume analysis of Hitchcock's work takes on the problem of the moral implications of Hitchcock's work in several places. Cohen, Tom. *Hitchcock's Cryptonymies: Vol. I Secret Agents, Vol. II: War Machines*. Minneapolis and London: University of Minnesota Press, 2005. Finally, many of the essays collected in Žižek (1992) deal with a range of moral and philosophical questions in Hitchcock's films. Žižek, Slavoj, ed. *Everything you Always Wanted to Know about Lacan (But were Afraid to Ask Hitchcock)*. London and New York: Verso Books, 1992.

to take the discussion of moral and ethical themes in Hitchcock's work beyond conventional ethical precepts that are occasionally presented as being central to understanding his moral position, such as the theory of retributive justice. This is not to argue that justice, retribution, and punishment are unimportant motifs in Hitchcock's films. This is plainly untrue. But in the present chapter I want to resist the temptation to bifurcate Hitchcock's moral world into good and evil, or guilty and innocent, in order that I might highlight an overlooked element of moral thinking represented in his work. This is the view that Hitchcock's films frequently present moral agency in the context of concepts like indeterminacy, undecidability, and anti-foundationalism. Moral agency, I want to suggest, is a more complex problem – and a more ambiguous state – than is ordinarily recognized in the more conventional "redemptive" readings of Hitchcock's work. Conceptions of justice and punishment, whether these are presented as being meted out by the law or by fate, introduce a teleological scheme to the evaluation of the moral conundrums with which Hitchcock deals, a scheme that can often be a rather negligible aspect of his narratives. I believe it is important to recognize Hitchcock's tendency to privilege the inherent appeal of moral obligation at the expense of unreflective fidelity to ethical rules. To move the analysis of Hitchcock's moral theorizing beyond the hegemony of ethical certitude is one of the goals of this chapter.

By arguing that the idea of the moral impulse is distinct from the sphere of ethical responsibilities, I am following a line of thinking derived from writers such as Zygmunt Bauman, Emmanuel Levinas, and Dwight Furrow who present a radical interpretation of ethical philosophy that challenges the priority of ontology.[4] Levinas once commented, "My task does not consist in constructing ethics. I am simply trying to find its meaning."[5] So too, my principal concern in this chapter is to reflect on the notion of moral agency as it is presented in Hitchcock's work rather than to develop a theoretical edifice into which his moral thought can be neatly placed. Thus, to a considerable extent I follow philosopher John Caputo's observation that "undecidability does not

4 Two volumes from Zygmunt Bauman are especially relevant to this discussion. See Bauman, Zygmunt. *Postmodern Ethics.* Oxford and Cambridge: Blackwell, 1993; and Bauman, Zygmunt. *Life in Fragments: Essays in Postmodern Morality.* Oxford and Cambridge, 1995. Dwight Furrow's critique of moral thought can be found in Furrow, Dwight. *Against Theory: Continental and Analytic Challenges in Moral Philosophy.* New York and London: Routledge Books, 1995. An interesting account of how Levinas's philosophy can be placed in the context of contemporary communication studies is Pinchevski, Amit. *By Way of Interruption: Levinas and the Ethics of Communication.* Pittsburgh: Duquesne University Press, 2005.

5 Levinas, Emmanuel. *Ethics and Infinity*, translated by Richard Cohen. Pittsburgh: Duquesne University Press, 1985, p. 90.

detract from the urgency of decision; it simply underlines the difficulty."[6] It is the ontological difficulty in being a moral agent rather than the specific challenge of determining right from wrong that provides my entry into the films of Alfred Hitchcock. This is because I look at Hitchcock's films as documents dealing with the problem of moral agency per se, and not as expositions of specific ethical problems; hence my focus in this chapter on a single illustration rather than on a survey of a range of particular moral challenges as these might appear in different films. Ethical rules, I suggest, are one aspect of our moral experience that often runs directly counter to our moral intuitions. In this respect, I follow Bauman in distinguishing between ethical rules and moral impulses, even as I examine the utility of this distinction in relation to the issue of moral agency in Hitchcock's work.

The Moral Universe of Hitchcock's Films

That Hitchcock's films are predicated on the proposition that moral forces are at work in our most ordinary affairs is clear; indeed, his work frequently manifests the problem of moral agency even as it seeks to problematize the impetus for ethical conduct. It is no surprise that many writers have found it useful to think through Hitchcock's work in relation to the sphere of morality.

Perhaps the earliest work to make this theme an explicit feature of its approach to the study of Hitchcock's films was Eric Rohmer and Claude Chabrol's *Hitchcock: The First Forty-Four Films* (1979).[7] This volume is conventionally seen as one of the groundbreaking works on Hitchcock's films for two reasons. First, the authors were pivotal figures in the construction of Hitchcock's public image as an auteur, a description Hitchcock would come to embrace as a kind of secular canonization even as it provoked a serious and ongoing debate in film studies.[8] Second, Rohmer and Chabrol provided a methodical if overly schematic reading of Hitchcock's films that suggested the central place the theme of exchange played in his work. Exchange is a broad concept with diverse representations, but Rohmer and Chabrol provided a concise and logical framework, conceptualizing exchange in terms of a moral expression (transferability of guilt), a psychological dynamic (the doubling or doppelgänger motif), a dramatic form (suspense), and a concrete or formal

6 Caputo, John. *Against Ethics: Contributions to a Poetics of Obligation with Constant Reference to Deconstruction.* Bloomington and Indianapolis: Indiana University Press, 1993, p. 4.
7 Rohmer, Eric and Chabrol, Claude. *Hitchcock: The First Forty-Four Films.* New York: Frederick Ungar Publishing, 1979.
8 On the canonization of Hitchcock as a bona fide auteur, see especially Kapsis, Robert. *Hitchcock: The Making of a Reputation.* Chicago and London: University of Chicago Press, 1992.

articulation (the to-and-fro movement of parallel editing, for instance). Each of these forms of exchange was plainly a dialectical adventure emphasizing the dynamic and processual nature of Hitchcock's films. However, it is the first of these modes of exchange, transferability of guilt, that is of particular interest to me. Transfer of guilt suggested to Rohmer and Chabrol that moral agency, as depicted in Hitchcock's films, was often presented as having an accidental or fortuitous quality insofar as the ascription of guilt could have an essentially random nature. Indeed, guilt could be assumed as readily as it could be ascribed, and it was this attribute that made transferability a crucial part of their analysis of Hitchcock's moral vision.

Subsequent writers treating the theme of morality in Hitchcock's work both followed and diverged from Rohmer and Chabrol's theories of exchange. Robin Wood recognized Rohmer and Chabrol's text as "a very serious attempt to account for the resonances [Hitchcock's] films can evoke in the mind," but Wood was also concerned by the teleological way their analyses were carried out.[9] The problem, he argued, was that Rohmer and Chabrol had determined in advance the moral limits of Hitchcock's work: Hitchcock's Catholicism. This presupposition, though illuminating in certain respects, was "ridiculous," Wood argued, when applied uncritically to each of Hitchcock's films. The predetermination that Hitchcock's Catholicism was the sole source of his moral vision, Wood pointed out, sometimes led Rohmer and Chabrol to force an interpretation where the fit was suspect. The result, Wood said, was an unfortunate tendency to "distort the film drastically."[10]

In *The Films of Alfred Hitchcock* (1993), David Sterritt argues that investigations of Hitchcock's work are incomplete if they fail to consider "the culminating fact of Hitchcock's universe: the transcendence of physical conflict over psychological and even moral confrontation with evil."[11] Thus, Sterritt's detailed analyses of Hitchcock's films are carried out in terms of what he calls the "broad moral vision than runs through Hitchcock's work," though the vision to which Sterritt points is not always clearly articulated.[12] Similar arguments concerning the importance of moral ruminations to Hitchcock's work run through several of the director's biographies. For example, Donald Spoto's biography of the director argues strongly in favour of Hitchcock's moral universe as having been produced by his Catholic upbringing, telling

9 Wood, Robin. *Hitchcock's Films Revisited* [1965]. New York: Columbia University Press, 1989, p. 62.

10 Wood, p. 63.

11 Sterritt, David. *The Films of Alfred Hitchcock*. Cambridge: Cambridge University Press, 1993, p. 1.

12 Sterritt, p. 16.

us "He was a profoundly Victorian Catholic, a rigid moralist."[13] This interpretation, as indeed most interpretations that look back to Hitchcock's childhood, is bolstered by the filmmaker's own words, for in his interviews with Truffaut he claimed that the time he spent as a child at the Jesuit St. Ignatius College had a lasting influence on him: "It was probably during this period with the Jesuits that a strong sense of fear developed – moral fear – the fear of being involved in anything evil. I always tried to avoid it."[14] Self-assessments of this nature have helped to fuel an interest in the 'Catholic Hitchcock,' but the director's penchant for clever misdirection is well known, and it is certainly possible that his ethical presumptions were more bourgeois than they were theological, despite what Hitchcock's own reminiscences might suggest. It is true that many common motifs in Hitchcock's films such as the transferability of guilt (e.g., *The Wrong Man* [1956], *Strangers on a Train* [1951], *Shadow of a Doubt* [1943]) can be cast in religious if not strictly Catholic terms, and for that reason many of his moral attitudes would seem at least in part to be motivated by theistic impulses. But to approach the representation of ethical praxis in Hitchcock's films in this fashion tends to single out a common and somewhat limited range of factors: the rightness or wrongness of specific behaviours, the prospect of vengeance or retribution for those actions, and the likelihood of redemption for characters who have transgressed against the moral order.

It is precisely these sorts of preoccupations from which I want to distance my approach. I am less interested in moral rectitude as represented in the director's films than I am interested in what Zygmunt Bauman has called a postmodern ethics, the view that our moral impulse is an ambivalent ontological state that dismisses "the possibility of a non-ambivalent, non-aporetic ethical code."[15] In developing this position, it is necessary to set aside more traditional readings of Hitchcock's moral universe as a site of "redemptive" promises. This does not mean that I am ignoring the ethical problems he dissects or that I am unaware of the visceral evil depicted in his films. Rather, I am concerned with a reading of moral agency in his work not as a product of his religious upbringing, his concessions to bourgeois philosophy, or his psychological make-up and personal idiosyncrasies, but as a central problematic in understanding the ethical anxieties provoked by his narratives. No doubt Hitchcock's Catholicism played a role in giving shape to

13 Spoto, Donald. *The Dark Side of Genius: The Life of Alfred Hitchcock.* New York: Ballantine Books, 1983, p. 277.

14 Truffaut, François. *Hitchcock* (Revised edition). New York: Simon & Schuster, 1983, pp. 25–26.

15 Bauman, 1993, p. 9.

his ethics and his view of life generally, but it is difficult to ascertain the extent to which religiously based moral ideals influenced his films.

To frame the basic premises of this approach, it is useful to establish straightaway a distinction that guides my analysis from start to end, the distinction that can be drawn between our moral impulses and the various processes of ethical codification into which these are rendered. This distinction has been given an especially lucid explanation by Zygmunt Bauman:

> Only rules can be universal. One may legislate universal rule-dictated *duties*, but moral *responsibility* exists solely in interpellating the individual and being carried individually. Duties tend to make humans alike; responsibility is what makes them into individuals. Humanity is not captured in common denominators – it sinks and vanishes there. The morality of the moral subject does not, therefore, have the character of a rule. One may say that the moral is what *resists* codification, formalization, socialization, universalization. The moral is what remains when the job of ethics [...] has been done.[16]

To act ethically, then, is to abdicate one's responsibility for the Other to express fidelity to the code or the law. Ethics, Bauman argues, has as one of its most important tasks the job of relieving us of our responsibilities as moral agents. This is also one of the great ironies of his work in postmodern ethics. In place of these autonomous responsibilities, we are filled with heteronomous duties. Ethics, because it pretends to the illusion of universality, speaks with a single voice and celebrates the effacement of individual obligation. Ethics' duty, as it were, is to make duty itself the goal of ethical action.

Morality, however, is fraught with ambivalence and individual culpability; it acknowledges openly the pretensions of universal conventions of correct behaviour and repositions obligation within the relation to the Other. Whereas ethics is a negotiated treaty in which reciprocal obligations form the essential bases for enforcing contractual relations, morality is a nonreversible encounter with the Other, one in which reciprocity is not the essence of the relationship, but its annihilation. To do what I must for the Other *because* of a reciprocal agreement (or the expectation of reciprocity) is not to act morally, but to act from a different motive entirely. Therefore, when we are confronted with a moral challenge we may seek comfort in an appeal to the ethical code, but if our situation is such as fails to clearly match any of the rules outlined in that document, what then? And when we turn to Hitchcock's films we

16 Bauman, 1993, p. 54. Emphasis in the original.

discover just such situations – artificial and abstract, to be sure – in which human agents must weigh up their impulse to do what they believe is right all the while being equally unsure exactly what that right action might be.

Other Hitchcock scholars have made similar observations. Robin Wood, for instance, has referred to the "disconcerting moral sense" of Hitchcock's films.[17] Wood suggests that this disconcertion is more ethical than aesthetic; that the existential drama of making choices is more unsettling than the bewilderment produced by a disturbing artwork. The matter of moral agency can be central to his work. Indeed, Hitchcock often seemed inclined to the view that moral agency battled ethical principles to the same extent that it struggled with futural uncertainties; that the central dilemma was not how to arrive at moral correctness, but whether this goal was even achievable.

These are complicated issues, and I develop this argument in more detail in the next part of this chapter. My aim in these introductory comments, is simply to show that whereas we often find ourselves making an appeal to ethical rules so that we can resolve a challenging moral problem, we also occasionally run headlong into the fact that rules are not always the surest guide to the resolution we seek. Moral problems can be intractable, and thus the appeal of casuistry where ethical issues are treated on a case-by-case basis and not by looking to universal principles. This is also the appeal of Bauman's point mentioned already, that whereas rules are universal, our moral problems are deeply particular. The universal prohibition against stealing is widely acknowledged, but when the question is whether I should steal to feed my starving children the issue changes dramatically. Thus, I want to explore this dilemma in somewhat more detail as it has been described by several important thinkers.

From there I turn to one of Hitchcock's greatest British-era films, *Blackmail* (1929), to apply some of these insights. *Blackmail*, which was Hitchcock's first sound production, is a remarkable overview of the challenge of making the morally correct choice. Or, more properly, it is a remarkable representation of the endemic uncertainty we often face when trying to decide on the appropriate behaviour when trapped in a moral quagmire. When I screen the film for undergraduate students, I frequently find that they are distressed by the concluding scenes in that right and wrong – good and evil – have not been properly sorted out. Though they recognize that in a superficial way the film has arrived at the appropriate place – heterosexual coupling has again won the day – there is something morally disquieting about the film nonetheless, for the ethical dilemmas the principal characters face have not been adequately resolved. And, of course, discussion then turns to the question whether such

17 Wood, p. 67.

resolution given the narrative's circumstances is even achievable. *Blackmail* is a wonderful existential meditation on the problem of being human: We know that we must make choices, but too often we are unable to determine which choice to make. Indeed, this existential issue is where I want to begin.

The Myth of Moral Perfectibility

As moral agents each of us must deal with the problem of having to choose a course of action from a range of possibilities that conventionally includes incommensurable options. Knowing that we have made the right choice, the choice we deem most morally acceptable, is difficult, for choices always entail other agents, competing interests, and overlapping social contexts. One of the main difficulties with moral agency is that when we seek direction for making our moral decision, moral theorizing might serve to confirm our inclinations rather than to guide our choosing, our actual agency being subsumed within the narrative of a specific theoretical position. This is the view of philosopher Dwight Furrow, who says, "If we understand moral prescriptions to be worth endorsing only if they conform to a theory, our moral judgments are undecidable." According to Furrow, this is because "consistent and intelligent theorists can argue either side of a case without result."[18] Moreover, any one of us can be a consistent and intelligent theorist and at the same time be unaware of the extent to which our actions are guided by our theoretical frames. It is possible to be a neo-Kantian when faced with one ethical predicament, and an act-utilitarian at a later day when confronting a different conundrum, choosing whichever approach best suits our preferences and desires in either case. We can also switch theoretical frames across time as a single event unfolds. For example, at the start of a military conflict we might argue that even a single casualty is one death too many, but as the conflict persists and the body count mounts, we might be tempted to switch theories and argue that a greater good is being served by these accumulated, tragic fatalities. In other words, we can provide theoretically sound arguments pointing to antithetically opposed courses of action, but no hint of experiential continuity will necessarily tie the decision-events together in the moral domain. Such apparent inconsistency could raise questions about moral character, but psychologizing this way is rarely useful insofar as there is nothing especially aberrant in switching theoretical positions in order to preserve the outward appearance of consistency. Indeed, even in cases where theoretical consistency is preserved (as when one remains a neo-Kantian across all situations,

18 Furrow, p. xiii.

for instance), the result may be theoretical uniformity rather than persistent ethical correctness.[19] Hence Furrow argues for

> the contingency of moral experience and for the absence of any rational principles more fundamental than the moral practices by which we happen to live, that will justify those practices.[20]

This focus on the experiential and the practical is clearly a postmodern take on moral problems with its tendency to privilege indeterminate and liquefied subject positions.[21] As Zygmunt Bauman says, "We know now that we will face forever moral dilemmas without unambiguously good (that is, universally agreed upon, uncontested) solutions, and that we will be never sure where such solutions are to be found; not even whether it would be good to find them."[22] This might seem nihilistic to many, but as he writes elsewhere, Bauman is concerned with challenging the modernist illusion that "there is an end to the road along which we proceed, an attainable telos of historical change [...] [a] complete mastery over the future – so complete that it puts paid to all contingency, contention, ambivalence and unanticipated consequences of human undertakings."[23] Furrow makes a similar point. The problem of moral contingency, he points out, is historical as well as philosophical: people across the ages, in myriad cultures, have sought to act morally, but have frequently ended up performing (or acquiescing to) "monstrous acts of cruelty."[24] Injustice and brutality have been carried out by those who claimed (and possibly believed) that they were acting in the name of what is morally right, and who imagined that their actions would secure a more just

---

19 Of course, consistency could be regarded on its own as a moral virtue, but even here one should be careful to separate mode of conduct (consistency) from individual performances in order to recognize the contextuality of moral behaviour. One can remain consistent precisely because one changes one's position. Being consistent is a complex and multi-level performance.

20 Furrow, p. xiii.

21 On the question of postmodernism's tendencies for indeterminism, see Hassan, Ihab. *The Dismemberment of Orpheus: Toward a Postmodern Literature* (2nd edition). New York: Oxford University Press, 1982. Cultural liquidity is most commonly associated with Berman, Marshall. *All That is Solid Melts into Air.* New York: Simon & Schuster, 1988. However, I am relying here more on the views of Zygmunt Bauman's development of social and cultural liquidity. See, for example, Bauman, Zygmunt. *Liquid Modernity.* Malden: Polity Press, 2000.

22 Bauman, 1993, p. 31.

23 Bauman, 2000, p. 29.

24 Furrow, p. xv.

and compassionate world. According to Furrow, this "complicity of goodness and evil" suggests that "morality has a tragic dimension, that even our most cherished moral ideals can generate an extraordinary moral blindness."[25] Furrow does not propose that efforts to be morally accountable are utterly wasted although such efforts can produce the sorts of consequences they are intended to defend against. Furrow puts the point plainly by stating, "We can never be sure that our attempts to alleviate suffering will not lead to more suffering."[26] That good and evil collude in the production of the fantasy that strict attention to a code of ethical reasoning will yield the single, correct decision is tragic in the classic sense. Hence the myth that we can perfect ourselves as rational moral agents – and especially by the strict application of rationality – is belied by everyday practice (and the ontology of moral experience) though it is sustained by the desire to do right, a desire that occasionally feeds on a confused conception of the relation between logical reasoning and ethical precepts. This confusion is expressed in the belief that to the extent that we can reason correctly, so too can we conduct ourselves in a morally appropriate fashion, that moral conduct, in other words, is completely reducible to an empirical substratum, such that ethical rectitude can be produced from proper, logical reasoning. There is little doubt that in the realm of moral determinations some decisions are better than others, but moral perfectibility is a myth in that it holds out the promise not of better choices, but of the best choice, the single, univocal option that follows from a process of consistent, deductive calculation.

That it is difficult to know that the appropriate course of ethical conduct has been chosen hardly needs establishing. But although this is obvious, the impetus to behave in an ethically correct fashion performs an important sense-making function by establishing a coherent match among events, motives, and sentiments. Indeed, in the world of cinema this impetus for morally appropriate conduct can be an important component of conventional narrative structure where motivation is commonly concentrated in the protagonist's character and actions. In other words, if conventional accounts of the Hollywood narrative are carefully examined, the notion of ideological closure will be seen to be closely allied with the view that the triumph of good is a consequence of having chosen the right course of ethical action. Thus, narrative closure, ethical certitude, and ideology are woven together in the seamless cinematic realism that masks contradiction and makes a fetish of moral perfectibility. Sense-making, in this respect, has ethical as well

25 Furrow, p. xv.

26 Furrow, p. 192.

as empirical and aesthetic dimensions. If boy gets girl, if good triumphs over evil, if David brings down Goliath, then the ideological closure the film evinces will match neatly the ethical precepts common to the bourgeois audience. What is ethically appropriate is often marked by certain emblems of social and cultural acceptability.

Why is Hitchcock important to this discussion? Hitchcock problematizes the union of these narrative elements, showing us particularly the artificiality of closure, the fallacy of ethical certitude, and various fissures in bourgeois ideology. He shows us, to borrow again from Bauman, that "contingency, contention, ambivalence and unanticipated consequences of human undertakings" are the normal course of affairs, not the anomalies. Hitchcock's films are visually arresting accounts of human imperfection in which the impulse for goodness is forced to contend with powerful, countervailing forces. In his work we may indeed confront the impurities of our own desires, as Robin Wood says, but likewise do we glimpse the fragility of those desires as they are romanticized in the myth of moral perfectibility. Desire is the sine qua non of human motivation, an incorporeal spectre haunting the lives of his film's characters. At one moment transcendent and the next profane, desire is the internal (and eternal) dialogue with the soul animated so often in Hitchcock's work. And while desire is often most central when his characters treat it as peripheral, and most peripheral when they regard it as essential, rarely does this amount to outright moralism. Indeed, Hitchcock's films are didactic without becoming sermonic, principled without succumbing to sentimentality, brutal without necessarily surrendering to evil. We may wish to perfect ourselves by transcending the conditions that bind us to the material world, but the incessant pull of our corporeal nature – that matrix of human and social relations – makes apparent that genuine escape is itself a myth. We are condemned to our condition as moral beings, animated by desires that both constrain and enable. We are, as Kenneth Burke has said, "rotten with perfection."[27]

In addition, Hitchcock's films are open-ended readerly texts that render the disconcerting aspects of lived experience aesthetically appealing, and in doing so, invite us to consider the allure of those passions about which bourgeois sensibilities prefer repressed silence. To betray the bourgeois passion for social convention is a hallmark of many of the endings of Hitchcock's films, for his is an aesthetic of dissatisfaction through which we experience the frustration of our longings, requited or otherwise. The 'nagging doubts' that

27 Burke, Kenneth. *Language as Symbolic Action: Essays on Life, Literature, and Method.* Berkley: University of California Press, 1968, p. 16.

figure prominently in his work are openings into subjects for which satisfactory conclusions are commonly lacking.

The impulse to resist ideological closure is consequently one of the more pronounced features of what Wood calls Hitchcock's "disconcerting moral sense." This resistance, I believe, is produced from Hitchcock's tendency to see institutional modes of proscribing behaviour – including the cinema's institutional mode of representation – as inherently suspect. The resulting discomfiture produced by this resistance is both emotional and intellectual and can perhaps best be assuaged by accepting that social convention is too often represented as a panacea capable of warding off the evils of endemic uncertainty. But such evils are not easily swept aside. "The moral situation is one of inherent ambivalence," writes Bauman, "and it would not be moral without a choice between good and evil"[28] (Bauman 1995, p. 7). More importantly, Bauman goes on to say,

> We understand now that uncertainty is not a temporary nuisance, which can be chased away through learning the rules, or surrendering to expert advice, or just doing what others do – but a permanent condition of life; we may say more – it is the very soil in which the moral self takes root and grows. Moral life is a life of continuous uncertainty. [...] Moral responsibility is *unconditional* and in principle *infinite* – and thus one can recognize moral persons by their never quenched dissatisfaction with their moral performance; the gnawing suspicion that they were not moral *enough*.[29]

Bauman's analysis of the place of uncertainty in the moral life of the subject – an analysis shaped by the influence of the philosopher Emmanuel Levinas – suggests the endemic and foundational nature of uncertainty in the world of human judgement including, and perhaps most tellingly, the world of moral judgement and reasoning. Ideological closure under such conditions is clearly not feasible when critical reflection by moral agents reveals, as Bauman expresses it, "the gnawing suspicion that they were not moral *enough*." Decisions taken with the aim of resolving moral problems will translate metaphysics (the moral impulse) into epistemology (rules, codifications, ethical conduct), but when understood in terms of the knowledge of right and wrong ethical conundrums will be undecidable, as Furrow has noted

28 Burke, Kenneth. *Life in Fragments: Essays in Postmodern Morality*. Oxford and Cambridge: Blackwell, 1995, p. 7.

29 Burke, 1995, p. 287.

above. Hence no genuine closure is possible under such conditions because the end point is a judgement, and a judgement, as Derrida has argued, is never fixed on epistemological bedrock.[30] It is a judgement precisely because it is not an unassailable fact. In the end we must live with the consequences of our decisions.

This is not to say that there are absolutely no happy endings in Hitchcock's films, but even in those that conclude with traditional expressions of bourgeois, heterosexual fulfillment, there are frequently indications of an underlying anxiety regarding both the emotional condition of the central characters and the reliability of the narrative's concluding images. Narratological uncertainty, in other words, is often a way of denying the myth of perfectibility (living "happily ever after") by making closure arbitrary rather than natural ('natural' being understood as preeminently ideological). This is because closure, whether realized as a conscious or unconscious interpretive preference, is a sense-making practice that also frequently serves a conciliatory or inclusive function. In this respect it is generally seen as having an affiliative capacity that is at its most effective when interpolating its predetermined middle-class audience (to "live happily ever after" implies possession of the material and economic means to do so). But closure of this kind is often denounced – and even subverted – in Hitchcock's films, the result being a vertiginous destabilization of commonly cherished ideas about love, relationships, and even authority. This is because Hitchcock never tires of showing us just how difficult it is to be certain that we have made the right decision, and how, having once decided on a course of action, we might be forced to accept compromise in place of resolution. Moral agents must act, in other words, but what is there that can guarantee the moral appropriateness of their actions?

The Moral Tale of *Blackmail* (1929)

I want to put these admittedly abstract ideas in a more concrete form by demonstrating how Hitchcock actually makes use of certain of the principles of postmodern ethics. I propose to consider the concluding sequence in one of Hitchcock's early British pictures, *Blackmail* (1929), as illustrating some of the claims I have made about the manner in which Hitchcock's work refuses ideological closure, and the consequences of this refusal in relation to my

30 Derrida, Jacques. *Force of Law: The Mystical Foundation of Authority. Deconstruction and the Possibility of Justice*, edited by Drucilla Cornell, Michael Rosenfield, and David Gray Carlson. London and New York: Routledge, 1992, pp. 3–67.

discussion placing ethical duties in opposition to moral responsibilities. In particular, I want to relate my analysis of *Blackmail*'s closing moments to my earlier comments respecting the myth of moral perfectibility and Furrow's (1995) notion of the complicity of goodness and evil.

In the final scenes of *Blackmail*, Frank and Alice prepare to travel down a corridor at police headquarters toward the station lobby. They have just come from the chief inspector's office where an opportune phone call to the inspector moments earlier has prevented Alice from confessing her responsibility for the deaths of Crewe and Tracy. Distracted by the telephone, which is an important recurring motif in the film, the inspector, who has no inkling that Alice is responsible for these two deaths, instructs Frank to escort Alice from his office and deal with whatever is troubling her. Frank is, of course, Alice's boyfriend, and he is now overwrought with worry. For despite his affection for Alice, Frank is a competent police detective, and he has established in his own mind that Alice is indeed Crewe's killer. And they now stand huddled together outside of the inspector's office as Alice attempts in choked, inchoate sentences to admit her guilt to Frank even as she tries to offer reasons for her actions. They hold hands in a tight two-shot as the camera frames them from the front. Frank tells Alice that he knows of her guilt and partially pulls the glove she left at the crime scene from his pocket as evidence of his knowledge. The camera then follows them as they begin their funereal walk down the hallway, changing to a rear point of view as they approach the doors to the lobby.

At the lobby doors Frank drops his right hand lifelessly to his side; then both Frank and Alice release their grip on the other's hand simultaneously, as if by some internal cue they have come to a sudden and mutual realization about the nature of their relationship. This cessation of handholding comes a moment or two earlier than would be necessary for Frank to open the lobby door and suggests the recurring motif of a strained romantic relationship between them that has been developed throughout the film. Once in the lobby a rotund police officer steps forward to make a joke at Frank's expense. Referring to Alice's comment several minutes earlier that she had information relating to Crewe's death in a tone meant to playfully mock her alleged detection skills, the constable tells Frank, "Watch out, you'll be losing your job." Frank, Alice, and the policeman begin to laugh quietly at the officer's comment, but as the camera pans closer the laughing grows louder, continuing far longer than would seem merited by the quality of the joke. Alice glances nervously from one to the other, feigning appreciation of the gibe, when she suddenly catches sight of Crewe's painting of the laughing jester as it is being removed to storage. It is interesting that the film concludes here, ending at the moment the police investigation itself has ended, a neat illustration of the interpenetration of theme and presentation.[31] Alice stands transfixed by Crewe's painting as Frank and the constable continue their good-natured ribbing. The camera lingers on the painting as it is carried through the lobby doors and down the corridor from which Frank and Alice have just emerged. The joking and laughing continue. Our final image of Alice is of a terrified young woman whose unconvincing laughter seals within her the knowledge of her culpability.

The image, as Robin Wood (1989) would say, is disturbing, but Hitchcock so completely masters the articulation (or perhaps, manipulation) of viewer subjectivity as to make Alice the most virtuous of killers. Indeed, Hitchcock makes evident that natural justice has been served precisely because bureaucratic justice has been thwarted, for it is the justice system's ethicality rather its efficiency that Hitchcock places under scrutiny.[32] Indeed, if justice is the search for truth, then Hitchcock presents us with a dilemma, for it is clearly neither the truth nor justice that will make Alice free. The only possibility for emancipation would appear to lie in her (and Frank's) silence concerning the truth. Even here, however, the freedom Alice might have gained by her silence is markedly ambiguous, for secrecy procures security at the cost of full and honest openness. Alice is condemned in this sense to her secret (again, shared with Frank) in a kind of existential compromise. If the film is to have a satisfactory conclusion – satisfactory in the sense that the wicked are punished and the righteous go free – then deceit is the fitting mechanism through which reason and compassion can successfully coexist. Alice can

---

31 This was Hitchcock's first sound film, and the idea of "bleeding" sound from one source to another seems a rather sophisticated understanding of how sight and sound could be connected metaphorically. It is also remarkable that Hitchcock blends the laughter from the constable and Frank, who are no longer in the frame, with the image of the jester whose laughing face taunts Alice. This cinematic effect creates a peculiar distortion in conventional conceptions of diegesis, for though the men's laughter is diegetic, it is displaced onto the canvass depicting the visage of the laughing jester. In this respect, it is diegetic sound with a non-diegetic element. This displacement also helps to heighten viewer anxiety about Alice's plight by creating an eerie representation of her feelings of guilt, the laughter goading Alice for her inaction.

32 Hitchcock is well known to have been intrigued by the police procedural as evidenced, for instance, by the opening sequences of *Blackmail* (1929) in which he devotes several minutes of the film to a documentary style account of British police practices in tracking down a robbery suspect. Nevertheless, the heart of *Blackmail* is not a deconstruction of investigative procedures, but a critique of the interpersonal evil that is done when bloodless principles are animated and living human connections are vanquished. The strained tension that juxtaposes Frank's moral obligations as a lover with his ethical responsibilities as a detective is emblematic of the problems that arise when ethical principles are pursued to the detriment of moral responsibility.

perhaps only be freed by confession, but Frank's involvement in covering up her actions – behaviour especially questionable coming from a police detective – has greatly complicated the relation between confession and indictment. Mutual guilt more than love is what binds Frank and Alice together.

A form of intimacy that is common to many romantic couples now connects them, but the secret by which they are united challenges conventional thematic elements of the romantic film in powerful ways. The film also invokes the collusion of good and evil that I mentioned earlier. Alice appears to have acted in a morally responsible way, defending herself from Crewe's attack when her life was being threatened, but her subsequent behaviour has been to resist confessing her actions and taking responsibility for what she has done. And by bringing Frank into the orbit of her decisions Alice has set in motion a sequence of events that brings her and Frank into a private, conspiratorial union. Their relationship, in other words, is founded on a confidential knowledge, and the ethical status of this knowledge seems destined to contaminate all prospects of romantic fulfillment. It further threatens to privilege their individualist motives over the communitarian values by which the social order is maintained. Alice's spirited resistance to two transgressions – Crewe's assault and the offense that would be committed against her by the legal system – sets the stage for a difficult contestation between the moral impulse and the ethical code. As Bauman writes:

> Moral issues cannot be 'resolved', nor the moral life of humanity guaranteed, by the calculating and legislative efforts of reason. Morality is not safe in the hands of reason, though this is exactly what spokesmen of reason promise. [...] Reason is about making correct decisions, while moral responsibility precedes all thinking about decisions as it does not, and cannot care about any logic which would allow the approval of an action as correct. Thus, morality can be 'rationalized' only at the cost of self-denial and self-attrition. From that reason-assisted self-denial, the self emerges morally disarmed, unable (and unwilling) to face up to the multitude of moral challenges and cacophony of ethical prescriptions. At the far end of the long march of reason, moral nihilism waits: that moral nihilism which in its deepest essence means not the denial of binding ethical code, and not the blunders of relativistic theory – but the loss of ability to be moral.[33]

33 Bauman, 1993, pp. 247–248.

That Alice successfully escapes the judgement of the law likely strikes some viewers as signifying a rupture in the cultural order, a violation of the social contract, or perhaps, more simply, an indication of Hitchcock's oft-cited disdain for the police. For others however, Alice has eluded authoritarian violations of her liberties in going undetected by the police, and this is to be lauded as a victory over the machinery of inhuman bureaucracy. In her resistance to the instrumental reason that reveals itself in the "ethical prescriptions" that Bauman describes as manifested in the legal apparatus, Alice determines a life course that produces discontent and a doubly articulated guilt (guilt for Crewe's death and guilt for evading punishment for that death).

In addition, the function of the cinematic dénouement in the bourgeois mode of representation has been turned topsy-turvy in *Blackmail.* We can say that there is a form of closure to *Blackmail* because the picture does end, and the characters are shown to have at least tentatively resolved a specific problem. However, this narrative closure stands at some distance from the ideological closure that is traditional with the arrival of the final credits. In *Blackmail*, the concluding image speaks at two levels. Denotatively, the image tells us that Frank and Alice are now able to enter into a connubial union. But at the connotative level the image is carceral, not emancipatory. Alice is trapped in a relationship with a man for whom she appears to have extraordinarily mixed emotions, and though Frank has been a victim of Alice's emotional inconstancy at times in the film, he now maintains a firmer grip on her life than ever before. It is Frank who is now positioned to blackmail Alice into marriage since the would-be blackmailer, Tracy, has perished during a police chase. It is unclear whether love motivates Frank to protect Alice from his colleagues, or whether it is out of fear that his association with a woman who might publicly be accused of murder might badly affect his career, his social standing, and his masculinity. It is therefore reasonable to wonder if this ending is really a sly warning from Hitchcock that marriage is a form of prison. Indeed, if heterosexual pairing in the romantic cinema is ideologically equivalent to the establishment of a preferred mode of social order, upon what is this social order actually predicated?

By concluding on this unsettling note the film parodies the convention of the traditional heterosexual union by suggesting a semantic relationship to the traditional romantic thriller all the while making syntactic diversions away from that same convention. In other words, the requisite elements for the conventional heterosexual coupling are present in material form (boy does get girl, after all), but the tension produced by the mutual guilt that binds Alice and Frank together belies those material elements at a deeper level. Private knowledge shared between romantic partners can easily be characterized as a form of mutual guilt insofar as such knowledge commonly produces a sense of isolation that can further enhance feelings of mystery and uniqueness. In Hitchcock's films heterosexual pairing is frequently achieved only after a series of adventures (and misadventures) have been completed and the couple, in a figurative purgatorial cleansing, are now ready for romantic closure. In *Blackmail*, these elements are present only as emblems of what might have been – they are semantically appropriate to the context but only in the most superficial of ways. From a syntactic point of view, they are inversions of matrimonial realization, serving instead to parody the very idea that intimacy is an essential state in which romantic partners might successfully isolate themselves from the social order. Romance is always and already infected by the suppositions of its surrounding culture. Shared longings and conspiratorial silence make *Blackmail* a remarkably curious kind of romantic thriller.

Blackmail gives us an ending that defamiliarizes viewer anticipation by mocking the prospect of moral perfectibility. Alice and Frank may be united by the film's end, but rather than provide answers the final image provokes many unsettling questions. Will their relationship survive the deceit they are practising? Have they achieved a level of moral comfort such as will allow the pangs of guilt to be washed away? Will Frank's professional code of ethics eventually overwhelm his sense of moral responsibility for the woman he says he loves? As a concluding motif, such unanswered questions are an unconventional cinematic strategy in the romantic thriller tradition, for rather than "tying things together" they further unravel the narrative. The open-ended nature of the film's narrative may parallel the open-ended problem of moral ambivalence, but it leaves a disquieting sentiment, nonetheless. Though Alice has acted on her own initiative it is hard to see *Blackmail* as a meditation on free will. Rather, the narrative has a haunting claustrophobia that is owed in part to its conditions of production (Hitchcock's first use of sound equipment demanded numerous close shots) and to the tightening of the moral noose in which Alice has been snared. Twist and turn as she might, the prospect of a fitting moral dénouement is denied to her, and though this can be read as a subversive assault against male privilege it is clearly also a universal situation in which Alice is caught. In Bauman's words, the "contingency, contention, ambivalence and unanticipated consequences of human undertakings" is writ large in Hitchcock's film.

Ultimately it is Hitchcock's representation of moral ambivalence that makes *Blackmail* a rewarding and serious document of human striving. Whether or not the film is serious art is far less important. Alice and Frank are swept along by circumstances which, to paraphrase Marx, were not entirely of their own choosing. The weight of their actions may weigh like nightmares on their minds and on their consciences, but this is the price that freedom exacts of all moral agents. The freedom to choose, Hitchcock reveals, is paid for in consequences whose ramifications can often only dimly be recognized. Moral agency makes willing blackmailers of everyone.

Chapter 6

HITCHCOCK'S DEBT TO SILENCE: TIME AND SPACE IN *THE LODGER*

Introduction

In this chapter I offer a scene-by-scene analysis of one of Hitchcock's most important films, his 1927 silent classic, *The Lodger*. This type of analysis is different from the approaches pursued in the other chapters in this book, but I have in mind the same ambition despite the shift in method. I want to illustrate several of the broader issues at work in Hitchcock's films as these are revealed not by placing the work under a specific philosophic or ideological lens, but by adhering strictly to the task of describing the film's various tableaux in sufficient detail as makes apparent the underlying principles on which the narrative is based. In other words, I construct my argument as a sequence of scenic analyses. However, rather than train my eye on a single scene, or mise en scène, I consider the film as Hitchcock might have described it: the arrangement of individual elements in the style of cinematic montage. The relative brevity of the film makes this a more feasible approach than is possible with one of his later, and thereby more complex, films. Moreover, the fact that the film is silent eliminates the need to consider the relevance of sound as a contributory element in the design of the production.

Yet I would be guilty of misdirecting my reader should I be understood as saying that these are the only reasons why I have selected *The Lodger* for this form of analysis. There is a further reason for choosing this film over the later, more mature works, and that is the fact that the argument can readily be made that *The Lodger* is the first of his films to define for Hitchcock the cinematic aesthetic that would come to signify his style, his narrative interests, his directorial preoccupations – in short, his artistic vision.

This proposition is not an original proclamation. In 1966, Hitchcock himself commented that *The Lodger* "was the first time I exercised my style [...]

you might almost say it was my first picture."[1] In offering this description, Hitchcock was hinting at the idea that with this early, black and white, silent picture he had come to understand his role as a filmmaker; that is, he could look back to 1927 and see, in nascent form, the formal properties of all his later works. Indeed, at a rather pedestrian level *The Lodger* is a veritable collection of Hitchcock firsts. Consider that *The Lodger* is

- the first film in which Hitchcock made a cameo appearance. Some writers claim that he actually made two cameo appearances in the film, an argument I examine later in this chapter.
- the first film in which Hitchcock introduced an unnamed central character. The most famous of his films to repeat this strategy was *Rebecca* (1940).
- also the first film in which the police were depicted as occasionally inept, and perhaps even as untrustworthy as the villain. This theme repeats itself across many later films, including, *Blackmail* (1929) *The 39 Steps* (1935), and *Rear Window* (1954).
- the first Hitchcock film in which brandy was taken for "medicinal" purposes. This motif was repeated in every subsequent Hitchcock film.
- the first of his movies to feature a rather Hitchcockian visual effect. This occurs in the scene where the sound of the lodger's footsteps is illustrated visually using a glass floor as a prop. There is also a scene where the film's detective, Joe, has his ruminations regarding the case reflected back to him in the lodger's footprint in the soil. Hitchcock would later come to pioneer many special effects such as occurring in *Foreign Correspondent* (1940), *Vertigo* (1958), *The Birds* (1963).
- the first Hitchcock film to be loosely based on a novel about a real-life serial killer (Jack the Ripper). Hitchcock repeated this with *Psycho* (1960) which was based on Robert Bloch's novel about Ed Gein. He also focused on a serial killer very much like the murder in *The Lodger* in his much later film, *Frenzy* (1972).
- the first film to depict the relations among the major characters as triangular. I will explain this in more detail later, but it is important to recognize that triangularity has both spatial and thematic qualities in this and other Hitchcock films. In *The Lodger*, Hitchcock even used stylized triangles on his title cards for the film.

---

1 Cited in Spoto, Donald. *The Art of Alfred Hitchcock: Fifty Years of his Motion Pictures.* New York and London: Anchor Books, 1982, p. 5.

- the first of Hitchcock's film to portray the consequences of evil being brought into the safe refuge of the middle-class family. This is a crucial aspect of his late film, *Shadow of a Doubt* (1943).
- the first Hitchcock film in which lovers are linked together with handcuffs. Hitchcock repeated this rather banal trop in *The 39 Steps* (1935) and again in *Saboteur* (1942).
- Hitchcock's first film in which a male character attempts the transformation of a woman by dressing her in clothing of his choosing. This was later done more famously in *Vertigo* (1958), and again in *Marnie* (1964).
- the first film in which Hitchcock was forced by studio pressure to alter his intended ending, for he wanted the lodger to be guilty – or at least to leave his guilt or innocence unresolved. He offered the same complaint about his 1941 film, *Suspicion*, claiming that the studio prevented him from showing Cary Grant as a killer.

I suspect that the list could be extended further, but this gives some evidence of the significance that *The Lodger* came to assume in Hitchcock's cinematic development. With *The Lodger* Hitchcock established the foundations for an artistic vision – and a philosophy of technique – that was to sustain his cinematic work for the next five decades. Indeed, there are few technical or thematic elements of Hitchcock's mature work that cannot be found in nascent form in this black-and-white, silent film. Hence Rothman's contention that "*The Lodger* is not an apprentice work but a thesis, definitively establishing Hitchcock's identity as an artist."[2]

But even as *The Lodger* prefigures much that was to form the core of Hitchcock's cinematic sensibility, the film is a product of a developing mind, and should not be taken as an inflexible template for the subsequent evolution of Hitchcock's imagination. Its artistry lies not merely in the way in which one can read into its images and style evidence of Hitchcock's later techniques, but in the way Hitchcock revealed his talent for exploiting the potentials of the cinematic medium. Unlike *Citizen Kane* (1939), which established a high-tide mark to which Orson Welles was forever forced – unsuccessfully – to reach, *The Lodger* established a kind of cinematic framework within which Hitchcock would hone his artistry. *The Lodger* was Hitchcock's arrival, not his departure.

2 Rothman, William. *Hitchcock: The Murderous Gaze.* Cambridge, MA: Harvard University Press, 1982, p. 7.

History of *The Lodger*

For all its artistic ingenuity, however, *The Lodger* was an exercise in frustration, for although he completed the picture with relative dispatch, Hitchcock was faced with several obstacles in releasing the film. A nearly vindictive lack of support from C. M. Woolf, who headed the distribution company for Gainsborough Pictures, and the personal jealousies of a rival director at that studio were formidable impediments standing between the film and the public. Even though the work had excited critics at a special screening in September 1926 – *The Evening News* described it as "an essay in film technique" (20 September 1926) – Woolf declared the film "too 'highbrow', and too involved with 'art'" to be suitable for theatrical release.[3] This was hardly the sort of criticism that was to be Hitchcock's fortune over the years. Nonetheless, it is important to point out that Woolf highlighted early in Hitchcock's career a theme that was to accompany and perhaps plague his career every step of the way: the conflict between high art and popular culture. It is easy today to forget that despite the mass appeal of films like *North by Northwest*, *Psycho*, and *To Catch a Thief*, a profound artistic perception was firmly in control of the production.

The Lodger is an exceedingly artistic film, combining the eerie, atmospheric aspects of German expressionism in its mise en scène, with the conventional narrative of the British murder mystery. Ivor Novello's somewhat campy performance hampers the film in some respects, but as an historical allusion to the traditions of live theatre his acting has a peculiar charm, nonetheless. And the occasionally heavy-handed staging in some sequences such as the lodger's initial appearance at the Bunting's home, in which Novello emerges as a ghostly apparition with vampiric intents, clearly dates the movie.

Working from Eliot Stannard's screenplay of Marie Belloc Lowndes's novel, Hitchcock and an illustrator sketched out each scene of the film in advance of shooting, indicating on paper everything from set design to props.[4] This penchant for preplanning – some might call it an obsession – would characterize Hitchcock's work forever after. But when Woolf decided the film was too artistically pretentious to warrant studio support, the production crew's labour appeared to be a waste of time – and a waste of 12,000 pounds. Woolf, who simply did not appreciate Hitchcock's sense of cinematic exposition, was concerned chiefly with ensuring that his films were structured according to conventional narrative intelligibility. Hitchcock's style was unconventional,

3 Kapsis, Robert. *Hitchcock: The Making of a Reputation*. Chicago and London: University of Chicago Press, 1992, p. 18.

4 Lowndes, Marie Belloc. *The Lodger*. London: Methuen Publishing, 1913.

however, and involved the pursuit of interpretive complexity that pushed the film in several directions at once. Hitchcock biographer, John Taylor, says the problem was easily identified: Woolf simply did not understand the film.[5] Where Woolf wanted explicit signposts directing the viewer, Hitchcock strove to multiply the different levels of meaning in the film, creating a more deeply textured work than Woolf thought necessary. Hitchcock, too, wanted to tell a story as much as Woolf, but not at the expense of excluding the unique style of narrative the cinema permitted. "My models were forever after the German filmmakers of 1924 and 1925," Hitchcock told Spoto. "They were trying very hard to express ideas in purely visual terms."[6] In like fashion Hitchcock laboured to present his ideas *cinematically* – to make the film's visual aspect the major component of the storytelling. Hitchcock prized the disequilibrium that could be achieved with unusual camera angles, intense contrasts in lighting, and the way that characters could be placed in the cinematic frame – the way, in other words, in which the art of the cinema could be used to evoke (and perhaps manipulate) the audience's emotions. In his quest to produce art, Hitchcock was unwilling to accept that his audience could understand nothing of the nuances of cinematic reality. "Isn't it a fascinating design?" he once said to Truffaut speaking of *Strangers on a Train*. "You could study it forever."[7] C. M. Woolf, however, had no interest in distributing pictures an audience might wish to study.

That *The Lodger* was eventually released was due chiefly to the interventions of the film's producer, Michael Balcon. Recognizing Woolf's intractability, Balcon enlisted the assistance of Ivor Montagu, who, though only 22 years old at the time, was a founding member of the Film Society in Britain. Montagu suggested reshooting several scenes and helped Hitchcock to pare the intertitle cards from nearly three hundred to around eighty. The result was a leaner film than the one Hitchcock had shot, but one that was superior in its dramatic narrative. It was not by Montagu that Hitchcock was introduced to the idea that a purely cinematic methodology was possible, but the experience with Montagu (about whose contributions Hitchcock was less than generous in his later reflections) consolidated the young director's growing appreciation for the discursive potential of a visually driven narrative. Even today the film transcends the putative limitations of silence with its typically Hitchcockian

---

5 Taylor, John. *Hitch: The Life and Times of Alfred Hitchcock*. New York: Da Capo Press, 1996, p. 73.

6 Spoto, 1982, p. 75.

7 Truffaut, François. *Hitchcock* (Revised edition). New York and London: Simon & Schuster, 1983, p. 195.

motifs and innovations. As Spoto comments, *The Lodger* "may be the noisiest silent picture ever made."[8]

The Film Scene by Scene

The film begins with a lengthy montage. A brief glimpse of a hand appears, and then the screen fills with a close-up of a young, blonde woman screaming in terror before a third cut brings us to the flashing lights of a theatre marquee. As with many of Hitchcock's films, there is an immediate joining of the "real" action of the film – the woman's murder – with the artifice of the theatre. The lights of the marquee that flash out the words "To-Night, Golden Curls" hover in the blackness, disconnected visually from anything but the young woman's panic-stricken face. We cannot be certain, in fact, that the flashing lights are a part of a theatre marquee until some minutes later, for no context is offered for interpreting the words that illuminate the otherwise blackened screen. Hitchcock then cuts back to the woman who now lies dead on the ground, a victim, we learn, of a serial killer who has been terrorizing London, preying only upon blonde women. His card has been left on the body, the words "The Avenger" framed within a triangle. Triangular configurations will come to play a conspicuous role throughout the film.

The montage carries us forward through the police interview with a witness, the mocking of her report by a bystander who mimics the killer's description, and the subsequent reports on the killing filed by reporters. In this latter sequence Hitchcock shows the mass media's operations in detail, with images of reporters, newspaper production, and radio broadcasts (there is some stock footage included here, as well as Hitchcock's first cameo appearance as an editor – or possibly news director – at the newspaper office). This fascination with detail will later be repeated in *The Wrong Man*, and even in *Psycho*, underscoring Hitchcock's lifelong interest with documentary film.

We then cut to the interior of the theatre mentioned already to find a group of young women returning backstage from an evening's performance; each woman wears a curly blonde wig, a detail that explains the illuminated words on the marquee while forcing a further connection between the Avenger (who preys only on blonde women) and the theatre. The chorus girls' jovial mood dissolves, however, with the appearance of a late edition of the paper and its headline announcing that the avenger has struck again – as he does every Tuesday evening. This weekly performance by the killer can be read as a strained kind of expediency, a sign, one might argue, of a poorly contrived

8 Spoto, 1982, p. 5.

plot. Yet in suggesting an additional relation between the serial murderer and performance, the homicides assume a theatrical quality. Just as certain programmes might be staged or aired on a weekly schedule, so too, the Avenger follows a schedule. And as his murders are fodder for the London papers, his performances have a morbid entertainment value.

Indeed, the cyclical repetition of the crime on a weekly schedule also provides a deliberately measured pace not only to the killer's behaviour, but also to the rhythm of the film's suspense. In *The Lodger*, Tuesday's approach brings with it not the surprise of the unknown, but the suspense of inevitability. Indeed, the inevitability of evil, rather than the shock of the unexpected, is the primary structure for Hitchcock's suspense. The inevitability of the Avenger's attacks reaches out not only into the audience's field of expectations but folds back again into the narrative of the film, for it is the Avenger's orderly movement across the geography of London that eventually suggests to the police a means for his apprehension. The nightmarish quality of predictability overshadows the fear of uncertainty.

None of the chorus girls featured in the backstage scenes is a major player in the subsequent drama, although one of the performers does become a victim of the killer later in the film. However, their varied reactions to the tragic news are a central part of Hitchcock's montage, giving us an important glimpse into their lives, and revealing in candid fashion their fears and insecurities. Several of the women joke about the Avenger to disguise their fear; one even conceals the lower portion of her face with a scarf in imitation of the witness's description as told by the news report. Another shows how she will camouflage herself by tucking two false ringlets of brunette hair beneath her hat. These acts of deflection neatly encapsulate the women's position in the urban world where they are first positioned as entertainers – or, perhaps, as entertainment – and second as potential victims. In the first instance, the women have adorned themselves with blonde wigs as part of a production number to appeal to their male audience. In the second instance, however, they contemplate disguising themselves with different wigs to be protected from a serial killer outside the theatre; again, the anonymous male, whether in the role of theatregoer or as killer, must in some way be appeased. Putting on and taking off make-up, wigs, and costumes to make themselves presentable/invisible to the anonymous male gaze has become a defining activity of both theatrical production and the production of everyday relations for the women. The tension that is developed in the juxtaposition of these competing motives – attracting and repelling the male Other – accounts in part for the obvious expression of powerlessness as displayed on the faces of the women who pass through the montage. As Spoto writes:

> The whole film has a delicate poise between this kind of repulsion and attraction, between paranoia (the murderer is on the prowl) and laughter at that paranoia (people in the street, and in the chorus girls' dressing room, frighten each other for fun and for the sense of relief). There is an underlying fear of the little things of everyday life, which are seen as menacing.[9]

The opening montage thus establishes the film's problematic with economy and wit. The combination of terror and morbid humour underscores the public's psychologically varied responses to the Avenger. Moreover, the consequences of the killer's actions are revealed primarily in the way that these actions affect those who have become victims of fear. Whereas we never actually witness the Avenger at work nor dwell on the immediate results of his actions, we are given a lengthy montage in which mass-mediated versions of the killer's activities are recounted.

The fear to which we are introduced is produced not simply by the Avenger's brutality, for a significant role in the manufacture of fear is taken up by the mass media. Indeed, the news media are curiously dependent on the Avenger and his weekly ritual, a fact that is revealed in the words of one newspaper vendor who proclaims Tuesday to be his "lucky day." Images of paper vendors clamouring the latest grisly headline appear throughout the film, as do scenes of the film's main characters gathered about the newspaper. Even the lodger, at that point in the film where Hitchcock is stoking audience suspicion that he is the actual killer, is troubled greatly by the sound of a newspaper seller announcing the evening's murder from the street below the lodging house window.

Despite the film's opening montage featuring a quick glimpse of the latest murder, and the subsequent response to that tragedy as it is relayed in the media's reporting, the film's action has virtually nothing to do with the Avenger's stalking of his victims, nor with the police effort to track him down. Indeed, that all action involving the avenger happens off-screen suggests that *The Lodger* is not so much a film about murder or police work as it is a film about insecurity, fear, and suspicion. And these insecurities, fears, and suspicions are more directly the results of mass-mediated information than they are the products of the actual slayings. As Lesley Brill has commented:

9 Spoto, Donald. *The Dark Side of Genius: The Life of Alfred Hitchcock.* New York: Ballantine Books, 1983, p. 101.

> Hitchcock devotes the opening of the film – second in rhetorical importance only to its end – to social reactions because the murders have great significance for the whole society; they are not represented as an isolated aberration. [...] London's response to the murders is to make of them entertainment, a source of titillation for the idly curious. Details both in the opening and in later sequences indicate that the amusement of the people of London find in the Avenger's murders is related to the voyeurist pleasures they take in fair-haired young women more generally.[10]

Brill's analysis is made more complete by the additional observation that Hitchcock's film is itself directly implicated in the realm of the mass media's tendency to transform the macabre and the horrific into entertainment; *The Lodger* is precisely just such an act of transformation. Furthermore, to insist that we must respect the difference between the film as fiction, and the representation of the murders *within* the film as fact, is to fail to acknowledge the way in which Hitchcock has shown us that the news is *produced*; in other words, the point of the opening montage, one might argue, is to erase the boundary between fact and fiction – not so that we might confuse *The Lodger* with a documentary film, but so that we will be drawn into the film as subjects and as spectators. The London crowds pore over the newspapers feverishly, and they stare at the outdoor news marquee in rapt attention. So too, our gaze at the screen is directed by the director – recalling, for the moment, that Hitchcock has made his first cameo in the film as an editor at the newspaper office, directing his underlings to their various duties. In our role as filmgoers, it is easy to criticize the throngs of Londoners who treat the killer's atrocities as though they were merely entertaining diversions from the humdrum of their everyday lives. However, as viewers of the film we are equally guilty of this attitude.

After her introduction as a fashion model, the film's heroine, Daisy Bunting, arrives home to find her parents discussing the newspaper report of the Avenger's latest murder. Her boyfriend Joe, a police detective, is there, too, waiting her return. As Daisy reads the newspaper account, Joe suggests an immediate affinity between himself and the Avenger, telling Daisy that, like the Avenger, he is himself fond of blonde hair – a direct reference to Daisy. This is the first of three jokes that Joe tells, a practice he will only

10 Brill, Lesley. "Hitchcock's 'The Lodger'." In *A Hitchcock Reader*, edited by Marshall Deutelbaum and Leland Poague. Ames, Iowa: Iowa State University Press, 1986, p. 72.

abandon when he returns from the scene of the Avenger's eighth killing, horrified by what he will see. From that point forward, Joe neither jokes nor smiles for the remainder of the film.

Early in the film, however, Joe is a happy-go-lucky character, whose cavalier attitude toward the Avenger suggests that he treats his police duties with less than serious attention. In drawing a parallel between his own attraction to Daisy (symbolized by her blonde hair) and the Avenger's fetish for golden-haired women, Joe articulates a triangular structure that will lie back of most of the film's subsequent action (the three-way relation between Joe and Mr and Mrs Bunting precedes the expression of the triangular relations between Daisy, Joe, and the Avenger, but this trilateral configuration is less important). Daisy is represented clearly as a potential victim of the Avenger, given that the three qualifications of being a woman, of being young, and of being blonde have already been related in the film's opening sequences. And Joe's status as police detective (though yet not assigned to the Avenger case) places him directly in the position of Daisy's guardian. Joe, we might reasonably conclude in these opening scenes, will stand between Daisy and the Avenger. In this respect Joe emerges in the narrative's introductory moments as the film's probable male lead.

And yet, Joe is quickly reduced in stature. His inappropriate joke comparing himself to the Avenger is rejected by Daisy who rolls her eyes in disgust, and his subsequent effort to make amends by surreptitiously presenting her with two hearts he fashions with the aid of a cookie cutter receives a mock rebuff from Daisy who tosses his heart back at him. Disconsolate, Joe tears his cookie heart in half and gazes forlornly into the camera. Daisy's reaction is only mild amusement.

The scene is curious for several reasons. In the first instance, it is unclear what we are to make of their relationship. Mrs Bunting shows obvious pleasure in Joe's efforts at affection, perhaps delighted in seeing her daughter matched with a police detective. Mr Bunting, expressing the stereotypically dull-witted oblivion of a cinematic father, remains noncommittal regarding matters of the heart. Hence our sense of Daisy's reaction to Joe's protestations of love is equally ambivalent. He appears to be genuinely attached to Daisy, but here and in later scenes she seems to be distant from him and disinterested in his actions. Moreover, his tasteless attempts at humour leave her more annoyed than amused, suggesting that although she tolerates his attentions – and accepts that Joe is the best she is likely to do – she has loftier ambitions in respect of a lover. Joe is a pedestrian sort: low, vulgar, obsequious, and cloying. His suit is cheap and rumpled and his manner generally brusque. Furthermore, as Brill points out, the fact that Joe relates as easily to her parents as he does to Daisy suggests that he may also be too old for her.[11] In short, Daisy's rejection of Joe's cookie heart is itself a heartfelt rejection even as it is apparently meant in jest. Indeed, although the scene is played for laughs the serious undertow is inescapable: Daisy reads about a murderer of blonde women and her boyfriend suggests that he and the killer are alike. It is hard to ignore the fact that Joe is a rather insensitive romantic male hero.

The climax of this domestic interlude is the lodger's arrival at the Bunting house. Two symbols suggest his imminent appearance, including the dimming of the lights (the electric meter requires money) and the sounding of the cuckoo clock. The first event may seem inconsequential, but the symbolic intimations of darkness as a prelude to a character's appearance hardly need explaining. Moreover, that the darkness is a consequence of a meter calling out for payment is a subtle indicator of the Bunting's lower-middle-class status. We also soon discover that the Buntings have advertised a room for rent. Hence, the fact that their financial situation is somewhat insecure makes their decision to let the room to a stranger understandable.

That the man at the door will turn out to be someone bringing them further income in the form of rent suggests that while he may usher in darkness of one sort (the suspicion of his being a murderer), he will bring light of another kind. It is true that the lodger's wealth is only revealed at the close of the film, but it is hinted at in his appearance in the story when he pays for a month's rent in advance with neither hesitation nor negotiation. Later we are shown that he is inclined to leave money lying about his room, a practice that distresses Mrs Bunting for whom money is far too important to be left unattended.

In the second instance it is difficult to ignore Hitchcock's use of birds as symbols of chaos. Perhaps the cuckoo, a bird that displaces others from their nest, is especially significant in this film, for as events will show, the lodger will initiate a series of displacements and disruptions. He will disrupt the apparently smooth operations of the Bunting home and displace Joe from his station in Daisy's affections. In addition, as many of Hitchcock's interpreters have pointed out, birds are outwardly soft animals, yet they have pointed beaks and sharp claws; many are predators. The lodger, too, conceals something dark and potentially sinister behind his affected exterior. The lodger's arrival is thus signalled by everyday events, which, though hardly significant to the characters within the narrative, are intended to be more than accidental occurrences to viewers of the film.

---

11 Brill, p. 70.

The structure of the lodger's entry has already been briefly mentioned. Mrs Bunting opens the door and as the London fog swirls about, a tall, dark, and menacing figure is revealed to us. Seen from Mrs Bunting's perspective, the stranger at the door immediately conjures up recollections of the witness's description of the Avenger including the detail of a scarf covering the lower half of his face. When he steps into the light and slowly removes his scarf, his actions are stilted, artificial, and deliberate. His face is a study in intensity, and he gazes about the room furtively. Mrs Bunting has difficulty collecting herself, but when the man points to the sign advertising a room for rent, she offers to show him upstairs to inspect the quarters.

The lodger inspects his room, finds it adequate, and dismisses Mrs Bunting to bring him a sparse meal. While she is out of the room, he seeks for a place to hide a small black valise, eventually locking it in a cupboard and pocketing the key. When Mrs Bunting returns, she opens the door to discover that he is turning around the room's artwork so that the pictures face the wall. These pictures are of young, blonde women in various poses, including one scene of bondage. The lodger explains to Mrs Bunting that he finds the pictures disturbing and would like to have them removed. She calls downstairs for Daisy to come and assist her.

Daisy enters the room, sees what the lodger has done, and bursts out laughing. This is the second time he has heard her laughter, for when he first entered the house, she was laughing at her father who had fallen from a chair while putting a coin in the meter. Here, standing in the doorway, framed in soft focus, Daisy is unaware of the lodger standing only several feet away, but the sound of her voice on him is hypnotic, and he is plainly startled out of his stupor. Then, in a remarkable take, the lodger, shot from Daisy's perspective, turns about to see her. He is facing the mirror and Daisy is to his left. Yet rather than make a simple 90-degree movement, the lodger turns to his right, sweeping around the room a full 270 degrees. His gaze comes to rest gaze on Daisy, a look that evinces surprise, attraction, and, I would argue, recognition. In Daisy, I believe, the lodger first sees the image of his murdered sister, though this information has not yet been revealed in the narrative. Nonetheless, this fact helps explain why he is entranced by the sound of Daisy's laughter, for we will eventually learn that the last thing he heard from his sister's lips at her coming-out ball was her laughter. The lodger's filial affection will, of course, be transformed into romantic love, but his first sight of Daisy carries him back into the dance hall, and memories of his sister fill his mind.

That the lodger is caught up in a painful memory may also account for a curious directorial decision, the fact that we have no subjective shot of Daisy immediately following the lodger's view of her. Instead, we cut to a shot of the room, where Hitchcock shows the lodger and Daisy eyeing one another hesitantly. The absence of the opposing subjective shot seems at first an editing oversight: What does he see in Daisy's face, and how is she returning his stare? Hitchcock withholds the answers, increasing our curiosity just as the lodger's extended turn increases our anticipation of his first view of Daisy. Not knowing what the lodger saw in Daisy's eyes at that moment of their first meeting increases the mystery of his intentions.

Mrs Bunting arrives and symbolically pushes Daisy across the threshold into the lodger's room. They gather up the offending pictures and Daisy carries them downstairs. Waiting for Daisy downstairs is Joe who follows her into the parlour. Inside, Joe sweeps Daisy into his arms and kisses her, the abruptness of his actions standing in stark contrast to the deliberate and extended movements of the lodger upstairs only moments before. This contrast is especially significant considering the way in which Hitchcock provides no touches of cinematic intimacy to the scene, and Joe's actions seem clownish and even juvenile. Indeed, most of Joe's and Daisy's embraces and kisses are shot from a medium distance. This structure establishes them as mere objects of our gaze, and the absence of close-ups as would come to characterize Hitchcock's style in romantic encounters lends a voyeuristic character to their intimacies. When Daisy and the lodger commence to kindling their romance, the camera itself turns more intimate, providing a sequence of powerful subjective shots to heighten the audience's emotional engagement with them.

Joe's physical impulsiveness stands in for a deeper examination of his immaturity, adding further evidence to our growing suspicions that he is unsuitable for Daisy. The lodger, by contrast, seems bereft of this sort of childish impulsiveness. True, he also exudes arrogance, and while this may be off-putting in the initial stages of the film, it is quickly evident that for Daisy his haughtiness has a captivating and even seductive quality. Joe is a more superficial character whose visceral responses betray an impetuosity he struggles to control. The lodger, on the other hand, is a man of far greater depth and complexity, whose tortured and anguished appearance hints at darker mysteries. With Joe, there is little to explore other than the surfaces; with the lodger, a world of possibilities opens to Daisy.

Mrs Bunting enters the parlour and Joe and Daisy cease their embrace and inspect the pictures the lodger has just rejected. Joe is puzzled that the lodger is upset by pictures of attractive blonde women hanging on his wall and suggests that the lodger is not "keen on the girls." The reference is double-edged, for the role of the lodger was played by Ivor Novello, who was known to Hitchcock and others working on the film to be gay. In the context of the narrative, though, it suggests that Joe's investigative instincts are utterly untrustworthy. The lodger, as things will turn out, is indeed "keen on the girls" – and especially keen on Daisy – though in a way the story has yet to make evident. The viewer cannot but be struck, however, by Joe's capacity to jump to precisely the wrong conclusion.

The scene with the pictures concludes with Hitchcock's first cinematic special effect. As Joe, Daisy, and Mrs Bunting huddle in the parlour discussing the lodger, an overhead shot brings the chandelier into view. It begins to sway, drawing their attention to the ceiling. They gaze at the chandelier and then the ceiling fades into transparency (Hitchcock used a glass floor). Through the ceiling we now see the lodger, as if shot from the parlour below, as he paces across his room, his movements causing the chandelier to sway. The effect is startling, though perhaps somewhat clumsy (Hitchcock later regretted it). Nonetheless, it serves to establish an important symbol for the rest of the film: the chandelier – with its three lamps – is now a symbol of the lodger, and when the Buntings gaze at the chandelier it is as if we are peering into their minds as they imagine the lodger and his murderous impulses.

With the lodger now firmly entrenched in the Bunting household, the storyline unfolds quickly and with a calculated predictability. Daisy and the lodger become friends, and we see her spending more time visiting in his room. They play chess together and display all the cinematic signs of an emergent romance. But there are still indications that we are not yet to trust the lodger fully. When Daisy brings him breakfast, for instance, a curious sequence of edits makes it appear as though he is about to threaten her with a knife (shades of *Blackmail* and *Psycho*), and during their chess match, he reaches for a poker as they sit near the fireplace with a menacing look as Daisy retrieves a chess piece from the floor. Both events are ruses, of course, but the *possibility* that the lodger is the Avenger is reinforced, nonetheless.

On the night when they are playing chess in the lodger's room, Joe arrives in the Bunting kitchen to announce proudly that he has been assigned to the Avenger case. Upstairs, the chess game has proceeded to the stage of incipient courtship with playful banter, plenty of giggling, and smiles. The lodger and Daisy then exchange a sequence of glances suggesting a combination of seduction and uncertainty. The intimate close-ups suddenly end, however, with a long shot of the lodger and Daisy drawing back from one another in response to a knock at the door. When Mrs Bunting enters to announce Joe's arrival, Daisy's expression is an unqualified look of disappointment, and she leaves the lodger's room reluctantly. She enters the kitchen to find Joe dangling a pair of handcuffs in front of her father and explaining, "When I've put a rope around the Avenger's neck" – and here he impersonates a hanged man – "I'll put a ring around Daisy's finger." This is the second time Joe has forged an alliance between himself and the Avenger, again making the nature of his relationship with Daisy dependent on his association with the murderer. It is also the first instance in a Hitchcock film of a connection being drawn between murder and marriage, a trope he returned to in later films.

Daisy leaves the kitchen and Joe follows her, continuing his joke about handcuffs and marriage, finally pinning her playfully near the bottom of the stairs and locking the handcuffs on her. However, when Daisy realizes what he has done she screams frantically. Mrs Bunting and the lodger rush out from his room at the sound of Daisy's cry. The camera then cuts to a low angle shot in which Daisy's struggle to free herself from the manacles is shown only in the shadows along the stairwell wall. This image darkens the implications of Daisy's struggle considerably, accentuating the terror she feels and negating the humorous intent lying back of Joe's actions. Shot only in the shadows, Daisy's efforts to free herself clearly suggest that she is fighting to release herself from something far more sinister than a boyfriend's prank. Perhaps, as both Brill (1986) and Rothman (1982) suggest, she is fearful of the idea of her impending matrimonial bondage to Joe.[12] From the top of the stairs the lodger looks down at the spectacle in disgust before returning to his room. Finally freed from the handcuffs, Daisy is comforted by her mother who escorts her into the parlour.

This is the first time in the film that the lodger and Joe have been in the same scene, though Joe remained oblivious to the lodger's presence. From this point in the film, one might almost think of *The Lodger* as a series of studies in the movement of Daisy across the emotional spectrum and across the screen. In this scene, she is drawn from the lodger's room by Joe's arrival (and moved from a state of sexual arousal to one of disappointment), and then taken into the parlour by her mother following Joe's sadistic prank with the handcuffs (where her reluctance to meet with Joe has given way to virtual terror). Once inside, Joe follows and offers apologies for placing her in handcuffs. Daisy apparently accepts his apology, albeit with some reluctance, replacing her anger with a look of resignation. But once she and Joe have hugged and exchanged a kiss, Daisy darts from the room and literally skips back up the stairs presumably to rejoin the lodger. Joe and Mrs Bunting are puzzled by her behaviour, and Joe reflects in what must be the most ominous intertitle card in the film, "Does this lodger of yours mean any harm to Daisy?" Mrs Bunting's laughter and her assurance that the lodger is not "that sort" do nothing to assuage Joe's concern – nor do they do much to deflect our attention from the possibility that the lodger and the Avenger are one. The fact that Daisy's symbolic emancipation from Joe is followed by her immediate

12 Brill, p. 72. Rothman, p. 7.

return to the lodger quickens the viewer's concern over the meaning of the lodger's dalliances.

Daisy has now begun a sequence of movements between the lodger and Joe that is sustained until the final stages of the film. Her departure from Joe following his apology in the parlour has also solidified the link between Joe and the lodger, and Joe's suspicions about the Avenger, and his suspicions about the lodger, begin to coalesce into a mutually reinforcing apprehension about his own place in Daisy's life. Indeed, Joe's investigation into the Avenger case, and his concerns about Daisy and the lodger, becomes an inseparable, overriding worry for him. Thus, Hitchcock continues to present the major relations of the film in the triangular motif described earlier, and with each subsequent scene in which the lodger, Joe, and Daisy are shown, the meaning of the action can be read from Daisy's movements across the frame, from Joe to the lodger and back again. This becomes especially pointed in their next encounter.

The Tuesday night following the lodger's arrival the Avenger's next victim appears in the person of one of the chorus girls who was shown in the opening montage. She has argued with her boyfriend and commenced to walk home alone through the London fog. At the same time, the lodger has begun preparations to go out for the evening, sneaking his way out of his room and down the staircase. His departure sequence contains several atmospheric touches, including low angle shots of the lodger emerging from his room, an angle that suggests that we are peering up at him from some secret hiding place. This camera position reinforces audience suspicions concerning the lodger and the reason for his movements. There is also a remarkable overhead shot of the stairway in the Bunting home, showing only the lodger's white hand against the dark wood of the banister spiralling downward as though running in concentric circles down a drain. This shot carries us back to the brief opening shot in the montage where a man's hand appeared a split moment before the film's first murder. There are also intimations in this sequence of the famous shots in *Vertigo* (1958). Staircases are significant in Hitchcock's attempts to draw out the length of a scene for dramatic and mysterious effects.[13]

Mrs Bunting is alone in the house, as Daisy is out (with Joe, perhaps?), and Mr Bunting has taken a job for the evening as a waiter and is not expected in until very late. Mrs Bunting hears the lodger leaving his room and cranes her neck to detect his movement down the stairs. Then, peering out her window she spies him walking away from the house into the night. She rises, pulls on

13 See, for example, the entry for "staircases" in Walker, Michael. *Hitchcock's Motifs*. Amsterdam: Amsterdam University Press, 2005, p. 350 ff.

her robe, and creeps to his room. There follows a series of shots tracing her movement from her bedroom to the lodger's room where she snoops around to discover any secrets that might confirm or refute her growing suspicions about the man who earlier that evening she herself defended from Joe's suggestions of impropriety. The close-up shots of her face, however, make it unmistakable that suspicions have begun to grow in her mind, though it is unclear whether these suspicions are connected to her fear that Daisy's love life is about to be disturbed or that Daisy's life is at risk. When she hears the lodger returning to his room after midnight, however, it seems clear from her expression that it is the latter worry that has consumed her. The lodger, she has determined, is the Avenger.

The murder of the chorus girl echoes faithfully the film's opening sequences, but the significance of the killing is curiously blunted by the comedic imagery that follows when the film commences the following morning in the Bunting kitchen. Mrs Bunting yawns incessantly as she prepares breakfast, apparently tired after a night made sleepless by worry. Mr Bunting yawns constantly because of his late night working as a waiter. And as they try in their turns to stifle their yawns, the sight of one another, mouths agape, makes it impossible for them to stem the contagion of their fatigue. Daisy watches all of this and laughs heartily before taking the lodger's breakfast tray upstairs.

Joe's arrival at the Bunting home is typical. He blusters into the kitchen without knocking at the door and seats himself in what has become his customary chair. He literally orders Mrs Bunting to bring him tea. But aside from his swaggering attitude, he is a changed man in some respects, and when he utters, "The way that fiend did her in –" we realize that his attendance at the previous night's murder scene has transformed the Avenger from myth to reality, the brutality of the killing having had a significant effect on him. His attitude, we can assume, is a result of what he has seen at the crime scene, though his uneasiness over the lodger – who he has come to recognize is a rival for Daisy – also accounts for his changed demeanour.

Joe's account to Mr and Mrs Bunting of the murder is interrupted by a cut to a tray of food falling to the floor and a close-up of Daisy screaming. This close-up of Daisy's hysterical expression and scream is a perfect match for the images of the two women who were previously murdered. There is then a rapid cutaway to one of the pictures that was removed from the lodger's room falling to the floor. Has the lodger attacked Daisy?

Joe and the Buntings rush up to the lodger's room. As Joe opens the door, he is surprised to find Daisy and the lodger laughing and embracing by the window. Seeing them in one another's arms, Joe stalks across the room, the camera providing his viewpoint as the distance between him and the couple diminishes. It is here that Daisy's proximity becomes telling. Joe pulls Daisy from the lodger's arms and interposes himself between her and the lodger, forming a linear arrangement from left to right across the screen. Daisy's mother then pulls Daisy further away yet, so that both Joe and Mrs Bunting now stand between her and the lodger (somehow Mr Bunting has disappeared entirely from the scene). Joe and the lodger square off as if preparing to come to blows. Daisy takes up the task of cleaning the mess while explaining to her mother and to Joe that she dropped the breakfast tray after being frightened by a mouse. Hitchcock then moves Daisy toward the camera, so a triangle is formed between her, the lodger, and Joe, Daisy forming the centre of the line between Joe and the lodger from the viewer's vantage point. Mrs Bunting is now framed outside of the triangle. The argument continues with Daisy placed symbolically between them as both the source of their connection and the cause of their anger. Just as Joe joked about his relation to Daisy being predicated on a connection with the Avenger, so now Daisy has become the medial object both drawing together and driving the two men apart.

The lodger crosses the room, opens his door, and demands that they leave. Another shot of the room establishes the triangularity again, Daisy now closest to the camera at equal distance from both men. Joe moves to the door, collapsing the geometry. Catching himself up Joe returns into the triangle, steps around a chair, and pulls Daisy from her position and pushes her to the door. Mrs Bunting, of course, first introduced Daisy to the lodger by pushing her across the threshold into the room; now Joe symbolically revokes that introduction by forcing her retreat. With the three-way configuration undone, Daisy and the lodger speak to one another at the door. She apologizes for Joe's behaviour; the lodger accepts her apology. Then, having walked out into the hall, she pauses for a suggestive glance across her shoulder at the lodger who watches her leave. Joe follows her, but not before directing an angry glance at the lodger who then informs Mrs Bunting that he will tolerate no such further interruptions.

Downstairs in the parlour Joe and Daisy argue. He apologizes by way of explaining that there is something undefinable about the lodger he cannot stand. His violent and potentially abusive treatment of Daisy is thus justified by his belief that masculine jealousy, and the privilege of intimidating and controlling women, is beyond the need of further justification. Hence the manifest differences between Joe and the lodger are drawn even more starkly. Joe's bellicosity, and his desire to dominate Daisy, is countered completely by the lodger's sensitivity, and his gentler treatment of Daisy.

Joe pushes his apology, and eventually, Daisy relents. They embrace and exchange a kiss. Mrs Bunting who is eavesdropping outside the parlour door decides not to enter, determining that this is moment to leave Joe and Daisy unchaperoned. But her look is a quizzical combination of happiness at their reconciliation, and continuing worry about the lodger and what his presence in their house might mean. No doubt she is also concerned about Daisy's changed attitude toward Joe and her growing infatuation with the lodger. Inside the parlour, Joe and Daisy continue their embrace while the camera cuts to an overhead shot recalling the earlier scene of Joe, Daisy, and Mrs Bunting gazing up at the swinging chandelier. This time only Daisy peers up from her position in Joe's arms and stares (longingly?) at the gently swaying lamps. The sequence concludes with Mrs Bunting finally revealing her fears to Mr Bunting, explaining how on the night of the most recent murder the lodger had disappeared for several hours before sneaking back into the house. Could this mean that he is the Avenger? They resolve that Daisy must never again be left alone with the lodger. They then turn their gaze upward and stare at the chandelier as the scene fades out.

The stage would now be set for the final confrontation and resolution of the mystery, but Hitchcock includes an interlude that heightens the suspense even as it pushes the more artistic aspects of the film into the domain of fetishism. The events also anticipate two later films, *Vertigo* (1958) and *Psycho* (1960). The scenes advance the theme of intimacy between Daisy and the lodger though they might lead some viewers to question the appropriateness of his dalliances.

The lodger goes out during the day to attend the fashion show where Daisy works as a model. Immediately before Daisy steps on to the runway, a model in a wedding gown is finishing her walk, and she and Daisy exchange smiles as they pass, the marriage motif appearing once again in the film but in a far subtler and far more romantic context. It is reasonable to presume the proximity of a wedding gown is meant to act as a foreshadowing. As she parades past the potential buyers Daisy smiles at the lodger and as she crosses in front of him modelling an evening gown, they exchange coy nods of recognition. The lodger then calls to a salesclerk to make a purchase.

Hitchcock breaks this romantic mood abruptly by cutting to the local police station where Joe is holding court before his superiors alongside a group of detectives. By plotting the Avenger's murders on a map, he explains, it is possible to determine where the next killing will occur. Pointing confidently at his map, Joe says that the Avenger's murderous spree is slowly converging on a specific, London location: the Bunting's neighbourhood. At last, and thanks to Joe's ingenuity, the police may have the means to anticipate the killer's movements and apprehend him before he kills again.

As the camera lingers over Joe's map there is a lap dissolve to a second map, similar in sufficient respects to Joe's map to suggest that it represents the same series of events, but different enough from the police map to enable us to understand that it belongs to another person. Someone other than the police is following the killer's movements across the city and noting them on their own map. Naturally, audiences are likely to interpret this map as being in the possession of the Avenger who is scheming his next murder. This interpretation is neatly reinforced when a hand reaches into the frame to sketch a triangle on the map, apparently indicating the scene of the next killing. The camera then pulls back, and we peer over the shoulder of a dark-haired man holding the map. The image dissolves, however, before we can catch more than a glimpse of this man from behind. The lodger, of course, has similarly coloured and styled hair.

Hitchcock then brings us back to the Bunting kitchen just as Daisy returns home to discover that a package that was delivered for her earlier in the day contains the dress she was modelling at work. To their horror Mr and Mrs Bunting learn that the gift comes not from Joe but from the lodger, and despite Daisy's protests, Mr Bunting collects the parcel and carries it upstairs to the lodger's room where he coldly informs him that their daughter will accept no gifts from strangers. The lodger, who likely does not conceive of himself as a stranger at this stage of his relationship with Daisy, seems almost paralysed by Mr Bunting's admonitions and remains silent, deeply offended.

The choice of gift is itself suggestive on a few additional fronts and can easily be seen as a way Hitchcock devised to set us once again to wondering about the lodger's intentions. In the first and most obvious instance, the giving of clothing is ordinarily reserved for relationships that are far more developed than is the lodger's involvement with Daisy. Yet Daisy's delight in receiving the gift indicates that she may view their relationship as more intimate than outward appearances might suggest. Though Daisy and the lodger have been unable to acknowledge openly their mutual attraction, it is apparent from Daisy's reaction to the gift that she is already in love with the lodger and willing to overlook the presumptuous and sexualized nature of the present. It is not clear, however, whether Hitchcock wants us to perceive the dress as a mark of presumption on the part of the lodger or as a token of the advanced state of their relationship. There may also be a certain naiveté associated with Daisy at this point, and her enthusiastic acceptance of the present could indicate that she misunderstands its deeper implications.

There is also the fact that this gift is something neither Daisy nor her parents can afford, and the dress therefore underscores the Buntings' lower middle-class circumstances. Indeed, it is important to note that with the gift of an expensive dress, the lodger tries to elevate Daisy from her social and economic position to what we will shortly learn is his own, higher economic station. He seeks to transform her from the daughter of a backstreet lodging house owner who has only part-time employment, to a woman of sophistication and elegance, one who will be worthy of the comforts he enjoys in his world. Of course, the attempt to transform a woman to make her a suitable partner – and to effect control over her in that act of transformation – plays a significant part in Hitchcock's much later films, *Vertigo* (1958) and *Marnie* (1964). In *The Lodger*, the theme of patriarchal control suggests an additional if somewhat uncomfortable affinity between the lodger and Joe; both have romantic intentions concerning Daisy, and both are prone to express those aims in ways that reflect their mutual desire to dominate her. In Joe's case, this penchant for domination is depicted in a most literal fashion as he physically bullies her to suit his wishes, even using handcuffs in an ill-fated gesture meant to express his affections. But the lodger's efforts at domination have a more sensual if fetishistic quality, especially if we note Hitchcock's view that for the male character to dress a woman in a film (and here he was speaking principally of *Vertigo*) is really to undress her.[14]

But the refutation of his gift provides an opportunity for the lodger to approach Daisy and to inquire whether she shares the concerns her father holds. Thus, later that evening, while she bathes, the lodger comes to the bathroom door to speak with her. He first tries the handle (somehow, we are given to understand that he knows that it is Daisy in the bath) but does not open the door. Is it locked or has he changed his mind? It is unclear whether the door is, in fact, locked. Regardless, the lodger hesitates momentarily, withdraws his hand from the doorhandle, and then appears to decide to walk away. But he changes his mind, re-approaches the door and rather than try the handle he calls to her. Daisy steps from the tub, wraps herself in a robe, and carries on a conversation with the lodger through the door. The image is quaintly romantic, yet the lodger's initial intention to open the door charges the scene with sexual tension. He explains to Daisy his worry that she is angry with him about the appropriateness of the gift as was her father, but she assures him that she was not at all concerned. Daisy then laughs – the third time in the film she has laughed – when the lodger complains that her father believes she should not go out with him. The lodger is elated at hearing that Daisy is unconcerned about her father's response to the gift. But he seems particularly attracted to her laughter. Indeed, Daisy's laughter is a potent nonverbal sign of the truth and the depth of her affections, and we are given to understand in his satisfied look that the lodger may have reached a point of confirmation in his own feelings about Daisy.

What that conclusion might be is made complicated by a curious intertitle card that is interposed in the scene that reads, "But Daisy didn't worry." The viewpoint assumed by the card is confusing: Does it refer directly to

---

14 See Truffaut, p. 244.

the narrative, suggesting that, unlike her father (and mother) Daisy didn't worry about going out with the lodger, or does it suggest instead that we are being given privileged, directorial information? Is it Hitchcock who tells us that Daisy was not worried, and is it therefore a warning? The conflation of these two perspectives – the narrative perspective and the authorial/directorial perspective – is a deliberate means by which the suspense of the film is extended, and any questions viewers might continue to entertain about the lodger's identity are kept alive.

Why should Daisy worry? At one level, the answer to this question is plain: Daisy should worry because the lodger is really a serial killer. But there are secondary answers as well. Perhaps Daisy should worry chiefly because her parents and her boyfriend will be angry with her; perhaps virtuous young women do not accept invitations for an evening out from men they have known only for two weeks; perhaps Daisy should worry that she is jeopardizing her prior relationship with Joe for a fling that will prove transient if not dangerous. By the film's end, however, it becomes clear that the card is merely a description and contains no darker auguries. At this juncture, however, it achieves nicely the double effect of confusing and worrying the audience.

That same evening, a Tuesday night, Daisy and the lodger go out together. Mrs Bunting laments to her husband that she has "let Daisy go out with the lodger," though in what manner she is responsible for their going out is unclear. Daisy and the lodger sit beneath a streetlamp which looks ominously like the lamp under which the second murder in the film occurred, but the lodger's behaviour is far from sinister as he attempts to make plain his feelings for Daisy. However, his attempts at affection are cut short by the arrival of Joe who, presumably, has been assigned to work on the Avenger case given that it is Tuesday night. He pulls the lodger's hand from Daisy's shoulder and demands that he leave her alone. But Daisy is tired of Joe's jealousies, and jumping to her feet, she places herself between Joe and the lodger. This sequence is a re-enactment of the earlier scene in the lodger's room, but now Daisy stands between Joe and the lodger, just as Joe stood between her and the lodger earlier. Daisy angrily tells Joe she never wants to see him again and departs with the lodger apparently to return home.

Joe seats himself beneath the lamp dejected, staring at the ground. Then, as he gazes directly at the camera, a moment of illumination dawns, and he again casts his eyes downwards this time staring directly at a footprint made by the lodger's shoe. What follows is a series of images shown to the viewer from Joe's point of view as we momentarily take up his subject position as he works through the evidence he has collected. In a flash, images of the lodger and Daisy, images of the chandelier, images of the lodger's black valise, and images of the pictures being removed from the lodger's room pass through the footprint as if on a movie screen.[15] Joe thinks carefully about these things and continues to stare. His expression shifts abruptly from pensive to triumphant: At last, he puts the pieces of the puzzle together and deduces the inescapable fact that the lodger is the Avenger. He sets off immediately to procure a search warrant for the lodger's room.

Aside from the fact that this is the second time in the film in which Hitchcock has employed a clever visual stunt, the choice of the footprint as a screening device deserves a brief comment. The footprint is, of course, an indexical sign of the lodger, bearing both causal and existential relation to him. The footprint serves also as a staple symbol of police work, and Joe's deliberations are thus presented as a sustained piece of analysis in which disparate pieces of a puzzle are brought together even as they are linked in the traces of the lodger. Cinematically, the footprint also enables Hitchcock to retain our knowledge of the lodger throughout the scene; he has become an absent referent – much as the film is structured around the absent referent that is the Avenger. In other words, the lodger must disappear physically in order that the footprint might represent him, he must become absent from the scene in order that Joe's cogitations can achieve the potent symbolic and visual intonations Hitchcock wanted. That Joe is wrong is not necessarily a condemnation of the police, but an illustration of how emotional attachment can detract from clear-headed thinking.

Back at the Bunting home the lodger and Daisy have withdrawn to his room where their romantic desires begin to find realization in passionate kisses. Daisy draws back at one point, emphasizing for the audience that although a sexual encounter is certainly implied by the action, she retains the properly Victorian attitude of virginal hesitation and decorum. She overcomes her hesitancy, but in her attempt to resume their intimacy, the lodger suddenly draws away from her, adding further complications and depth to his character. This mutual dialectic of attraction and hesitation can seem hackneyed, but it may also be motivated by the narrative's fidelity to prevailing cultural codes. As Rothman has suggested:

> Though Daisy's hesitation is easily explained, the lodger's behavior is more mysterious. His resistance to her passion may reflect either innocence or inhumanity. Many different explanations are possible. He could be enraged, taking her to be a cruel exploiter of men's desires. He

---

15 That Joe visualizes the lodger's valise is a bit of subterfuge on Hitchcock's behalf for at this point of the narrative Joe would not know that the lodger owns a valise, never having seen it.

> could be remembering his gentleman's duty to respect her honour. He could be revolted by her sexuality and unable to go through with the act of making love to her. He could be afraid that he is monstrous, fated to destroy what he loves, and be struggling with himself to spare Daisy from falling victim to his curse.[16]

Each of Rothman's suggestions is reasonable in the context of the narrative, but a simpler explanation is available, for it may be that an involvement with Daisy would be a distraction from his purposes. This seems the more reasonable explanation, for we are shortly to learn as the story unfolds that the lodger is on a quest to avenge the death of his sister who herself perished at the hands of the Avenger. Thus, I would argue that the lodger is worried that his dalliance with Daisy, though pleasurable, has derailed his mission. This is an explanation to be added to Rothman's list, however, for whatever the case, the enigma of the lodger's momentary rebuff remains unexplained for a quite different reason. For even as they resume their ardent kissing, Joe arrives downstairs with two other detectives, intent on bringing the lodger to justice. "We have come to have a word with your lodger," he explains to the frightened Buntings.

Upstairs Joe finds Daisy and the lodger together, and, once again, a series of highly choreographed movements involving Joe, the lodger, and Daisy ensue. The detectives commence searching the lodger's room while Daisy alternates between clutching the lodger's arm and arguing with Joe that he has accused the wrong man. Once the black bag has been discovered the tension in the film reaches its climax. Joe places the bag on the lodger's table and, ignoring the lodger's protests, he goes through the valise, discovering a gun. When he triumphantly announces the discovery of a map of the Avenger's murders in the bag, the lodger answers plaintively, "Exactly," a response that can only heighten our confusion as to the identity of the real killer. Joe next discovers press clippings of the Avenger's murders and, finally, a picture of a young blonde woman. Brandishing this in the lodger's face he challenges him with the accusation "Your first victim, eh?" But the lodger replies calmly that it is a picture of his murdered sister.

The identification of his sister's picture points directly away from the lodger's guilt, although his romantic attachment to Daisy has also given us ample reason to want to see him innocent. Hence Hitchcock has mobilized our desire in service to the narrative, pulling us first in one direction, and then persuading us through a romantic entanglement that physical clues are

---

16 Rothman, p. 38.

not to be trusted. Now the lodger's guilt or innocence is cast before us again, this time in the deliberations Joe is forced to undertake. He carefully weighs the lodger's explanation as to the identity of the woman in the picture but is forced to consider this explanation in relation to the gun, the map, the press clippings – and perhaps most significantly, his alienation from Daisy. In the meanwhile, Daisy remains faithful to the lodger, her eyes providing firm evidence to the camera that she has now severed her connection to Joe entirely and given herself over completely to the lodger. Convinced that the evidence he has uncovered is sufficient, Joe directs his underlings to arrest the lodger who is handcuffed and taken from the room.

The descent down the Bunting's staircase is slow, funereal, and melodramatic. The lodger's measured pace down the stairs is intercut with subjective shots of the Buntings who wait at the bottom, staring up in obvious shock. When the entourage reaches the landing, Daisy whispers to the lodger that she will meet him on the bench under the lamp where Joe found them earlier that evening. Then, in a puzzling though convenient reaction, Mrs Bunting faints, drawing the detectives' attention momentarily away from the lodger who bolts into the night. The detectives chase after him with Daisy in pursuit.

Daisy and the lodger meet at the bench under the lamp precisely where Joe came to the "truth" about the lodger earlier in the evening. Here the lodger at last reveals the truth of his identity to Daisy.

The lodger explains in flashback that the picture found in his bag was indeed of his murdered sister, the Avenger's first victim. He recounts how his mother, who never recovered from the shock of her daughter's death, extracted from him a deathbed promise that he would not rest until the Avenger had been brought to justice. The map and press clippings are merely the tools he has assembled in his hunt for his sister's killer; the gun, apparently, the means by which he intends to carry out his mother's wish. He may not be a murderer, but in his heart the lodger is prepared to kill another man in pursuit of justice outside the law. But now, suspected of being the Avenger himself, the lodger laments that his promise must go unfulfilled, and he collapses in Daisy's arms.

Much has been made of the flashback sequence, including Rothman's (1982) observation that in the flashback, the lodger does not appear after the opening moments in which he is shown dancing with his sister at her coming-out ball.[17] The lodger's absence throughout the flashback may be explained because of Hitchcock's desire to continue the possibility that the lodger is really the murderer. In this respect, the lodger's absence may be a further

17 Rothman, p. 45.

instance of the director working his manipulations upon an unsuspecting audience. It is also noteworthy that the flashback, which is told from the lodger's perspective, includes subtle details that only the killer would know. For instance, there is a shot of a gloved hand turning off the lights moments before the murder of the lodger's sister occurs, an image only the killer would see in the way it is presented in the flashback. Given that the flashback is told from the lodger's subjective position and given that that perspective coincides with what we imagine the killer's view would have been, is it possible that Hitchcock is telling us that the lodger and the Avenger are one and the same? It is possible that Hitchcock means for us to conflate the lodger and the Avenger for these reasons, and some Hitchcock scholars endorse this interpretation. Despite the film's apparent happy ending, Rothman maintains that the lodger might still be the Avenger after all.

More pedestrian explanations of the apparent inconsistencies in the flashback are also possible. To begin, the gloved hand turning off the light, from a technical standpoint, is impossible in any event. Ivor Montagu, who helped Hitchcock with editing the film, admits that the shot was disconcerting because it showed the hand turn off the lights a second before the lights went out. In the real world this would be impossible, but it was necessary to shoot the sequence this way for cinematic purposes. Thus, while it is interesting to speculate on the details of the flashback sequence, it does not seem profitable to attempt a literalist reading of the flashback as Rothman suggests, for otherwise we would be forced to deal with the more surreal qualities demanded by Hitchcock's cinematic methods as though they could be accounted for in strictly objective terms. Moreover, because several scenes were reshot after Hitchcock completed the film, continuity may have suffered as a result. Mr Bunting's absence from the lodger's room at the scene of Joe and the lodger's first confrontation is another example of a major character's absence being unaccountable by the narrative logic of the film. Therefore, it seems most likely that we are to take the lodger's account of his sister's murder at face value. In movies, flashbacks enjoy the truth status of objectively grounded realism.[18] I believe that the flashback sequence in *The Lodger* must be taken as the sort of certified truth that cinematic conventions have guaranteed. I am not ruling out entirely the possibility that the lodger and the Avenger are the same, but I find it unlikely.

---

18 Of course, Hitchcock himself upset this convention in his 1950 film, *Stage Fright*, by showing a flashback that proved to be false, but this was an extreme aberration he was never to try again.

His recounting of events completed, the lodger is spent, and Daisy takes him to a bar for a recuperative drink of brandy, his hands still manacled but now concealed beneath his overcoat. Just as Daisy had been escorted by her comforting mother following Joe's attempt to handcuff her, so now Daisy assumes a properly maternal attitude to the lodger. But to keep the handcuffs hidden from the other patrons, Daisy is forced to hold the lodger's drink for him. These efforts at nonchalance are more clumsy than logical, and only serve to provoke some of the other patrons to try to see exactly what is preventing the lodger from handling his own glass. Concerned that they are drawing too much attention, Daisy and the lodger exit the bar just moments before Joe and several detectives rush into the establishment to use the telephone. The barmaid overhears their conversation about a handcuffed man and tells them that their suspect left the premises minutes earlier. An enraged crowd, now convinced that the Avenger is literally within their grasp, charge out into the foggy night.

As the mob storms out into the evening air bent on revenge, Joe remains at the bar to complete his telephone conversation to his commander. As he speaks with his superior his expression suddenly changes and he appears to struggle to understand what he is being told – not because he is unable to hear the captain's voice clearly, but because he cannot believe what he is hearing. But it finally becomes clear: the police commander tells Joe that the Avenger has been caught "red-handed" elsewhere in the city only a short time earlier. Joe mutters to himself that he must save the innocent lodger before the throng tears him apart, and he too disappears into the night.

Daisy and the lodger first hear and then see the pursuing crowd; Daisy takes the overcoat from his arms and exhorts him to flee. The chase scene is remarkably tense, the eerie lighting and darkened sets providing appropriately haunting touches to the action, anticipating the horror films of the following decade. Stopping in the centre of a small bridge, the lodger first gazes frantically at the onrushing throng, and then attempts to climb over the bridge's spiked metal railing. But in trying to scale the railing he slips, catching his handcuffs on the metalwork. In an agonizing close-up we see the lodger dangling from one of the dagger-like points of the railing, his handcuffs holding him suspended above the crowd. The angry mob converges both on and below the bridge and begins to beat him as he hangs suspended and helpless.

It is difficult to overlook the crucifixion theme implied here, just as it is difficult to suppress our disgust with the behaviour of the mob. Incited by rumour, they have descended to the Avenger's level, their murderous intentions horrifying us with the immediacy and the violence with which they are carried out. When at last Joe and the other detectives arrive, they must force their way through the crowd, exchanging blows with many of the attackers. At last, the handcuffs are undone, and they lower the lodger to the ground, just as a vendor for the *Evening Standard* newspaper arrives, shouting that the Avenger has been apprehended in a different part of the city. The crowd collects around the paper reading the details in embarrassed disbelief. Joe then proudly assumes credit for the rescue, exclaiming, "Thank God I was in time!" As the injured lodger lies with his head cradled in Daisy's arms, it is difficult to imagine a more ludicrous utterance. Joe's pomposity is a self-delusional defence against the growing awareness of his own inadequacies.

In any event, Joe is simply wrong: it is the arrival of the newsboy, and the report from the mass media, that have rescued the lodger from the clutches of the throng, not Joe's actions. Joe's role in this episode has been only to agitate the crowd to its frenzy, and his arrival might have been entirely in vain had not the newspaper headlines reached the crowd when they did. Once again, the mass media's relation to the Avenger, and the effect of the media on the public's emotions, has been decisive in the Avenger case. Furthermore, the conclusion to the serial killings is accompanied not by shouts of exaltation, but by feelings of shame and guilt. The crowd and the (invisible) Avenger have been fused, his murderous impulses revealed in the everyman and everywoman of British society. Anger has become a symptom of impotence, a substitute for security. Once the lodger has been revealed at last as innocent of the crimes the crowd is deflated, humiliated, and remorseful. But their anger is directed as much at the failure of the lodger to be guilty, as it is at the Avenger himself, who eludes their grasp utterly.

Rothman (1982) says that Hitchcock makes his second cameo appearance of the film during the climactic battle between the detectives and the crowd, and indeed, an overweight man generally answering to Hitchcock's description is visible in the scene.[19] But if Rothman is correct, there is something about Hitchcock's appearance in this sequence that he overlooks either because the man in the scene only resembles Hitchcock, or because Rothman chooses to ignore the significance of his actions.

As the lodger hangs helpless from the railing, the man Rothman identifies as Hitchcock enters from the lodger's right, just one face among many in a group of enraged citizens. But as the scene develops, and as Joe and his fellow detectives fight their way through the crowd to get near the lodger, this Hitchcock-double also battles his way through the crowd toward the point where the lodger hangs, pushing back the crowd in a rather ineffectual and comic manner. He is, however, the only person other than the detectives

19 Rothman, p. 50.

who is actively battling against the mob. A quick cut, and we now see that the Hitchcock-double has reached a position immediately above the lodger. By this stage, Joe and his colleagues have tried unsuccessfully to release the lodger from his manacles, the jostling and swinging fists making that task impossible. But following a cut in the film that positions the Hitchcock-double directly above the lodger we see that *he* is now in possession of the key to the handcuffs, and it is this Hitchcockian figure who actually unlocks the shackles. How he has come into possession of the key is not shown, for the cut in the film effaces that detail. Whether he was handed the key or magically produced one of his own is not revealed. It is possible that he is another detective who has arrived late to the scene, but his clothing makes him look far more like a fishmonger than a policeman. It is equally conceivable that he portrays a good Samaritan – though again, his possession of the key to the handcuffs goes unexplained. At the most literal level, however, it is Hitchcock who releases the lodger from the handcuffs, and Hitchcock who therefore controls the destiny of the characters. It is Hitchcock who releases the lodger so that he and Daisy can wed, and Hitchcock who ultimately resolves the narrative's most suspenseful episode – the lodger's suspense being embodied in literal fashion. It is Hitchcock who has the key to the film's conclusion.

And yet, I am unsure if the actor shown is or is not Alfred Hitchcock. John Taylor claims (1978) that the man shown in the final sequence is not Hitchcock, but an actor whose resemblance, seen from certain angles, is striking.[20] But whether the character in the scene is or is not Hitchcock, it remains somewhat of a mystery that he, rather than the detectives, releases the lodger from his handcuffs. It is possible that the director deliberately chose a performer who resembled him. Ultimately, it is unclear how to resolve the puzzle.

The lodger's release from the handcuffs sets in motion what Rothman (1982) has referred to as the first of three endings to the story – the number three continuing to play an important role in the film.[21] The first ending features Daisy poised over an apparently unconscious lodger with the police gathered about, the shamed and contrite mob consoling themselves in the background. For all intents and purposes, it appears that the lodger may have died in the assault, and that the film is to have a tragic ending.

An immediate fade-in to a hospital ward undoes this conclusion, however. This new scene reveals Daisy sitting by the lodger's bed while a grandfatherly doctor explains that while badly injured, the lodger's "youth and vigour" will

20 Taylor, p. 83.
21 Rothman, p. 54 ff.

see him through the trauma. The lodger and Daisy clasp hands, and the film appears to have ended here on a second, melodramatic note.

However, a third fade-in opens in the lodger's mansion. Daisy and her parents wait in a foyer, and then, from the top of the stairs, the lodger descends to greet them. He moves down the stairs in a curiously halting way, as if savouring a moment of victory. The scene recalls several other staircase movements in the film: the lodger's first ascent of the staircase in the Bunting home, his descent when sneaking out at night to look for the Avenger, and the descent he made while handcuffed in the custody of the police. Now he appears to relish the turn in fortune he has experienced, and he descends with an air of deliberate superiority.

At the bottom of the stairs, he hastens over to Daisy and, at her urging extends his hand to her parents, symbolically welcoming them into his home – and we may presume, into his life. Mr Bunting, unaccustomed to the mansion's plush carpeting, trips on a rug, a vaudevillian moment that plays against the grain of the narrative though it is consistent with Mr Bunting's general representation as comically loutish. Then Daisy and the lodger retreat to an inner room away from her parents where a window overlooking the city nightscape reveals the same flashing marquee shown in the opening montage: "To-Night, Golden Curls." The words retain their seductive charm, of course, but are now infused with sexual connotations as the lodger and Daisy exchange a passionate kiss by the window. The camera moves closer, and we fade out on the film's third, romantic conclusion. The film has ended.

Conclusion

Made in the waning years of Hitchcock's silent film career, *The Lodger* is often the film to which historians and critics first turn when explaining the origins of Hitchcock's style. Indeed, the film is a treasure trove for cinema sleuths in search of the Hitchcockian motifs and themes that would inflect his subsequent filmmaking. While the film provides us with near textbook examples of Hitchcock's penchant for privileging the individual shot over the logic of the narrative, however, there are other elements in the film equally important in the context of the stylistic touches and psychological complexities for which Hitchcock would become renowned. The major achievement of *The Lodger*, one might say, is its remarkable handling of such difficult themes as guilt, innocence, despair, and romance, and the technical virtuosity with which the young director confidently arranged the cinematic exposition of his narrative. Hitchcock transcended the limitations of the theatrical mannerisms of his principal players, and the abstractness of their motives and countermotives, by using the eye of the camera to peer deeply into their thoughts and feelings. *The Lodger* explores moral and emotional ambiguity with a candour that impresses and disturbs audiences today.

For instance, the film's exploration of romantic sentiment is developed in a manner, which, primitive in many respects, has a haunting and even lyrical quality to it. Love is never an easy experience in Hitchcock's films, and even early in his career, romance must be threaded through the tightly woven obstacles fashioned in both the plot and the conflicting emotions of the characters. *The Lodger* rarely compromises in its telling of the double-edged nature of our passions: Daisy risks everything in turning from Joe to the lodger, who in turn agonizes over abandoning her in pursuit of justice. And the lodger's courtship of Daisy is shown as a strangely traumatic affair for him, as he struggles with his long-standing commitment to his mother's deathbed wish, and his sexual and romantic attraction to Daisy. That he appears to have found happiness at the story's end in having secured Daisy's love is compensation for all he has endured.

The more significant relationship, in my view, is the nature of the attachment that has formed between Daisy and Joe, a bond that was formed prior to our entering the narrative, and whose foundations are occluded in the pre-history of the film. Daisy and Joe's relationship is depicted in the opening moments of the film as quietly strained by competing tendencies, Daisy trying to deflect his amorous overtures one moment, but then unwilling to cool his ardour entirely lest she be abandoned to spinsterhood. Joe's petty jealousies, of course, turn out to be fully grounded in their own way, for he is helpless at preventing Daisy from turning away from him toward the shadowy lodger. Joe's mettlesome professions of love, which stand in sharp contrast to the mysterious qualities of the lodger, leave him a rather pitiable figure in the end. His self-importance assumes an entirely different quality by the story's conclusion, the bravado and macho swagger of his earlier appearances having been held up to the audience for ridicule. Daisy's ascent is mirrored by Joe's decline, and he vanishes in the final moments a tortured character, declaring unconvincingly the important part he has played in the lodger's rescue – and, one might suggest, in the narrative itself. As a kind of practical functionary, Joe and his steady paycheque is enough to impress the Buntings as a suitable match for their daughter. In the conflict between reason and passion, however, it is passion fuelled by Daisy's willingness to risk her heart that ultimately pays off.

In concert with its calculated examination of the intricacies of human emotion, *The Lodger* equally deserves appreciation as a visual accomplishment. As I have already pointed out *The Lodger*'s atmospheric spirit owes much to Hitchcock's careful study of German filmmaking in the 1920s. Taylor writes that

> the German cinema [at the time of *The Lodger*] had a special corner in atmosphere, and had built up a repertory of visual language – mirrors and reflections, for example, are usually deceiving; stairs are inescapable, the movement of characters on them creating a feeling of elation or dejection, their spiraling up into the shadows strangely unsettling the spectator.[22]

This architecture of suspense is fully exploited in *The Lodger*, where structural axes of movement between the upstairs and downstairs of the Bunting home signal a series of narrative divisions. Movement upwards, into the lodger's quarters, is a movement into mystery, the unknown, and possibly danger. But it is also a movement into a realm of heightened sexuality and pleasure, and a movement away from the mundane amusements and activities of the Bunting household below. Daisy, it seems, is the only character in the film who is comfortably at home in both spaces, enjoying the company of her parents and Joe in the kitchen downstairs, but equally at ease in the lodger's room above. She forms a bridge between their worlds, metaphorically ascending to the heights of the lodger, but never entirely breaking with her family. Whereas the others in the film demonstrate a concentrated effort at retaining a life of horizontal movement across the screen, Daisy undertakes the vertical movement demanded of someone who seeks to become a different person, transformed by the challenges of the lodger's status, and by her willingness to peer into the mysteries from which the others shy away.

The Avenger, the unseen villain of the piece, is a quintessential Hitchcock MacGuffin. He puts the events of the story into motion and sustains them only by the malevolence that seeps from the shadows he casts across the story. In this respect he will reappear as the hold-up man 30 years later in *The Wrong Man* (1956), a criminal who is sighted in brief moments near the film's end. And *in Shadow of a Doubt* (1943), detectives also pursue a suspect who never appears on screen, and whose untimely death – also shadowed in the off-screen world – temporarily releases Charles Oakley from suspicion. Indeed, the fact that important action sometimes takes place off-screen in Hitchcock's work is a subject that deserves further attention.

As it unfolds, *The Lodger* transforms from its initial appearance as a police manhunt into a rather different kind of story. The principal enemy, the Avenger, becomes incidental to the main action of the narrative. As a cinematic MacGuffin he very nearly achieves the state of nothingness Hitchcock avidly sought.

---

22 Taylor, pp. 71–72.

Although it is not developed in the film, the prospect remains that one part of Daisy's attraction to the lodger issues from her awareness – and perhaps suspicion – that he may indeed be a serial killer. This is an unsettling point to suggest, but it is difficult to overlook. Hitchcock's opening montage includes images of Londoners whose salacious appetites are gratified by accounts of the Avenger's activities. Admittedly, Daisy evinces nothing of this attitude toward the macabre, but it is hard to imagine that she is utterly naïve concerning the suspicions that Joe and her parents have entertained even before the execution of the search warrant that turns up circumstantial evidence of his guilt. Much as Alice White is drawn to Crewe in *Blackmail* (1929) partly for the possibility of flirtation on the margins of forbidden sexuality, so too Daisy Bunting finds something awakened in her by the lodger that Joe's affections seem unable to kindle. That this something is erotic desire can hardly be doubted, but that it may include a thirst for the darker aspects of human nature is also possible. It is one thing to say that Daisy's love for the lodger conquers her fears that he means to do her harm, yet to what extent is her love intensified by the seductions of an illicit (and possibly) dangerous liaison? We should not ignore Hitchcock's intimations that the satiation of romantic desire can also entail the risk of uncontrolled passion. As Donald Spoto has said, *The Lodger* demonstrates "a delicate poise between paranoia and security."[23]

23 Spoto, Donald. *The Art of Alfred Hitchcock: Fifty Years of His Motion Pictures*. New York and London: Doubleday Books, 1976, p. 8.

Chapter 7

HITCHCOCK'S DEFERRED DÉNOUEMENT AND THE PROBLEM OF RHETORICAL FORM

Introduction: Rhetoric of Form and Narrative

Things don't always go as expected, though this fact probably owes less to the nature of things than it does to the power of our expectations. We are anticipatory by nature, innately hermeneutical creatures projecting our imaginations into the future to speculate about possible outcomes and lines of action. Indeed, our ability to speculate is contingent upon our sense of expectancy, an aspect of consciousness that phenomenology sees as essential to the nature of awareness itself. Hence it would be an error to imagine that our tendency to speculate is an idle, pointless practice. Though we often get things wrong, our efforts to discern form and pattern by way of anticipation are fundamental to our sense-making practices and abilities. It is with the anticipation of form that we take the initial step toward semantic completion.

I see this as an aspect of our rhetoricality because expectations are deeply influenced by the allure of structure and the seductions of form. In trying to anticipate particular outcomes we discern patterns that inscribe the shape of our expectations on otherwise shapeless events. And in seeking forms and patterns in the world, we can take comfort in the established conventions of the familiar, the expected, and what passes for common sense. So, when things don't turn out as expected, the disruption can come as something of a visceral shock. Because we establish, follow, and rely on forms so steadily that when those forms go unfulfilled, confusion and even disappointment may overtake us.[1]

1 I am using the word *form* to describe the patterned expressions of cultural practices in daily life. To this end, I rely on several of the ideas developed in Caroline Levine's masterful text, *Forms: Whole, Rhythm, Hierarchy, Network*. Princeton: Princeton University Press, 2015, where Levine defines form as "all shapes and configurations, all ordering

In this chapter I take up the issue of things not turning out as expected. My focus, however, is not with events in our everyday lives, but with occurrences in the world of film where form is usually understood as conventions and genres, and where expectations derive from audience familiarity with those same conventions and genres. There are certainly many films that surprise us with unexpected twists and turns, but my focus in this chapter concerns a narrative strategy that Hitchcock used in several of his films. My particular interest is in the way that Hitchcock would occasionally disrupt or destabilize his film's narrative form by deviating from the customary happy ending, a phenomenon that I refer to as the *deferred dénouement.* Putting to one side the philosophical position that sees closure as an ideological formation – a point with which I have sympathy – I want to posit a more literary connection, namely, that forms demand completion, and that completion can be taken as a kind of rhetorical satisfaction. Hence my question is rather simple: What happens when the satisfaction promised in the anticipatory nature of the form is denied? When form is intended to lead to a conventional, satisfying, ideologically approved conclusion, is the author or filmmaker under an obligation to provide the traditional dénouement?

Of course, not all works of art faithfully follow the contours of socially approved forms. Hitchcock told François Truffaut that "in some cases the happy ending is unnecessary," for if "there is sufficient entertainment in the body of the film, people will accept an unhappy ending."[2] As with so many of the pronouncements Hitchcock produced for public consumption, his view of the unhappy ending – his view that it is perfectly reasonable to deviate from audience expectation – is far from universally true, for audience attitudes are much more complicated than his austere syllogism suggests. When the conventional, expected ending is subverted – when viewers don't get the conclusion they bargained for – they may feel dissatisfied, as though the filmmaker has failed to keep a promise. Hence, ensuring that the film provides a healthy serving of entertainment to guard against the possibility of dissatisfied viewers is not always going to guarantee the success of an unhappy ending. The strategy can easily backfire if the viewer, carried along by the felicitous comfort of the familiar form, arrives at the final credits with the customary finale nowhere in sight. So, whereas Hitchcock is probably correct that in specific films the happy ending can be subverted if the main body of the film is wildly

---

principles, all patterns of repetition and difference" (p. 3). Certain aspects of Levine's definition of form will appear more plainly in later parts of this chapter.

2 Truffaut, François. *Hitchcock* (Revised Edition). New York and London: Simon & Schuster, 1983, p. 106.

entertaining, this simply isn't going to be the case with all films. And it is certainly not true in all of Hitchcock's films where endings were frequently deferred and neither critics nor audiences always pleased. It is important to keep in mind that one of the reasons viewer dissatisfactions can be so intense is because form frequently serves as a promissory note, and that artists – including filmmakers – leave this note unredeemed at their peril. The implicit agreement that form establishes can be a powerful bond between artists and their publics. Failure to deliver on a promise is often seen as a moral failing and thus the filmmaker who leaves the ending suspended will be treated to more scathing criticism than the filmmaker who makes no promise at all. Taking form as a promise, then, is to regard the relation between filmmaker and viewer as more ethical than contractual. If that transformation is granted, then the necessity of an acceptable dénouement is even more imperative.

My argument includes several elements, but fundamentally builds on the work of two important rhetorical scholars, Lloyd Bitzer and Kenneth Burke. Bitzer provides an interesting analysis of social settings he famously described as *rhetorical situations.* Although he did not apply his work directly to film, I take up that task in this chapter, showing how films, and Hitchcock's in particular, were often founded on the elaboration of rhetorical situations. I aim to show that films are rhetorically constituted, and that in its most elementary expression, persuasion is a central part of the formal pattern of many films. I am also interested in how the urgency of the rhetorical appeal is contingent upon the film narrative's exigence, that is, its central problematic. Indeed, one of the surprising ways in which rhetorical elements are part of the cinematic narrative is that filmmakers frequently represent rhetorical appeals as (1) essential to the storyline, and (2) integral to the process of developing a dialectic of tension. Thus, I show how *the rhetorical situation is often a cinematic situation.*

Kenneth Burke's work on rhetorical form provides the second theoretical basis for my analysis. Burke famously defined form as "an arousal and fulfillment of desires."[3] This definition along with other similar descriptions scattered throughout his numerous texts suggests the centrality of gratification in Burke's understanding of the rhetorical function of form and thereby connects our appreciation of form with the idea of the embodied viewer (or reader) experiencing satiation as a kind of intellectual nourishment.[4] One

3 Burke, Kenneth. *Counter-Statement.* Berkley and London: University of California Press, 1931, p. 124.

4 A somewhat different account of rhetoric as consonant with bodily appetites is developed in Stormer, Nathan. "An Appetite for Rhetoric." *Philosophy and Rhetoric*, 48, 2015, pp. 99–106.

might even suggest that Burke's ideas about rhetorical form suggest a turn to the body, and that the sated body resonates metaphorically with the intellectual satisfaction of a suitably resolved narrative, a situation Burke referred to as "proper form." Burke acknowledged that certain kinds of form are deeply connected and even performed bodily. Rhythm, for instance, "enjoys a special advantage in that rhythm is more closely allied with 'bodily' processes."[5] Burke's recourse to metaphors of bodily processes alongside accounts of audience experience indicates that form is successful when it is satisfying, and this will be an important part of my account of the deferred dénouement.

My presentation has three parts. First, I discuss the idea of the rhetorical situation in relation to film to establish a foundation for talking specifically about rhetorical form in Hitchcock's films. My main concern here will be to show how Lloyd Bitzer's conception of the rhetorical situation applies to many films, and in particular to works by Alfred Hitchcock. I argue that in dramatizing rhetorical situations in his films, Hitchcock also relied on the rhythm established by such situations to create the formal structures on which his stories were based. In other words, rhetorical situations, as Bitzer described them, involve certain aspects which, taken together, suggest a kind of form that helps to frame the plot in terms of audience expectancy.

Second, I take a detailed look at Burke's analysis of rhetorical form. Here I outline some of the salient aspects of Burke's ideas with a particular emphasis on what makes form "proper" and how deviation from properly constituted form would appear to work against the idea of audience satisfaction. Hitchcock, so far as I can determine, never spoke of rhetorical methods in filmmaking, but his concern with the architecture of his films was sufficiently encompassing that it is rather simple to draw from his views about cinema a nascent philosophy of form that would have interested Kenneth Burke. Indeed, Hitchcock was so consumed by matters of form that he told many interviewers down the years that he was largely unconcerned with the plausibility of his stories and was instead engaged chiefly by images and effects, the markers, and emblems of formal structure. "I only interest myself in the manner and style of telling the story," he once told an interviewer from *Cinema* magazine. "But as for the story itself, I don't care if it's good or bad, you know. If it serves my purpose."[6] Focusing on Burke's theory of form, then, also helps to illuminate aspects of Hitchcock's interest in cinematic style.

---

5 Burke, 1931, p. 140.

6 Gottlieb, Sidney. *Hitchcock on Hitchcock: Selected Writings and Interviews.* Berkeley and London: University of California Press, 1995, p. 299.

Finally, I turn to the specific problem of the deferred dénouement, and what this might mean in relation to a theory of rhetorical form that emphasizes properly constituted form as essential for audience satisfaction. When the film's ending is deferred or subverted, how do audiences accommodate themselves to this failure to achieve resolution, and can these moments of cinematic subversion be reconciled within the paradigm that Burke offers?

Rhetorical Exigencies in Cinematic Narratives

The rhetorician J. Killingsworth once suggested that imaginative fiction "both dramatizes rhetorical events and creates them," a process that he identified as involving two levels of discourse when applied to the study of cinema.[7] First, the dramatization of rhetorical events refers to the film's representation of specific acts of rhetoric. This way of thinking about dramatization, Killingsworth says, is concerned with the way the storyline often shows certain characters in the act of trying to persuade other characters of something which, while important in the context of the plot, also serves the purpose of moving the story forward. Whatever it is that necessitates this need for rhetorical action will usually be a central concern of the narrative's larger problematic, although there are times when the deployment of rhetorical activity plays a more ancillary role in the overall story. For example, in many romantic comedies the male lead assumes a rhetor's position as he tries to persuade a woman of the sincerity of his romantic intentions by declaring his undying love and claiming, for instance, that fate decrees they should be together. Thus, rhetoric is a motivating dimension of this simple, time-worn narrative, with the manoeuvrings of the young man sustaining the story from start to finish. On the other hand, a B-grade science fiction film may feature a rhetorical event which, though important in demonstrating a central concern of the story, is more contributory than foundational in relation to the overall narrative. As an example, we might see a soft-hearted and concerned scientist trying to dissuade a zealous military officer from using explosives to gain entry to a recently landed alien spacecraft. This scene will figure more incidentally than centrally in the narrative, though it is easily integrated into the general storyline as illustrative if not crucial. Various displays of rhetorical activity, then, are not necessarily equal in terms of how they add to, or advance, the film's plot.

7 Killingsworth, M. Jimmie. *Appeals in Modern Rhetoric: An Ordinary Language Approach.* Carbondale: Southern Illinois University Press, 2005, p. 7.

Of course, the romantic comedy's young suitor may fail to win the woman's heart, and the scientist's pleas will probably fall on deaf ears, but their respective failures are not the point. The key issue to which Killingsworth draws our attention is simply that film narratives frequently dramatize rhetorical events. Additionally, these rhetorical events often figure in the development of generic qualities, including suspense, humour, or romance. Films regularly depict peoples' efforts to be persuasive.

Killingsworth's second point about the creation of rhetorical events appears in the ancillary effect on the audience that follows from the primary narrative. While watching cinematic portrayals of rhetorical events, audiences are subject to the appeals the filmmaker has embedded in the film's narrative – what is colloquially known as the deeper meaning of the film. In the two examples above, audiences watching the young admirer trying to win the young woman's affections might enjoy his comedic displays of passion and the humorous repartee that is a mainstay of this genre. But they will likely also absorb something of the larger meaning of the sentimental nature of romantic relationships, including the common belief in an ideal and fated love interest. They might also glean something of the cultural hegemony of heteronormativity. In the second case, the viewer might read this science fiction storyline as a critique of the dangers of military hubris, or as a comment on our tendency to fear things that are unfamiliar, the problem of unreflectively judging what is culturally foreign as inherently dangerous. The concerned scientist's ill-fated efforts to prevent the destruction of the alien spaceship speak to the challenges of overcoming a tendency for reckless endangerment such as happens when prejudice is summoned ahead of experience. Thus, there are "messages" in films that speak to issues more universal than might initially be apparent in any individual movie's storyline, and these messages are what Killingsworth means in speaking of the cinema's creation of rhetorical events at this second level of discursive practice.

Killingsworth's ideas add a provocative element to film analysis, though it is slightly problematic that he doesn't offer a detailed definition of how we should understand the concept of a rhetorical event. I think, however, that the examples he provides generally make clear the point he is driving at. Reading his argument closely, it is apparent that with the phrase "rhetorical event" he is referring to narrative situations where conditions are such as to necessitate the use of persuasion as a means of resolving a problem, putting an end to a conflict, establishing bonds of sympathy or affection, overcoming an impasse, and so on. This description accords with rhetorician Lloyd Bitzer's well-known concept of the *rhetorical situation*, and though Killingsworth mentions Bitzer mainly in passing, the context of his analysis shows that he has some version of Bitzer's theory in mind.[8] Further, because Bitzer's model of the rhetorical situation directly matches Killingsworth's notion of a rhetorical event, I am going to speak of Killingsworth's arguments regarding imaginative fiction as a logical extension of Bitzer's theories on the situational aspects of rhetoric. I am certain I am doing no disservice to Killingsworth's arguments in drawing this link.

It would be helpful at this point to offer a more concrete example as to how cinema dramatizes and creates rhetorical situations. Fortunately, Killingsworth has done some of the work for me with a brief analysis of the science fiction film, *The Matrix* (1999). I will begin with his exegesis of this film before providing a separate example of my own to further develop his argument about rhetorical events as represented in cinema.

Killingsworth on *The Matrix*

In keeping with Killingsworth's approach, I am going to presume readers are sufficiently familiar with *The Matrix* to make a detailed overview unnecessary. As the people of Zion slowly work their rhetorical charms on Neo, he comes to realize that the world he thinks he lives in, the world he takes as undisputed reality, is an elaborate digital fabrication. Convincing Neo of this takes a good deal of persuasive energy and involves a few rhetorical techniques, several of which are only possible for people with access to the computer-enhanced technologies of a science fiction future. But eventually, Neo comes to accept that the people of Zion are speaking the truth, and that he is indeed, as the Oracle predicted, the One. This is the first level of rhetorical activity Killingworth refers to, namely the level at which the film *dramatizes* a rhetorical situation in that the plot focuses on how the people of Zion aim to persuade Neo of the unreality of his everyday life and the reality of the virtual world. At this level we are viewing rhetorical activity rather than experiencing it from our position as viewers of the film.

The second level of rhetorical practice in *The Matrix*, the *creative* level, identifies the way that we, as viewers, might come to realize the implications that this fictional tale holds for us. To this end we might argue that the "imaginative fiction" of the movie successfully persuades its viewers that we also live

8 In the book from which this discussion of imaginative fictions is taken, Killingsworth refers approvingly to Bitzer's ideas. Indeed, just pages further on from the passages cited above, Killingsworth speaks at greater length of Bitzer's theory though he doesn't overtly acknowledge any debt to Bitzer as it pertains to his ideas about rhetoricality and cinema.

in a world analogous to the film's eponymous matrix. We might conclude that in ways terribly similar to the people of *The Matrix*, our lives are a tissue of lies, and that the banal comforts of our consumer culture have blinded us to the secretive forces that actually govern the world. At this second level of rhetorical activity, viewers of *The Matrix* might recognize that Baudrillard's simulacrum describes all too well the premise of the film – or, perhaps, that the film faithfully reproduces the central idea of Baudrillard's theories about the precession of simulacra.[9] At this second level of rhetorical activity, we are exposed to messages in the film's narrative concerning the insidious and dehumanizing machinations of capitalism. As Morpheus and his associates employ their rhetorical skills to convince Neo that the world is not all it seems to be, the film employs its rhetorical power as a form of emancipatory discourse.

Killingsworth's example is good in presenting the essential points supporting his idea about the dramatization of rhetorical events in imaginative fiction like film, but his discussion covers only a few of the key elements found in Bitzer's work. To strengthen and further elaborate Killingsworth's position, I want to offer a more detailed illustration of this process of dramatizing rhetorical events by looking at a different film, Steven Spielberg's 1975 blockbuster, *Jaws*.[10] Following my discussion of *Jaws*, I will examine the theoretical arguments that support Bitzer's concept of the rhetorical situation in further detail. Then, I will turn to discuss several of Alfred Hitchcock's films and show that Hitchcock's work is a rich source of cinematic rhetoricality. Ultimately my goal is to argue that one of the most overlooked aspects of film has been the dramatization of rhetorical processes in the emplotment itself. I will begin with *Jaws* simply because the film is so widely known as to need little elaboration of its storyline.

The Rhetoric of *Jaws*

The central rhetorical situation in *Jaws* involves a dilemma facing Brody, the local police chief, as he tries desperately to persuade Amity's mayor and city councillors that an enormous white shark hunting in the town's local waters is a threat of such magnitude as to require that the city should prohibit access to Amity's public beaches. Right from the start, then, we are introduced to the importance of persuasion. Yet Brody's rhetorical appeals are stonewalled

9 Baudrillard, Jean. *Simulacra and Simulation* (orig. French, 1981), translated by Sheila Faria Glaser. Ann Arbor: The University of Michigan Press, 1994.

10 Jaws, 1975. Dir. Steven Spielberg, Universal Pictures.

by these same city officials who argue that because Amity has just entered its lucrative vacation season it would be in the best interests of the community to ignore the dangers posed by the shark and keep the regional beaches open. Their reasoning is driven by a cost–benefit analysis which, they have concluded, shows that there is more to be gained in the long term by prioritizing profit ahead of safety. Hence, the city council thwarts Brody's efforts to carry out his duties as the town's chief law enforcement official owing to their commitment to local businesses – their commitment to capital. Brody resorts to increasingly urgent pleas in his efforts to protect both the residents and the tourists flocking to Amity for their summer vacations. To accomplish this goal, rhetorical discourse is Brody's principal weapon.

Reading the film this way – that is, seeing it in terms of rhetorical pleadings – deviates from traditional interpretations of the story in obvious ways. In the conventional account, *Jaws* is not so much a story focused on the dramatization of rhetorical activity as it is about the efforts of a gallant and ragtag group of heroes trying to locate and destroy a great white shark even as the creature, gifted with uncanny intelligence, is able to turn the tables and make the hunters into the hunted. *Jaws* is a narrative drawn from that venerable tradition of man versus beast, an epic tale of adventure, hubris, and monsters. To frame the film as shaped by the theme of persuasion, some might claim, is to miss the point of the story.

However, although a rhetorical framework would be unsuccessful in analysing every aspect of the film, it is equally improbable that most viewers completely miss the narrative significance of Brody's attempts to persuade local government officials to act. And those viewers are unlikely to regard his efforts as utterly disconnected from the plot. This is because Brody is something of a literary and cinematic trope, a character who figures in the story as the traditional a voice of reason, a lone voice struggling to be heard above the chorus of doubters. His anxiety about the safety of the people he is charged with protecting is increased by the recalcitrance of city leaders to take any steps toward ensuring public safety, and it is largely in witnessing Brody's ever-mounting fear that the viewer is provided an entry point to the emotionally compelling sense of peril that pervades the story. Hence, it is possible for viewers to keep Brody's persuasive efforts in mind without reducing *Jaws* to a seminar on rhetorical theory.

In fact, Brody's efforts to sway the city's council are important to director Steven Spielberg's orchestration of the film's suspense, the dialectic of tension being formed partly in the back-and-forth discourse between Brody and city officials. His attempts to rouse the town administrators into action are important in creating and developing anxiety in the film, and the fact that his overtures are initially doomed to failure is equally important to the success of the narrative. It might seem odd to suggest that failure produces success, yet the pressing demands of any film's rhetorical situation are rarely resolved quickly or easily if we are to experience the heightened emotions such dramas evoke. This back-and-forth tension is only possible in the face of creditable opposition. In the case of *Jaws*, a compliant and responsible city council would be a far less interesting oppositional force. Hence, whereas Brody's primary antagonist would seem to be the shark, his battle with the mayor and city councillors is no less important in terms of preventing further deaths. Indeed, the mayor and councillors are ultimately surrogates for the shark in that the narrowness of their vision is an analogue for the shark's single-mindedness in pursuit of prey, a combination that guarantees the threat to human life will continue. The rhetorical situation Brody faces vis-à-vis the city council is no less important than his confrontation with the shark.

Amity's city officials indeed frustrate Brody, but this is not because of mean-spirited disinterest. Rather they are motivated by perfectly acceptable capitalist logic: the financial interests of the town. Amity's economic lifeblood is its tourist industry, and by asking council to close the beaches to save only a few people, Brody is perceived as acting against the town's long-range interests. The denizens of the council chambers value economic considerations above everything else, and therefore they find it rather easy to frame Brody's appeals for public safety as too radical, too extreme, and too severe. Further, as already suggested, this characterization also serves a second purpose in casting Brody as a classic illustration of the single, righteous man, the solitary voice calling for justice. Brody demands action from those with the power to save lives but finds they are not inclined to take the morally appropriate action. Or at least, this is the way it seems to Brody – and possibly the way it seems to most filmgoers. The main difficulty Brody faces is that his rhetorical appeals would be persuasive only in the case that they reached sympathetic ears, and the cultivation of sympathy is possible only if there is common ground shared by both rhetor and audience. As the respective parties to this rhetorical situation converge in their shared concern for the welfare of Amity, the ways in which they differ – the key positions on which they take opposing views – result not in urbane disagreement, but in invective and blaming. Theatre audiences probably side with Brody in this debate since the preservation of life will generally hold the upper hand in such moral disputes. On the other hand, had he won his argument in the opening scenes of *Jaws* there would be no story to enjoy.

There is a further issue in respect of the town's administrators pushing back against Brody's rhetoric, and that is the logic underlying their resistance. To put it plainly, it is not entirely fair to claim that the city fathers are inherently callous and unfeeling, that they are by nature an evil bunch. After all, while it is true that they may be more attuned to business values than the values of human life, they are not being illogical in their concerns for the town and its long-term prospects. As an important antagonistic force in the narrative, the rationale they invoke in turning aside Brody's pleas would certainly find support if circumstances were less "cinematic" and more true-to-life. Risk-taking has its acceptable measures, and when the payoff is great the risk may be worth the challenge.[11] This doesn't mean that I am advocating that as viewers we should side with the mayor against Brody, that we should throw our lot in with capital against the lives of innocent beachgoers. I simply mean that the narrative Spielberg develops works well in the context of ennobling the putative villains of *Jaws* since the reasons that support the decision they take can at least be understood if not admired. Driven by their interest in their town's well-being, the mayor and his followers have financial logic on their side in that there are times when short-term consequences are squelched in deference to long-term payoffs. Problems arise, however, when those long-term interests put money ahead of lives and the situation is framed as a moral rather than a strictly numerical problem. Then the argument for economic survival can be more difficult to make, especially in the context of a film which requires a rapid resolution. In a running time of 124 minutes, it is impossible to depict the long-range effects of the mayor's desire to ignore the shark in favour of vacationers' dollars. Thus, Brody's efforts to persuade the town's leaders of the imminent danger lurking offshore meet a formidable enemy not just in the ocean, but in the seductive, rhetorical power of capital.

This discussion of *Jaws* relies on several of Lloyd Bitzer's ideas about rhetorical situations. However, I have deliberately presented this analysis without constant reference to Bitzer to maintain the flow of the narrative. I have tried to set the stage for the next task, a more comprehensive delineation of rhetorical situations as formulated by Bitzer and as that phrase is used by rhetoricians today. This requires going over some ground already covered, but in doing so I will offer more extensive commentary concerning the central aspects of Bitzer's work and how they might be applied, as Killingsworth suggests, to imaginative fictions, specifically film. Once I have described Bitzer's ideas concerning rhetorical situations I will take a final, brief look at *Jaws* before turning to discuss several of Alfred Hitchcock's films.

11 As I am writing during the COVID-19 pandemic, the idea of balancing lives against the economy is a particularly salient concept. See, for example, Victor Greech, et al. "A Risk Balancing Act – Tourism Competition using Health Leverage in the COVID -19 Era." *International Journal of Risk & Safety in Medicine*, 31 (2020), pp. 121–130.

Understanding Rhetorical Situations

Commonly used by rhetoricians today, the phrase 'rhetorical situation' was first defined in a highly influential paper by Lloyd Bitzer in 1968. Though Bitzer's ideas have been criticized for the sin of theoretical narrowness, and though they have been subjected to the inevitable reformulation advanced by subsequent scholars, his basic insights remain productive in the field of rhetoric. As James Jasinski says, "more than three decades after its initial presentation, the idea of a rhetorical situation still occupies a significant place in both the rhetoric classroom and scholarly discourse."[12] Whereas the main features of the rhetorical situation are simple to grasp, their implications are far-reaching in being applied to a wide range of social settings and cultural contexts – including Killingsworth's views about imaginative fictions.

So, what exactly is a rhetorical situation as Bitzer theorized it? Although Bitzer doesn't mention the work of Erving Goffman in the article in which he first brought the idea to public attention, much of what he argues certainly articulates with Goffman's work on "defining the situation."[13] Goffman saw this process of definition as crucial to the task of social activity insofar as a correctly identified situation enables all parties to play their roles appropriately. According to Goffman, knowing the nature of the situation in which you find yourself is tantamount to knowing important facets of social context, including the expectations that come with adopting the role most suited to that situation. Sometimes the task the rhetor faces is establishing an atmosphere conducive to a particular understanding of the prevailing social conditions such as allow the rhetor to define the situation according to their interests; for Aristotle, of course, this is the province of *pathos*, the affective state of an audience as produced by the social context. However, matters are far from simple in this process of defining the social settings in which we find ourselves because situations are often intricate webs of social custom interwoven with the knotty uncertainties common in most encounters in interpersonal communication. In some cases, how to behave "properly" is a matter of detailed codification, as would be the situation in being introduced to royalty. In other situations, there can be greater degrees of uncertainty and ambiguity, and formal codes for consultation may not even exist. Although it is generally agreed that online interaction is not the same as face-to-face communication, there are no universally agreed upon rules to follow when switching from one

12 Jasinski, James. *Sourcebook on Rhetoric: Key Concepts in Contemporary Rhetorical Studies.* Thousand Oaks: Sage Publications, 2001, p. 514.

13 Goffman, Erving. *The Presentation of Self in Everyday Life.* Garden City, New York: Anchor Books, 1958.

to the other. Interactants must thread their way carefully at times even as they pick up the necessary cues for suitable conduct as they go. Social situations are thus multi-levelled sources of communicative complexity, replete with a range of possible social roles waiting to be taken up. There is the persistent problem of conflicting social expectations, too, especially as the procedures for defining a situation are not always perfectly transparent. In addition, even the simplest of social situations can be founded on formal and informal codes intended to outline acceptable behaviour but that don't necessarily align perfectly. And, of course, social situations frequently invoke rules prescribing organizational structures that seem beyond the ken of individual performers. Having the requisite tacit knowledge to successfully negotiate social situations was a central concern of Goffman's understanding of various forms of social intercourse.

Bitzer's work can be seen as a contribution to this sociological tradition in the sense that it expands Goffman's ideas by defining a rhetorical perspective as important to further refine our understanding of social interactionism. Like Goffman, Bitzer was interested in the idea that people often find themselves in situations demanding an appropriate response. For Bitzer, however, the key thing was to note that some social situations are such that by virtue of the prevailing circumstances, the response they demand is rhetorical, or discursive – or, at least, Bitzer's contribution was to single out the rhetorical issue for concentrated analysis. In many different social settings, a discursive response is needed to see that a problem is set right, to argue that an injustice is overcome, or to ensure that a challenge is defeated. There are social situations, in other words, that can be defined as rhetorical situations. Thus, Bitzer says the *rhetorical situation* is "a complex of persons, events, objects, and relations presenting an actual or potential exigence that can be completely or partially removed if discourse, introduced into the situation, can so constrain human decision or action as to bring about the significant modification of the exigence."[14] This definition is not easily parsed, but the key elements essential to a rhetorical situation are obvious. These are an *exigence* demanding attention, an *audience* toward whom discourse will be directed and which has the power or authority to effect change in the exigence, and various *constraints* against which the rhetor's discourse must contend.

I want to go back to Killingsworth's notion that cinema "both dramatizes rhetorical events and creates them" and take a second look at *Jaws* in light of Bitzer's theory. If we consider *Jaws* as representing a rhetorical situation, how do exigence, audience, and constraints appear in this film?

---

14 Bitzer, Lloyd. "The Rhetorical Situation." *Philosophy and Rhetoric*, 1 (1), (1968), p. 4.

In the first instance, we see that Brody has an exigence, a problem to be resolved in the fact of the shark, and an audience in the form of the city councillors and mayor. Significantly, this is also an audience Brody believes has the requisite authority and/or power to remove/resolve the dominant exigence (the shark) by taking appropriate action.[15] And, of course, there are myriad constraints that prevent the resolution of this exigence, the most obvious being the reluctance of the mayor and his council (the audience) to accept Brody's arguments because of their commitment to Amity's financial situation. Furthermore, discourse is Brody's chief weapon for overcoming these constraints, and he uses several rhetorical tactics to persuade his audience of the correctness of his analysis. The essential features of Bitzer's rhetorical situation are rather clear when worked out this way.

When viewed from this perspective it is obvious that rhetorical situations feature prominently in many movies. In films where characters are caught in sinister plots, or when they find themselves unjustly accused of criminal behaviour, they will attempt to resolve an exigence against constraining forces by the work of properly constituted discursive activity. A major problem must be resolved even as the protagonist/rhetor faces potentially significant constraints intent on blocking his or her attempts at resolution. And the principal force the rhetor employs – discourse – must be aimed at the members of an audience who are able to bring about the desired change: the successful resolution of the prevailing exigence.

The Exigence of Non-identity

The analysis of *Jaws* offered here provides a steppingstone for a further analysis of some of the films of Alfred Hitchcock. Hitchcock's work evinces a surprising number of movies in which rhetorical situations play a central role in the storyline, the nature of the relationship between principal characters, and the way suspense is presented and maintained. In the following section, I will apply the same analytic technique to a classic Hitchcock film, *North by Northwest* (1959), to illustrate how closely Hitchcock's work can be shown to conform to Bitzer's theories, and how Killingsworth's notion of the

15 Just to be clear, removing or resolving the exigence in the present case does not only mean that removing the shark, i.e., its literal death or destruction, is the only option. The exigence of the shark could potentially be resolved in other ways, such as closing the beaches to the public. It is helpful to keep in mind that the exigence is really the relationship between the shark and the beachgoers. To solve a problem can mean removing ourselves from the situation just as it can entail confronting and overcoming the object that we regard as the principal cause of the problem.

dramatization of rhetorical events is indeed an important component of this film narrative.

North by Northwest can be appreciated as turning on the dramatization of a rhetorical situation – in fact, more than one such situation can be found in this particular film – and this process accounts for the narrative's structure. The architecture of the film is a sequence of rhetorical pleas intended to move an audience to take steps toward resolving an exigence bedevilling the principal character. This way of framing the action of *North by Northwest* also explains certain of the sources of the underlying tension in the story as this also impacts the viewer.

Recall that Bitzer describes the exigence as the difficulty for which rhetorical discourse is required, that is, a problem requiring action. Specifically, Bitzer says that the exigence can be construed as "a defect, an obstacle, something waiting to be done, a thing which is other than it should be."[16] Applying this definition to the narrative of *North by Northwest*, the primary exigence is the fact that foreign spies operating in the United States have made a terrible and life-endangering blunder. These spies have erroneously identified an advertising executive named Roger Thornhill as someone these spies know by the name, George Kaplan. This act of misidentification has resulted in Thornhill being kidnapped by these enemy agents, an act that places the innocent Thornhill in mortal danger. Once the spies determine that Thornhill is going to remain uncooperative – a belief fuelled by their failure to realize that they have the wrong man – they decide to murder Thornhill/Kaplan.

The immediate exigence, then, is this act of misidentification, and to save his life Thornhill seeks to resolve the exigence through a discursive appeal – that is, via rhetoric. In Bitzer's words, he must bring about a significant modification of the exigence by discourse, for in mistaking him for someone named 'Kaplan,' the agents have created a situation in which "a thing is other than it should be." Thus, Thornhill must try to convince others (his captors) of his true identity, and in order to persuade his kidnappers Thornhill attempts a number of rhetorical strategies that include pleading, logical demonstration, incredulity, and even bluster, but all to no avail. The act of misidentification that initiates the problems Thornhill faces throughout the film is thus the controlling exigence around which lesser exigencies ultimately cluster.

To deal with this exigence rhetorically requires that Thornhill be able to identify and address an appropriate audience, the second element in Bitzer's theory, for the audience in a proper rhetorical situation, Bitzer says, is defined as those persons who have the power to alter events and neutralize

---

16 Bitzer, p. 6.

the exigence. "Properly speaking," Bitzer says, "a rhetorical audience consists only of those persons who are capable of being influenced by discourse and of being mediators of change."[17] In the case of *North by Northwest*, several different audiences appear to meet this criterion as potential mediators of change at different points in the narrative. Thornhill's first effort to resolve the exigence is to address the enemy agents who have kidnapped him. This audience, should they be persuaded by Thornhill's arguments, certainly has the power to realize their error and set him free. The enemy spies, however, are not persuaded by Thornhill's pleas, and their rejection of his rhetorical appeals leads directly to their decision to kill him. Moreover, in the face of Thornhill's efforts to persuade them of their error they grow increasingly convinced that the man professing to be Roger Thornhill is really the American spy they fear, George Kaplan. The elegance of Thornhill's oratory ultimately serves to further their opinion that Thornhill is really Kaplan since his protestations concerning his "true" identity are so convincing: "expert play-acting," the lead spy, Vandamm admires. In short, Thornhill's rhetorical discourse is so persuasive that the enemy agents conclude that his account can only be false.[18]

Of course, Thornhill is not murdered owing to several improbabilities that devotees of Hitchcock's films will accept as allowable, most notably navigating a car with no brakes down a steep mountain highway while utterly inebriated. Nonetheless, following his escape, Thornhill addresses his concerns to a second audience, the police, reasonably convinced that they, too, possess the capacity to resolve his difficulties. But for several reasons, including his inebriation and the fantastic nature of the story he relates, the police refuse to take his account of events seriously. This refusal to believe his account subsequently expands to a third audience, his own mother, when he later attempts to enlist her aid. She, too, is unconvinced of her son's claim that he was recently kidnapped and almost murdered by foreign spies. In addressing these different audiences, Thornhill appears to be defining the correct individuals as appropriately positioned to assist him. His failure to gain their

---

17 Bitzer, p. 8.

18 A situation in which the rhetor's eloquence serves to condemn rather than exonerate is not unknown and suggests that the principle of ethos can be more complicated than it is sometimes envisioned. Thornhill's rhetorical appeal from ignorance strikes Vandamm as mockery, and this both frustrates and angers Vandamm since he is convinced his associates have nabbed the right man. The scenes where the two men debate Thornhill's identity also show how the confirmation bias can overrule other considerations such as reason and logic such that all pieces of evidence – confirmatory and disconfirmatory – become semantically equivalent.

support – or more precisely, his failure to convince them of the truth of his narrative – should not be taken as an indication that we are not in a properly constituted rhetorical situation, however. Rather, Thornhill's efforts fail for the simple fact that, as Bitzer admits, "many questions go unanswered and many problems remain unsolved."[19] Addressing yourself to the correct audience – the audience with the capacity to bring about a solution – is not a guarantee that they will choose to do so. The rhetor's credibility does not always nor automatically overcome the audience's disbelief in every case.

Finally, every rhetorical situation comes with constraints that hamper the resolution of the exigence. Bitzer suggests that while constraints can be physical, as when the rhetor must overcome considerable distance to reach their audience, they are more usually cultural, or psychological, as in the case of audience members holding certain attitudes, beliefs, or presuppositions that work against the rhetor's interests or against aspects of the rhetor's message. Political affiliation to a particular party, for instance, might constitute a constraint against which the speaker must struggle in trying to present an opposing point of view, just as unfamiliarity with the specific concepts used by the speaker might operate as a constraint against successful persuasion. Properly constituted *ethos* is often sufficient to overcome many constraints, but even this is not a guarantee of successful persuasion.

In the case of *North by Northwest*, Thornhill must find a way to overcome several different sorts of constraints particular to the different audiences he addresses. These constraints include the lead spy Vandamm's confidence that Thornhill is lying and that the enemy spies have correctly identified the man they know as George Kaplan. The reasons supporting this confidence are admittedly flimsy, but they serve the purposes needed to suture the story together in making the act of misidentification plausible. Further constraints also include the doubting attitudes expressed by the official authorities, such as when the police refute Thornhill's account of his abduction owing to his obvious intoxication. Another constraint is the recalcitrance of the American intelligence bureaucrats to alter their scheme to capture Vandamm. Relying on moral consequentialism, the principle that more good than harm will come should they intervene, these intelligence officials behave in a way consistent with Hitchcock's usual depiction of authority figures as bureaucrats operating on questionable morals. Whereas they could take action to remove Thornhill from the obvious danger into which fate has placed him, they determine that he is useful to them in keeping their enemies off balance, and therefore they allow Vandamm and his associates to continue in their misidentification in

19 Bitzer, p. 6.

the hope that this confusion will serve the aims of American intelligence interests even though Thornhill's life remains in grave danger. The constraints further include the patriotic loyalty shown by Eve Kendall, a double agent with whom Thornhill falls in love along his journey. As she has infiltrated Vandamm's gang, she is also in a position to assist Thornhill, but in order to keep her identity secret and her life safe, she ignores Thornhill's pleas and even assists the spies with a scheme that puts Thornhill's life in considerable jeopardy. This act of pseudo-loyalty maintains the secret of her double agent status, and although Hitchcock reveals her regret at "playing along" with the enemy spies, her behaviour clearly constitutes a constraint on Thornhill's efforts to extricate himself from danger. All of these and more are constraints on Thornhill's ability to resolve the exigence(s) he faces. In some cases, this doesn't mean that the audience – that is, the audience as defined by Bitzer, not the audience sitting in the theatre – is unaware of the constraints. For example, it emerges that Eve Kendall has developed strong feelings for Thornhill to match his infatuation with her, but she believes that allegiance to her country takes precedence over romantic inclinations. Thus, Thornhill pleads with her for assistance without success. It is also worth noting that the different constraints in the film operate at various sociocultural levels, running from macro-level political machinations embedded in national agencies, to individual predilections shaped by romantic and sexual interests. Issues of political constancy also enter the rhetorical situation of *North by Northwest* as constraints on Thornhill's ability to modify the exigence (and ancillary exigences) against which he must battle.

Thornhill's dilemma, then, can be conceptualized as a problem in the domain of rhetoric. From the moment he is first kidnapped by the foreign agents he finds himself in a rhetorical situation. He must convince a range of audiences of several things, including at different times his innocence, his ignorance, his identity, and his love. Each of these is a subsidiary to his larger ambition to convince his audiences of the truth. The film's suspense is anchored on the fact that each audience Thornhill addresses – the spies, Eve, the police, his mother, the American intelligence services – proves unwilling for various reasons to yield to his pleas despite his discursive creativity. And as the narrative develops, each of the audiences to whom he directs his discourse changes from those with the power to induce the necessary change that will obviate the exigence, to an audience comprised principally of opponents – or, at least, an audience of persons disposed to reject his arguments and deny the legitimacy of his experiences.

Naturally, the film resolves in classic Hollywood fashion. The enemy spies are vanquished, and Thornhill is rewarded in the consummation of his romantic feelings for Eve. Thus, two exigences are resolved with those successes explained largely by Thornhill's ability to identify and address the appropriate audience in terms that bring matters to conclusions satisfactory to his wishes. And, of course, those of us taking in the picture for its entertainment value are also subject to Killingsworth's second discursive practice, the creation of a rhetorical event, for we are given to understand that whereas good usually vanquishes evil, the good will occasionally look very much like evil if it is to triumph in such extraordinary circumstances. We also learn the importance of the formation of the heterosexual couple, or perhaps that love will also triumph in the end. Discourse properly applied to the appropriate audience results in resolutions highly desired by our moral guardians.

Hitchcock's Films as Rhetorical Situations

Cinematic portrayals of rhetorical situations such as I have described in relation to *North by Northwest* appear with surprising frequency in many of Hitchcock films. Main characters in his movies frequently find themselves facing rhetorical situations where they try to discursively motivate other characters in order to prove their innocence; elude capture by villains or police; dissuade people from speaking to the authorities; convince the police that a crime has taken place; demonstrate their moral character; assure strangers of their mental soundness; persuade their paramours of the sincerity of their love; convince sceptics of their actual identity; inveigle against a scheme of which they disapprove; and in some cases, persuade themselves of the correctness – and occasionally the incorrectness – of their own interpretations of events. Sometimes the rhetorical situation is blatant, as when Professor Michael Armstrong must convince an East German scientist, Dr Gustav Lindt, that he is a trustworthy recipient of important technical information in the 1966 political thriller, *Torn Curtain*. The rhetorical situation is also front and centre in *Rear Window*, where Jeffrey must convince his detective friend, Tom Doyle, that he has credible evidence that a murder has been committed in an apartment just across the courtyard. In other cases, the rhetorical situation is kept in the background, shaded by the significance of other concerns more crucial to the audience. In some films, there is a combination of these overt and covert rhetorical situations embedded in a single plot. In *Shadow of a Doubt* (1943), for instance, Charles Oakley must convince a range of people in Santa Rosa of the genuineness of both his charm and his philanthropic character, while his niece and namesake, Charlie, ultimately becomes the foil to this exigence – Charlie, in Bitzer's terms, is a constraint working against Charles's ambitions. But then, Uncle Charles is an obstacle for Charlie, too, in that he threatens the domestic peace and order of her beloved family. Indeed, family is a curious part of the rhetorical situation in this film, for the fact of their familial connection, a bond that should be celebrated, ends up being an important constraint that ties Charlie to a situation from which she would prefer to escape. This sense of family obligation is why Charlie initially refuses to believe Detective Jack Graham's suspicions concerning her uncle, her belief that she has a spiritual connection with Uncle Charles rendering Graham's story simply unbelievable. Charles recognizes this fact, and in his threatening speech to Charlie in a famous scene at the *Til Two* tavern he relies explicitly on appeals to the family bonds Charlie so cherishes. As a fear appeal it is a masterful piece of rhetorical discourse.

While there are many other examples in Hitchcock's films, in the following section I am going to provide brief synopses of just four of his films that dramatize a rhetorical situation. This is not a comprehensive account of all the incidents in Hitchcock's catalogue where rhetorical activity can be found. It does, however, represent the significance of rhetorical situations in the fashioning of his plots. Following these short summaries and analyses I conclude with some observations of the importance of thinking of Hitchcock's films in terms of their rhetorical dramatizations. From there I turn to the final portion of the chapter by considering how Kenneth Burke's notions of rhetorical form are at work in Hitchcock's films as well.

Strangers on a Train

Strangers on a Train (1950) was famously cited by Hitchcock for the intricacy of its plot and the brilliance of its doubling motif, both in its visual realization and in the doppelgänger design drawing characters and scenes into alliance. However, rhetorical activity is also present right from the opening dialogue. The chance meeting between Guy and Bruno is immediately followed by the latter's soliloquy aimed at procuring Guy's favour and respect. And in seeking to ingratiate himself in Guy's estimation Bruno crosses the border separating enthusiasm from derangement, engaging several rhetorical strategies to convince Guy of the feasibility of a plan to exchange murders. His rhetorical overtures, which include a range of ethical and emotional appeals, ultimately fail as Guy refuses to take the plan of swapping murders seriously. The fact that Bruno is convinced of the soundness of his scheme, and that he attempts through consubstantial identification to enlist Guy's cooperation, is crucial to the narrative if Bruno's failure to persuade Guy is to ratchet up the tension, in part because it enlists the theme of the doppelgänger so effectively.[20]

20 "Consubstantial identification" is the rhetorician Kenneth Burke's phrase for what is more colloquially known as identification. The idea in the present context is that

Bruno identifies Guy as an audience with the power and the motive to help him remove the main constraint in his particular situation, his domineering father. Thus, an exigence and prevailing constraint are central to Bruno's decision to present his scheme for Guy's approval.

Guy, of course, must make his own rhetorical appeals because of the suspicions entertained by the police following Bruno's murder of Guy's estranged wife, Miriam. And these rhetorical pleas to the authorities follow directly from Guy's unsuccessful efforts to convince Miriam to grant him a divorce so that he can marry Ann Morton. Miriam, in other words, is an enormous constraint on the exigence that underlies the motivations of one of the central characters: Guy's desire to end an unhappy marriage to a resentful and unloving woman to be with a woman to whom he is passionately devoted. Even Bruno's insane proposition to trade murders is contingent on his knowing of Guy's predicament from reading the society pages in the newspapers.

This is the predominant exigence motivating the rhetorical overtures central to the story. However, many other rhetorical appeals pervade the film, including Ann's visit to Mrs Antony during which she attempts to persuade Mrs Antony that her son, Bruno, is mentally unstable; Guy's attempts to persuade Professor Collins that they met on the train, a meeting that would provide Guy with a substantial alibi for Miriam's murder; and Senator Morton's several efforts to convince his younger daughter, Barbara, that her conduct and manner of speaking are unbecoming for someone of her social standing. However, the film chiefly turns on the back-and-forth rhetorical practices in which Bruno and Guy engage, each seeking to persuade the other in respect of Bruno's murderous scheme. Even as Bruno seeks to persuade Guy that they can exchange murders and neither will be caught, Guy tries to convince Bruno of the madness of the scheme and the inevitability of failure. Guy even makes a late-night visit to Bruno's family estate in the forlorn hope of persuading Bruno's father that his son requires psychiatric help. And in the closing moments of the film, it is the fact that Guy's lighter is in Bruno's possession at the very moment of his death that turns the tide of persuasion in Guy's favour and convinces the police of his innocence. Thus, objects as well

---

Bruno hopes to persuade Guy to agree to his plan by demonstrating how he and Guy are really very much alike – that is, they are consubstantial, or of the same essence. Studies show people are more likely to be persuaded by others that they believe to be most like them, and thus Bruno is actually on solid psychological ground. As Burke wrote, "You persuade a man only insofar as you can talk his language by speech, gesture, tonality, order, image, attitude, idea, identifying your ways with his." (Burke, Kenneth. *A Grammar of Motives* (orig. 1945). Berkeley, Los Angeles, and London: University of California Press, 1969, p. 55.)

as people – or objects as well as discourse – can play a valuable role in bringing about a resolution to a rhetorical situation's exigence.

Suspicion

In the1941 film, *Suspicion*, the central character, Lina McLaidlaw, alternates between trying to convince her new husband, Johnnie, to carve out a respectable career and put aside the profligate habits of his youth, while also striving to persuade herself that Johnnie will ultimately find a useful career and bring financial and emotional stability to their marriage. These turn out to be parallel tracks insofar as Lina tries to convince Johnnie to mend his ways all the while she seeks to convince herself that her efforts to convince Johnnie will meet with success. Along this journey Lina appeals to several different audiences as she struggles to convince her parents, various friends, and even the police that Johnnie is an upstanding citizen. What is especially notable about her efforts is the way these rhetorical efforts are accompanied by a corresponding internal struggle. Lina is beset by self-doubts regarding Johnnie's capacity to reform. This externalization of her inner turmoil in the interests of reconciling herself to the perils of her situation is an apt illustration of what Jean Nienkamp has called "the rhetorical self," an aspect of our psychical lives that

> consciously and unconsciously practices rhetoric within itself, among its constituent voices, both to maintain a fragile equilibrium of personal identity and to resolve ambiguous or conflicting imperatives for attitude, decision, and action.[21]

Lina's efforts at this kind of self-persuasion aimed at resolving ambiguity provide many of the film's most engrossing moments of gothic suspense as her paranoia slowly becomes the basis for her growing belief in conspiracies.[22] To face down her paranoia, Lina must alter her actual circumstances. Having tied her life irrevocably to Johnnie's public image, and further having real-

21 Nienkamp, Jean. *Internal Rhetorics: Toward a History and Theory of Self-Persuasion.* Carbondale and Edwardsville: Southern Illinois University Press, 2001, p. 128.

22 Characters in other Hitchcock films are also seen engaging in internal rhetoric or self-persuasion. Take as an example the iconic character of Marion Crane from *Psycho* (1960). Marion engages in an extreme session of introspection following her conversation with Norman Bates, finally convincing herself that she must return the stolen money. Her successful appeal comes too late, of course, but it is often the delays in, and failures of persuasion, that make for good stories.

ized how his behaviour continues to devalue her social standing, Lina pushes Johnnie in the direction of bourgeois decency, hoping that he will eventually seek out a respectable station of his own accord. If she can only accomplish this dream, she will finally banish her conspiratorial fears.

But as these rhetorical efforts meet with failure, Lina begins to imagine her new husband must be harbouring terrible secrets. She eventually comes to fantasize that he is capable of murder, even envisioning herself as a future victim. However, despite dabbling in such dark fantasies Lina remains a romantic at heart, and because she believes that love is the rhetorical antidote needed for Johnnie's particular affliction, she spends an inordinate amount of screen time trying to determine the necessary dosage for his recovery.

The prevailing exigence, convincing Johnnie to join the world of middle-class sobriety through perseverance and hard work, is beset by constraints that are both material and psychological in nature. Johnnie's reformation becomes Lina's project, but his reluctance to conform serves as her most formidable constraint. He has carved out a life to which he is thoroughly attached, comfortably installed in a world of spendthrift debauchery. When Lina suggests that he finds meaningful employment shortly after returning from their honeymoon, Johnnie is aghast. The prospect of gainful work has never struck him as an agreeable way to while away the hours – not when there are racetracks to attend, friends to entertain, and poker games to join. This exigence raises special problems in respect of an identifiable audience with the power to quell the constraining forces and solve the problem. Lina comes to realize there are very few others she can trust and to whom she might turn for support, that an audience to whom she might direct her rhetorical appeals is hard to locate. Johnnie's friend, Beaky, seems a possibility at first, someone who loves Johnnie as an old and dear friend, and who might therefore respond to Lina's rhetorical pleading with an intervention of his own. But Beaky turns out to be more spineless than supportive, casually informing Lina that any effort to change Johnnie would inevitably end in failure. In a memorable scene he explains to her that it would be something of an injustice to the natural order of things should she succeed in reforming Johnnie. Purged of his foibles, ridded of his illicit yearnings, and set on a narrow path to respectability, Johnnie would be nothing but an empty shell. "You mustn't mind Johnnie cutting up," Beaky explains, "that's what makes him Johnnie."

In a surprise ending that left many critics profoundly dissatisfied, Lina is ultimately successful, and Johnnie comes to agree that he must change his ways if their marriage is to survive. This conclusion can be taken as signifying rhetorical success, though a more cynical reading might see Johnnie's promise to reform from a more sceptical point of view. However, it is not necessarily the successful application of discourse to the problem of the rhetorical situation that interested Bitzer. His focus was on the fact that when people find themselves in such circumstances, they need to determine the most likely rhetorical procedure to achieve their aims. Lina engages in this exact task in *Suspicion*, trying to work out how it might be possible to influence Johnnie to accept the value of a neoliberal identity. Whether she succeeds in the film's final frames is a question that film lovers will debate endlessly.

Notorious

The plot of the 1946 war thriller, *Notorious*, is structured around American agent Devlin's efforts to convince a young socialite, Alicia, that she must persuade a man named Alexander Sebastian, a Nazi living in Rio de Janeiro, that her romantic feelings for him are genuine. This is all rather sordid and complicated, but if Alicia can succeed in persuading Sebastian that her affections are real, if she can gain his trust and confidence, it will then be possible for her to gather information about his nest of post-war Nazi comrades. This information will then enable the American government to devise a way to prevent whatever plan Sebastian and his associates are concocting. To complicate matters, however, Devlin has fallen in love with Alicia, and to maintain the professional façade necessary for this caper's success, Devlin must struggle to convince Alicia that he has no romantic feelings for her. Two remarkable situations frame the story: Alicia must convince a Nazi agent that she genuinely loves him if she is to continue her espionage activity, while Devlin, who is now in love with Alicia, must convince her that he has no romantic feelings for her. This might be sufficiently complicated so far as movie plots go, but to further the complications, Alicia has fallen in love with Devlin. She is tormented by the thought that her love for Devlin is unrequited, that his sole interest is in advancing the ambitions of his government supervisors.

Rhetorical situations appear often in Hitchcock's film because much of our time is spent in the drama of rhetorical practice. "The world presents imperfections to be modified by means of discourse," says Bitzer, "hence the practical need for rhetorical investigation and discourse."[23] The rhetorical situation, when dramatized in film, becomes a kind of container for Todorov's equilibrium theory and can be understood as a formal structure by which expectancy is mobilized in the interests of resolution.[24]

---

23 Bitzer, p. 14.

24 Todorov, Tzvetan. *The Poetics of Prose*. Oxford: Wiley Blackwell, 1977.

Hitchcock, Burke, and Matters of Form

Critical reactions to the theory of rhetorical situations most often focus on its prescriptive quality. Bitzer suggested that rhetorical situations often "dictate" appropriate responses, and this idea invited criticism for its apparent promotion of a teleological interpretation of human activity. We find ourselves faced with a situation that demands a discursive response, Bitzer says, and we seek out the "appropriate" response, a response that is decreed by the situation itself. Bitzer's critics, in other words, sometimes attacked his theory for its apparent disavowal of the prospect of human agency. However, the examples of Hitchcock's films I have presented to illustrate Bitzer's work show that there is no single, univocal interpretation entailed in treating these narratives as rhetorical situations. The idea that there is one and only one fitting response to a rhetorical situation is not a necessary conclusion to which that concept drives us. What I prefer to focus on here is that if we accept – even if only provisionally – that there is a rhetorical dimension in play in Hitchcock's films, then it would be useful to go the further step of asking what sorts of resolutions follow from that fact. In other words, how does Hitchcock ultimately resolve the rhetorical situations his narratives construct? Are they always informed by the principle of ideological closure or do they deviate from that procedure in certain cases? I suspect that my response is implied by the nature of the question, for Hitchcock might be described as notorious for ambushing his viewers with dénouements that violated cinematic form in several ways. Hitchcock was not always an advocate for happy endings.

To explain the process of the deferred dénouement, I rely on the work of Kenneth Burke, whose attention to form as a rhetorical principle is one of the hallmarks of his method. Following this account of rhetorical form, I discuss Hitchcock's work in detail to show its way of evading customary formal conclusions, and how these decisions created the kinds of cinematic tensions that solidified his reputation as a filmmaker. Burke's emphasis on "proper form" and Bitzer's work on "appropriate resolutions" come together in demonstrating how, for Alfred Hitchcock, the deferred dénouement was a form of creative destruction.

The Forms of Burke's Rhetoric

Kenneth Burke understood form as "the creation of an appetite in the mind of the auditor, and the adequate satisfying of that appetite."[25] Whereas infor-

25 Burke, 1931, p. 31.

mation may resolve uncertainty that arises from ignorance, form exploits uncertainty arising from expectations. A key aspect concerning form in the context of cinema, then, is how the formal structures of genre and convention whet our appetites and how the narrative, engaging us in the various tropes and strategies that constitute emplotment, leads us toward a conclusion that will satisfy those desires which have been aroused.

While Kenneth Burke argued that form and content are indissociable, he nonetheless separated them conceptually in order to explain how the form in which information is presented can be understood from a rhetorical point of view. Burke understood form to be an essential complement to the informational component of the message; indeed, without form there really is no information.[26] And form, taken as an organizing principle for information, was mainly understood in Burke's view in terms of its anticipatory qualities. That is, form is the invocation and expression of patterns that lead to expected conclusions.[27]

Burke divided form into five aspects: progressive form, which comprises both syllogistic and qualitative form; repetitive form; conventional form; and minor or incidental types. The first aspect, syllogistic progressive form, involves a step-by-step, logical movement as when we move from premise to premise to arrive at the inevitable conclusion. In syllogistic form, as Burke says, "certain things must follow, the premises forcing the conclusion."[28] Syllogistic form thus takes interpretive activity partly out of the hands of the reader/viewer, by turning the process into a matter of conviction and

---

26 One might see this point as Burke's way of framing (or reframing) Aristotle's claim that rhetoric is the counterpart of dialectic. (Aristotle, *On Rhetoric*, 1354a).

27 Burke was certainly not the first writer to take note of the way that form helps to establish the logic of specific interpretations and enlist the aid of audience expectations. A much earlier illustration of this understanding of the anticipatory effects of form can be found in Wordsworth's Preface to *Lyrical Ballads*. Wordsworth noted that writing in verse was a kind of invitation to the reader, even suggesting that in picking up a book of verse poetry, the reader was entitled to entertain certain expectations arising from the formal nature of versification. The reader was especially justified in believing these expectations to be produced in part by the implied agreement, or promise, the author had contracted with his or her audience. As Wordsworth wrote:

> It is supposed that by the act of writing in verse an Author makes a formal engagement that he will gratify certain known habits of association; that he not only apprizes the reader that certain classes and expressions of ideas will be found in his book, but that others will be carefully excluded.

See Wordsworth, William and Coleridge, Samuel. *Lyrical Ballads* (1798 and 1802). Oxford: Oxford University Press, 2013, p. 96.

28 Burke, 1931, p. 124.

understanding. In syllogistic progressive form, in other words, logic rules over interpretation.

Progressive qualitative form is more complex, and is the only kind of form, Burke concedes, where we do not encounter form's "anticipatory nature." Qualitative form usually entails a backward glance as we come to realize that certain qualities from earlier scenes, conversations, and events served to prepare us for similar qualities and feelings in later scenes. Thus, with qualitative form, Burke says, we tend "to recognize its rightness after the fact."[29] In their book on rhetorical analysis, Foss, Foss, and Trapp illustrate the notion of qualitative progressive form by referring to Hitchcock's film, *Vertigo* (1958). They point out that first-time viewers likely have no idea that the two women with whom Scottie falls in love, first Madeleine and then Judy, are really the same person, and that Judy's death in the film's final moments makes sense only by considering Madeleine's staged death from earlier in the narrative. In other words, *Vertigo*'s form is subtle to the point of requiring a retrospective analysis to be properly discerned. Qualitative progressive form thus has none of the logical rigour (and temporal precision) of syllogistic progressive form, but retains the latter's focus on the linear connectivity by which disparate scenes are linked.

Repetitive form, unsurprisingly, is "the restatement of a theme by new details."[30] Of course, each restatement can vary from its predecessors in salient particulars but only so long as the underlying principle is maintained. In *Counter-Statement*, Burke describes repetitive form as it might appear in a single text, as, for instance, when "each detail of Gulliver's life among the Lilliputians is a new exemplification of the discrepancy in size between Gulliver and the Lilliputians."[31] But, of course, there will be other times when repetitive form is carried over across different texts. Hitchcock's persistent use of birds and bird motifs in films separated by several decades would be one illustration. Generally, however, repetitive form is restating "the same thing in different ways" within a single text.

Burke says that we have conventional form when form is presented *as form*. So when an author begins a limerick, for instance, the form is unmistakable and establishes conditions Burke calls "categorical expectancy."[32] Whereas "the anticipations and gratifications of progressive and repetitive form arise during the process of reading [or viewing], the expectations of conventional

29 Burke, 1931, p. 125.
30 Burke, 1931, p. 125.
31 Burke, 1931, p. 125.
32 Burke, 1931, p. 126.

form may be anterior to the reading."[33] This means that sometimes we recognize form from a point distant from its beginning, as with qualitative form when we look back to note the pattern that has unfolded over the course of the text, film, or artwork, while there are also occasions when form is introduced at the opening, the classic illustration being the phrase "once upon a time." Here the invitation is presented in the clichéd structure of the form, and while it is rather elementary, its allure is equally apparent. The effect of such weathered but durable forms is to procure immediate assent to the invitation and, very often, to attenuate a cynical or resistant attitude. If we are to have a fairy tale then certain predispositions are best brought forward at the outset, and intellectual defences against improbability put to one side.

Finally, Burke describes minor or incidental forms such as "metaphor, paradox, disclosure, reversal, contraction," and so on.[34] Burke says rather little about minor or incidental forms, focusing mainly on the idea that their chief function will be determined by their place in the text. To begin a sentence a certain way – for instance, to begin a sentence with the word *therefore* – is to engage in minor form insofar as the opening word sets up a certain (though minimal) degree of expectancy in the reader, the idea of a provisional summation, in this case. Minor forms are generally said to be parts of larger formal patterns and work their effects in somewhat incidental though clearly important ways. But the mere fact that even at the level of the sentence we can identify form as integral to the rhetorical function of the utterance shows how deeply our understanding of texts (including films) is embedded in formal patterns and the consequent expectancies of everyday discourse.

Whether form is made apparent in the opening words, or whether it becomes clear retrospectively, form is always an invitational strategy for establishing meaning through pattern. In Burke's account of form, the ideas of invitation, expectation, and gratification are key aspects of the rhetorical constitution of appeal.[35] And gratification is achieved ordinarily when completion is made conspicuous. This might involve minor form, as when the narrator concludes that the personages "lived happily ever after," or syllogistically, as when the preceding events are said to lead explicitly or implicitly to a single, inevitable conclusion. However, our sense of satisfaction when the form is correctly constituted is often experienced imperceptibly, being discerned in the sensation of completeness if not in the recognition of moral or aesthetic order. For this reason, Burke concedes that the principle of gratification can sometimes "be

33 Burke, 1931, pp. 126–127.

34 Burke, 1931, p. 127.

35 Indeed, Burke says that "form *is* the appeal." Burke, 1931, p. 138.

better revealed by our dissatisfaction with an uncompleted thought than by our satisfaction with a completed one."[36] That is, we are more likely to be aware of improperly constituted form in the experience of dissatisfaction than we are to recognize proper form in the experience of contentment. When the novelist fails to bring their book to a conclusion we were expecting, we might experience a sense of dissatisfaction greater than the pleasure we note when the book ends as we wish.

The invocation of an invitational quality is apparent in virtually all the major works in which Burke considers the concept of form, and it is elaborated in various ways though always with the same essential principles in mind. In addition, Burke was aware that by an appropriate use of form the author (or filmmaker) could establish identification between author and reader, and in doing so could gather the assent of the reader to the content of the properly constituted form. Burke offers a few examples, but one of the illustrations cited most frequently is found in his text *A Rhetoric of Motives* (1950):

> 'Who controls Berlin, controls Germany; who controls Germany controls Europe; who controls Europe controls the world.' As a proposition, it may or may not be true. [...] But regardless of these doubts about it as a proposition, by the time you arrive at the second of its three stages, you feel how it is destined to develop – and on the level of purely formal assent you would collaborate to round out its symmetry by spontaneously willing its completion and perfection as an utterance.[37]

Burke's point is that agreement with the content of the proposition is at least partly contingent on agreement to the correctness of the form, a fact that helps to explain why, when the form is not adhered to faithfully, the content is regarded with disfavour. The idea of proper form thus suggests that the appeal of form, whether syllogistically, conventionally, or repetitively articulated, is concerned with the idea of satisfaction, a tacit approval of the proposition enunciated in the content. The audience enjoys the narrative because it has commenced in ways consistent with cinematic conventions, developed its plot in accordance with anticipated events, and concluded with a dénouement that harmonizes with our beliefs: it is a satisfactory and gratifying experience. But when form is subverted, the incorrectness of the form may be transferred

36 Burke, 1931, p. 140.

37 Burke, Kenneth. *A Rhetoric of Motives*. Berkeley: University of California Press, 1950, pp. 58–59.

to the interpretation of the actual message and interfere with the expectancy of gratification. An improper form may result in a discredited message.

The Deferred Dénouement versus Proper Form

I want to pick up on this point of formal correctness as a way of engaging with the question of the deferred dénouement. To reiterate what I said at the outset, Hitchcock occasionally subverted his film's narrative by putting off or deferring the customary ending and thereby frustrating audiences by denying them the conventional pleasure of a satisfactory resolution. This was the case perhaps most famously with *The Birds* (1963), which was initially received by critics and fans as a failure (or at least a seriously flawed effort) because the film provided no indication in its closing scene as to where Mitch, Melanie, Lydia, and Cathy might turn for salvation. Hence the film was dismissed by some for its refusal to follow the dictates of its thriller genre. It was, as Burke might have said, victimized by an improperly constituted form.

In addition, the critics, who dismissed *The Birds* as a lesser effort, argued that it interpolated its viewers to a subject position that it was unable to completely satisfy, a claim that tended to overvalue and perhaps essentialize the idea of form as reductively determinative. This was the view of well-known British film critic, Penelope Houston, who penned an influential essay arguing that *The Birds* was largely detached from the usual plot formations that constituted suspense, and that its ending therefore represented a failure of cinematic vision in the way it left the audience hanging.[38] Other critics over the decades have shared in this assessment. Many commentators have regarded *The Birds* as an excessively "arty" indulgence, the product of a filmmaker with ambitions that exceeded his talent. Others have said that the film is pretentious, chiefly because it lacks the requisite narrative weight expected by the art-house crowd. Indeed, when traditional form is subverted in the popular cinema, a common explanation is that the filmmaker has lapsed into the abyss of artistic pretentiousness.

38 Houston, Penelope. "The Figure in the Carpet." *Sight and Sound*, Fall, 32 (4) (1963), pp. 159–164. I might add that one might read *The Birds* as a text concerned preeminently with resolution failures. Not only does the film fail to resolve the central exigence of the birds' attacks, but as Margaret Horowitz has observed, so too the film contains no resolution for the Oedipal relationship that is commonly seen as crucial to the film's underlying meaning. Thus, the deferred dénouement of *The Birds* is part of a larger thematic failure to achieve resolution more generally. See Horowitz, Margaret M. "'*The Birds*': A Mother's Love." In *A Hitchcock Reader*, edited by Marshall Deutelbaum and Leland Poague. Ames, Iowa: Iowa State University Press, 1986, pp. 279–287.

Of course, not all film scholars would agree that *The Birds* ends badly because it closes without fulfilling traditional expectations. Although many critics focused on the lack of resolution as preeminent among the reasons for dismissing the work, Robert Kapsis has argued that the film's deferred dénouement was likely part of a larger strategy Hitchcock adopted to solidify his growing reputation as an auteur. As Kapsis notes, whereas Hitchcock wanted the script for *The Birds* to be suspenseful from start to finish, "the gloom, the tentativeness, and lack of resolution of the film's final scene are indications that Hitchcock also wanted the film to appeal to a more high-culture audience." The deferred dénouement, then, can be overdetermined by a combination of aesthetic, economic, and even legacy issues, three considerations to which Hitchcock's ego often made him liable.[39]

Furthermore, *The Birds* is only one of many films in which Hitchcock refused to follow the dictates of conventional form. It may be that *The Birds* is the most widely discussed Hitchcock film in which form was subverted, but equally interesting examples of deferred dénouements can be found in several of his other films. Recall our earlier discussion of Hitchcock's first sound feature, *Blackmail* (1929). The plot is simple. Alice White argues with her detective boyfriend, Frank Webber, over dinner and leaves the restaurant with a man named Crewe. Frank disconsolately watches them disappear into the night, apparently resigned to the belief that his relationship with Alice has ended. Crewe guides Alice through foggy London streets to his flat where, after some music and flirtatious dialogue, he tries to rape her. Alice kills Crewe with a knife and flees for home only to discover the following morning that Frank has been assigned to the case. Having discovered one of her gloves in Crewe's apartment during a search of the crime scene, Franks has rightly deduced that that Alice is the killer. The blackmailer of the title, Tracy, who saw Alice leave Crewe's flat the evening prior, enters the scene. By a series of twists and turns, Tracy winds up being suspected of Crewe's death. He attempts to flee but ultimately falls to his death (in the British Museum, no less) trying to evade capture. Alice is consumed by guilt and wants to confess to Crewe's death, but Frank, worried that his decision to conceal Alice's involvement will jeopardize his career, prevents her from doing so. The film ends on the sight of Alice's anguished face, the sound of Alice's hollow laughter, and the knowledge that she and Frank will forever be bound not by romantic love but by the nightmare of their mutual guilt.

39 Kapsis, Robert. *Hitchcock: The Making of a Reputation*. Chicago and London: University of Chicago Press, 1992, p. 93ff.

Hitchcock told several interviewers he would have preferred *Blackmail* to have ended with Frank arresting Alice for Crewe's murder, but he was overruled by the studio, leaving the film with what Thomas Leitch has described as "a technically happy ending," though one profoundly marked by pathos and irony.[40] Other film analysts have made similar observations. David Sterritt argues that *Blackmail* ends on a note of extraordinary moral ambiguity and narrative ambivalence,[41] while Robin Wood's feminist analysis suggests that the coherence of the classical narrative is shattered by an ending that leaves questions of guilt and innocence unsettled.[42] In short, the film avoids the sort of resolution expected from a romance thriller.[43] The conventional form is violated.

Films like *The Birds* and *Blackmail* lack resolution in the sense that while the films arouse audience desires, they subsequently leave those desires unfulfilled in terms of conventional narrative patterns. In this sense, it would seem that both films misfire as rhetorical works in respect of Burke's argument for the centrality of form in meaning-making practices. And indeed, some viewers find these films deficient precisely because they challenge specific notions of ideological closure, such as the importance of punishing the wicked, reestablishing equilibrium following a major disruption, or even the idea that heterosexual coupling is the definitive way of resolving the romantic thriller.

But are they failures, or is form inherently malleable? Perhaps audience expectations are not always an appropriate measure of rhetorical success? One might suggest, for instance, that the violation of rhetorical form is actually a revolutionary artistic impulse, and that in subverting the expected conclusion, Hitchcock wanted to break the artifice of cinematic tradition in favour of a different sort of affective experience. This raises the question of the extent to which audience expectations dictate artistic license.

Furthermore, not all viewers feel the same discomfiture that critics of the deferred dénouement see as emblematic of a cinematic failure. For my part, I find that the ending to *Blackmail* is eminently satisfying precisely because it dispenses with the formulaic images of fanciful bliss. But that experience is

---

40 Leitch, Thomas. *The Encyclopedia of Alfred Hitchcock.* New York: Checkmark Books, 2002, p. 36.

41 Sterritt, David. *The Films of Alfred Hitchcock.* Cambridge: Cambridge University Press, 1993, p. 50.

42 Wood, Robin. *Hitchcock's Films Revisited.* New York: Columbia University Press, 1989, pp. 273–274.

43 I might add that the film differs significantly from the Charles Bennett play which ends with the police discovery that Crewe actually died of a heart attack and literally fell on his knife! This ending, of course, completely exonerates Frank and Alice.

still predicated on the prevailing structures of form; that is, it is in the deviation from accepted custom that the subverted form is permitted to succeed, for if there is no traditional principle to begin with there is nothing from which the artist can deviate. I realize that it is obvious to point out that the form must pre-exist the anti-form for the latter to have any sort of value. But I think the argument is important regardless, for as Burke explains in terms of its rhetorical function, form is a powerful inducement to audience acceptance of the correctness of the narrative events conveyed when the form is deemed correct. That is, we use forms to guarantee – as much as is possible – that the narrative will be accepted as "proper" in the way that audiences feel a sense of satisfaction. The reasoning here is plain: if the form is improper then audiences are unsatisfied; and if audiences are unsatisfied, they will reject the story along with the form. Proper form is thus very often a guarantee of narrative success as well as a matter of appropriate structure.

This is a complicated problem, nonetheless, because there are limits to both form and expectations, and knowing how to manage the degree of latitude an audience might be willing to tolerate is itself more art than science. To illustrate this point consider Hitchcock's 1950 psychological thriller, *Stage Fright.* Hitchcock opens the film with a flashback in which Jonathan is speaking with Eve, recounting events concerning a murder for which he claims he is being framed. But at the film's conclusion this entire flashback is shown to have been false. We discover that Jonathan is the killer and not the victim of the elaborate conspiracy he related in the flashback. It is an unsettling moment, and the film was largely unsuccessful. So where did Hitchcock go wrong?

It turns out that audiences and critics were outraged because they believed that Hitchcock had no right to play so brazenly with an accepted form: namely, that movie flashbacks must always be true. Without the guarantee that flashbacks reveal objective facts, it was argued, audiences would be unable to make sense of the story, never knowing for certain which characters can faithfully be relied upon. What is particularly notable about this response is that this concern is motivated solely by the power of the form, for there is nothing inherently truthful about a cinematic flashback. The flashback is merely a convention, a cinematic technique in which an omniscient narrator positioned outside the diegesis temporarily transcends the narrative. Hence the idea that flashbacks must invariably reveal empirically reliable information is maintained not by conditions essential to that particular cinematic practice, but by the rhetorical traditions that fashion the flashback as a particular kind of form. But the power of this time-honoured form, Hitchcock learned, was not something to be trifled with. Whereas he regarded *Stage Fright* overall as a good film, Hitchcock had to accept that the production was undermined by his refusal to follow the conventional form of the flashback technique. As he recalled years later:

> I did one thing in that picture that I never should have done; I put in a flashback that was a lie. [...] Strangely enough in movies, people never object if a man is shown telling a lie. And it's also acceptable, when a character tells a story about the past, for the flashback to show it as if it were taking place in the present. So why is that that we can't tell a lie through a flashback?[44]

No doubt Hitchcock was aware that audience expectations can overpower artistic creativity. Although they cannot do so absolutely, forms can certainly constrain interpretive activity, and to violate a form – even an incidental cinematic form like the Hollywood flashback – is to risk the loss of audience pleasure by denying viewers the satisfaction of an expected resolution. In addition, the more familiar viewers are with the prevailing form, the more difficult it may be to ask them to allow for departure from the customary patterns established by that form.

How do Kenneth Burke's ideas about proper form figure in the case of the deferred dénouement? Throughout the book, *Counter-Statement*, Burke explains the value of form as a rhetorically significant organizing principle. However, there is one brief section where he addresses the fact that artists occasionally deviate from customary formal practices. And in order to explain how these moments of subversion can be accommodated to his ideas about form, Burke provides an interesting if potentially tautological explanation of the meaning of the deferred dénouement. So, the final question I want to address is how Hitchcock's theory of the unhappy ending can be measured against Burke's account of improperly constituted form.

As with Hitchcock, Burke recognizes that when artists arouse but then fail to satisfy, they must appeal to some larger principle for exculpation. Recall that Hitchcock argues that unhappy endings will be tolerated if there is "sufficient entertainment" in the body of the text to compensate for the denial of satisfaction that comes with the deferred dénouement. For Burke, the matter is slightly more complicated, though he, too, appeals to the necessity of a higher purpose:

> In violating a convention, an author is undeniably violating a major tenet of form. For he is disappointing the expectations of his audience;

44 Truffaut, p. 189.

> and form, by our definition, resides in the fulfillment of an audience's expectations. The only justification which an author may have for thus breaking faith with his audience is the fact that categorical expectations are very unstable and that the artist can, if his use of the repetitive and progressive principles is authoritative enough, succeed in bringing his audience to a sufficient acceptance of his methods.[45]

Burke's comment reflects certain aspects of Hitchcock's position. An artist might be able to persuade their audience to accept deviation from traditional form precisely because (1) form is inherently unstable, and (2) because the artist possesses sufficient authority (or ethos) to do as they wish providing their motivations for subverting expectations are aesthetically justified. Burke goes on to strengthen his claim by suggesting that in reviewing the history of art we note that if "changes in conventional form are introduced [...] to produce a kind of effect which the violated convention was not well able to produce, but which happens to more apropos to the contemporary scene, the changes may very rapidly become 'canonized' in popular acceptance and the earlier convention may seem the violator of categorical expectancy."[46] Whereas Hitchcock argues that there must be sufficiently engaging entertainment in the text to permit the filmmaker to deviate from traditional form, Burke suggests that there must be sufficient value in the way the violation permits new meanings suitable to the present context to be established. In other words, form can be violated successfully when there are adequate compensatory pleasures to be had. However, as I suggested earlier, this argument might be read as tautological in that Burke suggests that in failing to satisfy the audience owing to having violated the expectations aroused by the form, the artist manages to satisfy the audience nonetheless as the new form is "more apropos to the contemporary scene." This suggests that form is violated successfully if the artist sacrifices their allegiance to proper form in the interests of another type of form that may eventually be canonized to the detriment of the earlier form it replaces. Audiences will dispense with the comfort of the form when it is in their interests to do so.

It is a bit challenging to make complete sense of the problem this argument raises in terms of Burke's understanding of the notion of proper form when he has apparently accepted two kinds of satisfaction as simultaneously operative. In other words, if form is defined as being proper to the extent that audience satisfaction is achieved, then violations of form will automatically be failures

45 Burke, 1931, p. 204.
46 Burke, 1931, p. 204.

if the initial act of arousal goes unfulfilled. But Burke then offers a qualified addendum: it is true that an audience might well be dissatisfied when form is violated, but they might also be satisfied if they appreciate the novelty of the conclusion by accepting what Burke calls the artist's methods. Some filmgoers might be dissatisfied by the ending to *The Birds* because it violates the convention of the happy ending, even as other viewers might be satisfied by that ending for precisely the same reason: the subversion of traditional form. Hence, we might speak of the deferred dénouement as a potential metacommentary; that is, by attending to the way in which satisfaction has been put off or deferred, a viewer might derive satisfaction from the aesthetic and social values attached to this strategy. And if the lack of satisfaction is to be experienced as satisfying, it would appear that the unhappy ending must be balanced against the happy ending in order to be appreciated in the broader conception of form that Burke advances.

Burke argues in *Counter-Statement* that "in expecting how things *will be*, we expect by implication how they *will not be*."[47] Thus, the unhappy ending is ordinarily precluded by the invitation of form, and in order to overcome the seduction of form – which would seem in this instance to require an extra-diegetic movement – the viewer must also overcome the expectation for a certain ordering and closure. And this conclusion is allowable, one might say, to the extent that we agree to Burke's claim that "categorical expectations are very unstable," and that audiences will occasionally be persuaded by a subversive organization of the narrative.

Hitchcock frequently told interviewers that his films set out patterns and associations that could be appreciated only after multiple viewings, that they were deliberately qualitatively progressive, in Burke's terms. For some, this argument was motivated by a wish for greater box office returns, but most critics agree that there are often labyrinthine aspects to his films that indeed demand repeated viewings. So, when, in one of Alfred Hitchcock's films, things don't turn out as expected, this may well be expected owing to the complexity with which his plots were developed. More to the point, the viewer might be wisely advised to look to the rhetorical function of form as a potentially disabling constraint. For this reason, it is fair to think of the deferred dénouement as a kind of creative destruction. The "modern delight in happy endings," Burke wrote, may simply be a way to "indulge our humanitarianism in a well-wishing which we do not permit ourselves towards our actual neighbors."[48] Or as Hitchcock loved to remind his critics, it is, after all, only a movie.

47 Burke, 1931, p. 209.
48 Burke, 1931, p. 41.

Chapter 8

MORALIZING UNCERTAINTY: SUSPICION AND FAITH IN HITCHCOCK'S *SUSPICION*

> Suspicions amongst thoughts are like bats amongst birds, they ever fly by twilight.
>
> – Francis Bacon[1]

> For the interpreter to "perform" the text, he must "understand" it: he must preunderstand the subject and the situation before he can enter the horizon of its meaning. This is that mysterious "hermeneutical circle" without which the meaning of the text cannot emerge.
>
> – Richard Palmer[2]

In a discussion of the hermeneutical problem of symbolism, Paul Ricoeur draws attention to the double-sided nature of discourse. Multivocality or polysemy, Ricoeur points out, is a constitutive feature of all human communication. Meaning is a plurality, a kind of semiotic surplus. "When I speak," Ricoeur says, "I realize only a part of the potential signified." This condition, as Derrida famously argued, is the "indefinite referral of signifier to signifier [...] which gives the signified meaning no respite."[3] Meanings are excessive, spilling beyond the perimeters delimited by dictionary definitions. The problem of symbolism, according to Ricoeur, is how communicants make sense out of signs which are duplicitous by their very nature, for if "only a part of the potential signified" is realized in a communicational event, then what passes the outskirts of our understanding undetected is an infinity of interpretative

1 Bacon, Francis. *Essays* (orig. 1597). London: J. M. Dent & Sons Ltd., 1972.

2 Palmer, Richard. *Hermeneutics: Interpretation Theory in Schleiermacher, Dilthey, Heidegger, and Gadamer.* Evanston: Northwestern University Press, 1969.

3 Derrida, Jacques. *Writing and Difference.* London: Routledge & Kegan Paul, 1978, p. 25.

possibilities. When we communicate, it is by virtue of our capacity to limit ourselves to partial conceptions of the world that any comprehension can occur.

Yet despite this semantic partialness, our communications are intelligible, a consequence of the astonishing collaboration between symbols, reference, and contexts. But the fact that our semantic intentions are accomplished at all indicates that we manage to arrive at mutual understanding in the face of persistent alternative interpretations. Our concentration on a single intended meaning does not neutralize other potential interpretations, Ricoeur states, but is facilitated by the individualizing focus of specific units of speech, such as sentences. Indeed, Ricoeur maintains that

> the rest of the semantic possibilities are not cancelled; they float around the words as possibilities not completely eliminated. The context thus plays the role of filter. [...] It is in this way that we make univocal statements with multivocal words by means of this sorting or screening action of the context. It happens, however, that a sentence is constructed so that it does not succeed in reducing the potential meaning to a monosemic usage but maintains or even creates a rivalry among several ranges of meaning. Discourse can, by various means, realize *ambiguity*, which thus appears as the combination of a lexical fact – polysemy – and a contextual fact – the possibility allowed to several distinct or even opposed values of a single name to be realized in the same sequence.[4]

Hence discourse realizes ambiguity at the point of intersection between lexical fact (words) and context. Ambiguity is an inherent aspect of discourse, and therefore is a foundational matter for anyone concerned with interpretation, however quotidian the circumstances. Contexts are filters we use to screen out as many of the competing interpretations as is reasonable. We do this, as Ricoeur suggests, because we need to produce univocal meanings from multivocal symbols. Although this implies that ambiguity attends all efforts at interpretation, the appeal to socially and culturally relevant contextual information enables us to bracket this chorus of alternative significations to make immediate sense of our experience. Or such is the supposition we make when we claim to have understood.

4 Ricoeur, Paul. "The Problem of Double Meaning as Hermeneutic Problem and as Semantic Problem." In *The Conflict of Interpretations*, translated by Kathleen McLaughlin. Evanston: Northwestern University Press, 1974, pp. 62–78. Passages quoted from p. 71.

If ambiguity is never eliminated but continues to "float" about our discourse, it is always possible to recapture one of these ethereal alternatives and render it the centre of our attention. There are many reasons one might do so. One might choose this course of action owing to feelings of unease produced by nagging doubt or suspicion. Or one might find that a stated intention is at odds with one's prevailing beliefs or faith. We might have good cause to be wary of the univocal interpretation to which culture and common sense pushes us – indeed, suspicion is very often produced out of the very semantic density to which Ricoeur refers. Suspicion, as Kenneth Burke might suggest, is a terministic screen that deflects attention from some aspects of the world in order to draw out attention to other aspects and to other interpretations.[5] Suspicion may seem irrational, but it can also produce the sorts of interpretations that permit us to find our footing.

In this chapter I offer a phenomenological account of a specific mode of uncertain interpretation. I argue that suspicion can be conceptualized as an interpretive framework whose principal function is to bring order to circumstances that otherwise would remain confounded by uncertainty. This is not an entirely original idea, of course, as the relation between the practices of textual demystification and cultural interpretation has been argued by a variety of commentators, such arguments focusing occasionally on the role of suspicion as an underlying analytical principle. Taken as such a principle, suspicion can be viewed as integral to the modernist project of a rational, deconstructive understanding. The "hermeneutics of suspicion" which is commonly associated with Marx, Nietzsche, and Freud can suggest both method (the dialectic; depth psychology) and ideological commitment.[6] We are driven by our suspicion, in other words, to discover the hidden truths, the contradictions, and the traces of false consciousness that constitute the reality of social relations, political economic practices, and even psychological

---

5 Burke defines terministic screens as follows:

> We must use terministic screens, since we can't say anything without the use of terms; whatever terms we use, they necessarily constitute a corresponding kind of screen; and any such screen necessarily directs the attention to one field rather than another. Within that field there can be different screens, each with its ways of directing the attention and shaping the range of observations implicit in the given terminology. All terminologies must implicitly or explicitly embody choices between the principle of continuity and the principle of discontinuity.

Burke, Kenneth. *Language as Symbolic Action: Essays on Life, Literature, and Method*. Berkeley: University of California Press, 1966, p. 50.

6 Ricoeur, Paul. *Freud and Philosophy: An Essay on Interpretation*, translated by Denis Savage. New Haven and London: Yale University Press, 1970.

fixations. Thus, suspicion can be seen as a Janus-faced figure: it is a form of uncertainty motivated by unclear, equivocal, or doubtful perception. But so too it is a form of certainty that draws its subject onward by the seductive allure of what is already suspected. And it is this latter aspect that inspires advocates of the hermeneutics of suspicion to pry free the deceitful masks of social convention in search of an underlying reality.

However, arguments of this sort can suggest that suspicion is a teleological endeavour, one in which the subject finds his or her interpretations matched up in the final moments against a truth that has been predetermined by the same sources from which the conditions of mistrust first arose. I am not suggesting that all forms of analytical inquiry prefigure the conclusions to which they come. My point is more modest, for what I want to do is to look at suspicion itself instead of focusing on the results of a suspicious inquiry. What is it to be suspicious? Suspicion may indeed be an important motivational force, but can we say more than that by examining suspicion as an interpretive gesture? If we were to treat suspicion as a kind of interpretive filter – a contextual element, as Ricoeur would say – can we examine it in the same fashion that subjects are scrutinized in the field of cultural studies?

If my main ambition is to put forward the claim that suspicion constitutes a kind of interpretive framework, my method is to accomplish this analysis with a reading of one of Alfred Hitchcock's early American films, the aptly titled *Suspicion* (1941). When Hitchcock took up Frances Iles's 1932 novel *Before the fact* for adaptation, he was fresh from the bittersweet success of *Rebecca* (his first film in America and the Academy's selection for Best Picture of 1940), though yet a novice in the ways of Hollywood. His experiences with American actors had been less than uniformly pleasant, and his dealings with the politics of production had been mixed. Many in the film industry in the United States accused Hitchcock of laziness, a director who took much longer to complete his work than was usual with more seasoned American filmmakers. He was regarded as an eccentric, and an outsider, a director whose working methods were unfamiliar in the Hollywood studio system. Hitchcock's strategy of "cutting in the camera," which permitted him extraordinary control over his production, had frustrated and angered David O. Selznick, his first American producer. The major studios had made evident their suspicions about Hitchcock's abilities to adjust to the Fordist mentality in Hollywood from the moment it was announced that he was relocating to America.

For his part, Hitchcock was suspicious of authority, a feeling that could transmute into dislike when he discovered that his plans were being interfered with from above. Hence when Selznick loaned Hitchcock to RKO Studios in 1941 to work on *Suspicion*, Hitchcock relished his release from Selznick's controlling gaze and welcomed the opportunity to take command of a film from start to finish. However, several problems interfered with the film's production, including illness and interruptions in the completion of principal photography. In addition, Hitchcock's use of time once again proved to be something of a concern to studio executives. The meticulousness of the *auteur* was unappreciated by those in Hollywood whose vision of the film business tended to be circumscribed by a single value: efficiency. Hence suspicions in the industry about Hitchcock's *Suspicion* circulated as the production lurched from one delay to another.

The result of the various setbacks that plagued the production, according to commentators who judge the film unkindly, was a compromised narrative. Many critics have suggested that the film betrays Hitchcock's inexperience with the American culture industries in several ways, most notably in its ending. For instance, in an otherwise enthusiastic essay about the film, Mark Crispin Miller is blunt in his condemnation: "The ending is, indeed, a disappointment," he writes, before going on to say that

> In a hurry to prepare the film for a summer premiere, Hitchcock quickly worked out and shot this ending after another version [...] was hooted down by a preview audience. While Hitchcock's unwonted haste will explain the ending's general shoddiness, however, the scene's fundamental weakness is not technical but dramatic: Hitchcock simply was unable to devise a strong conclusion. [...] By locating *Suspicion* within its heroine's mind, Hitchcock had written himself into a corner.[7]

While Miller's overall analysis of the film is engaging and insightful, I would contest his view of the film's conclusion. My disagreement is not with his evaluation of the film's ending from an aesthetic or formal point of view, and I have no intention of offering an assessment of the merits or demerits of *Suspicion*'s dénouement. Rather, I believe Miller's claim that Hitchcock had written himself into a corner is motivated by a commitment to narrative resolution that aims to be faithful at an elementary level of textual interpretation but that overlooks consideration of the film's psychological dimensions. In that respect, the resolution Hitchcock decided upon enhances the poignancy of the story which is, after all, a tale of suspicion. Indeed, as viewers we are left in doubt at the story's end about several key points in the plot; we come away, in other words, somewhat suspicious of the reliability of what we are shown. Thus, many critics of the film, including Miller, overlook the fact that

7 Miller, Mark Crispin. "Hitchcock's Suspicions and Suspicion." In *Boxed in: The Culture of TV*. Evanston: Northwestern University Press, 1988, pp. 274, 275.

the film deals with a phenomenological approach to suspicion per se, and not only with the suspicions of the film's heroine. I believe that we must attend to *Suspicion* in terms of what it offers us as *a text about suspicion* to recognize more fully the film's intricacies. If we are willing to accept that the heroine of the film, Lina, is more emblematic than literal, we arrive at far more interesting question: How does suspicion operate in *Suspicion*?

The Film

With Cary Grant and Joan Fontaine in the starring roles, *Suspicion* was the title eventually chosen for Hitchcock's adaptation of *Before the fact.*[8] Cast in a role that contrasted sharply with his usual screen image, Grant plays Johnnie Aysgarth, a dissolute but charming spendthrift whose convention-flouting escapades initially shock a young woman with whom he falls in love, the socially reserved Lina McLaidlaw (Fontaine). But Lina's shock is short-lived, and against her better judgement she is beguiled by Johnnie's roguish ways. His devil-may-care attitude is an irresistible force, and Lina, captivated by Johnnie's rakish demeanour, rewards him with her heart.

The contrasts between Johnnie and Lina are important to the film's plot on several levels. Notable is the difference in Lina's and Johnnie's social standing. A prim and proper young woman, Lina is used to a sedate, bookish, and uneventful life. Her wealthy and uptight parents oppose her burgeoning relationship with Johnnie, but they are powerless to stem the tide of her desire. Long stifled by their stodgy ways, Lina sees in Johnnie's carefree manner the prospect of romance, adventure, and excitement. His freewheeling approach to life, so opposed to Lina's upper-class sense of propriety, sets off pointedly the plodding and predictable course of her own existence, and this contrast arouses her spirit for escape as much as it inflames her passion. Johnnie is an emblem of all that her parents reject – and even resent – and their contempt for Johnnie colours Lina's affections with a sensual longing for the forbidden fruit, the taboo liaison. Johnnie is the outlaw who will rescue her from spinsterhood boredom.

Hitchcock establishes the contours of this relationship with remarkable cinematic economy. The film opens in blackness with only the sound of a moving train situating the story. We then hear a man's voice (Johnnie's) as he apologizes for having bumped into a woman's (Lina's) leg: "Oh, I beg your

8 Donald Spoto reports that other titles Hitchcock considered included *Search for tomorrow, Men make poor husbands,* and *Girl in the vise.* See Spoto, Donald. *The Dark Side of Genius: The Life of Alfred Hitchcock.* New York: Ballantine Books, 1983, p. 255.

pardon, was that your leg? I had no idea we were going into a tunnel." The sparse and clipped dialogue, which reflects Hitchcock's enthusiasm for double entendre, also suggests something of Johnnie's obliviousness to the concerns of other people. Then, as the train emerges into the daylight, Hitchcock commences to sketch the contrast between the two characters in chiefly visual terms. Johnnie, apparently, is hung over. Lina is fully alert and reading a book on child psychology. Johnnie is tired and dishevelled, an obvious victim of his own weaknesses and passion. Lina is restrained and quiet, dressed in an expensive overcoat, with matching hat and gloves. These visual contrasts, which speak loudly of the pair's differences in terms of social class, intellectual interests, and lifestyle, are made with a series of visual juxtapositions characteristic of Hitchcock's penchant for "pure cinema." The opening sequence, with its emergence from darkness into light, is a potent stylistic motif for the theme of suspicion, for Lina will shortly find herself plunged into alternating moments of doubt (darkness) and clarity (light) in the course of the film. In addition, the train is an effective symbol suggesting the freedom that Johnnie will come to represent for Lina, even as it indicates the sense of confinement she will experience in her marriage.

In this opening sequence Johnnie and Lina are merely two strangers on a train, but Hitchcock contrives to present them as an incipient couple by manufacturing a circumstance requiring their collaboration. And because matters of trust and uncertainty will come to figure prominently in the course of the narrative, it is hardly surprising that this circumstance involves a confrontation with authority. The conductor enters the compartment and discovers that Johnnie is riding first class with a third-class ticket. At first, Johnnie tries to argue his way out of the predicament with hopelessly convoluted and comedic logic, but the conductor's impassive gaze makes it plain that he is immune to Johnnie's persuasive charms. Convinced of the conductor's intractability, Johnnie abruptly asks Lina for money so he can make up the difference between his ticket and the first-class fare to which, significantly, he appears to believe himself entitled. When Lina begins to explain that she hasn't sufficient change in her purse, Johnnie unexpectedly leans forward, reaches directly into her purse, and removes a stamp which he hands triumphantly to the conductor. Lina is understandably shocked by the audacity and the suddenness of Johnnie's actions, but Hitchcock's camera lingers on her long enough to show us that she is plainly captivated as well. Lina's text on child psychology is given fresh meaning considering these events, for Johnnie's impulsive and immature conduct would seem to constitute the very sort of behaviour in which Lina is apparently interested. Johnnie is also a subject against which her academic insights might be measured. In any event, Hitchcock's initial cinematic exposition provides reference points for a good deal of the subsequent character development upon which the story will rely.

This brief sequence is also important in terms of deeper narrative development. First, Hitchcock's arrangement of the mise en scène suggests a visual foundation for the theme of suspicion. Lina knows almost instantly the sort of person that Johnnie must be, but her knowledge provides her with no protection from her desires. Again, the book on child psychology is a significant symbol on this point. Lina's studious approach to interpersonal relations suggests a tendency to reduce emotional complexities to scientific principles. However, her attraction to Johnnie is impulsive, almost instinctual. When Lina later overhears her father explaining to her mother that Lina is "not the marrying sort," she rushes immediately into Johnnie's arms and kisses him on the lips, an overdetermined response, to be sure, but a response that makes evident Lina's wish to constitute herself in opposition to her parents' image. Moreover, her dash into Johnnie's arms is not the studied and deliberative action of the scholar, but a performance that Lina stages for herself as a means of self-persuasion. The dichotomy of mind and emotion is developed throughout the film in such a way as to raise continual questions about Lina's perception of events and her perceptions of other people.

Richard Allen has defined this aspect of Hitchcock's work as a mode of "metaskepticism" which recognizes ambiguity as a narrative ploy for heightening audience uncertainty.[9] This ambiguity colours not only individual scenes, of course, but shapes the intertextual resonance that brings apparently disparate parts of the story into unison. Nothing in the film is accidental, and each scene is meant to echo other scenes across a spectrum of cinematic elements. The movement from the darkness of the tunnel into the daylight is just one illustration of the self-referential structure of the narrative. Hence while some commentators see the initial meeting between Johnnie and Lina as an innocent and unmotivated staging, this sort of reading overlooks the foreshadowing that permeates the opening. For example, Joel Finler has said that "the picture is almost half over before the central theme, of 'suspicion', first begins to emerge."[10] Nothing could be further from the truth. In these first scenes the viewer is made keenly aware of Johnnie's irresponsible nature, and of Lina's attraction to him, nonetheless. Hitchcock strives to raise

---

9 Allen, Richard. "Hitchcock, or the Pleasures of Metaskepticism." In *Alfred Hitchcock: Centenary Essays*, edited by Richard Allen and S. Ishii Gonzalès. London: British Film Institute Publishing, 1999, pp. 221–237.

10 Finler, Joel W. *Alfred Hitchcock: The Hollywood Years*. London: b. T. Basford Ltd., 1992, p. 49.

audience suspicions about Johnnie, about his motives, and about any future liaison with him that Lina might be contemplating. Finler is correct only if we limit ourselves to overt displays of suspicion on the part of Lina, but as a central interpretive problematic, suspicion enters the film even as the train enters the tunnel. Simply from the fact that the film opens in confusion and in darkness we can infer that the theme of suspicion is an important interpretive frame for the narrative.

A second element that makes this opening sequence both prescient and thematically important is the way that Hitchcock organizes spatial relations as metaphors for class and gender. This is accomplished in part using cuts between Johnnie and Lina who are seated on opposite sides of the train car. The invisible boundary that separates them is made evident in the medium two-shots Hitchcock combines with alternating close-ups. But he also reveals the permeability of this boundary in the transgression committed by Johnnie in bumping into Lina's leg. This event suggests a sexual contravention, just as his literal raid upon Lina's purse, which furthers the sexual symbolism, also transgresses the boundary of social propriety. Indeed, Johnnie's actual movements in this sequence are figurative movements as well. He has already breached conventional and economic boundaries by placing himself where he has no right: in a first-class car with a third-class ticket. And he has violated boundaries of appropriate sexual conduct (and unspoken codes of civility) in brushing against Lina in the dark. Finally, his theft of the stamp needed to pay the train conductor shows his impetuosity and his disregard of social conventions. Johnnie is privileged and apparently accustomed to getting his way. But his actions in this opening sequence go at least one further step by infantilizing Lina, rendering her subordinate to Johnnie's whims. His tendency to deprecate her wishes and to substitute his concerns and interests for her desires is a theme developed to considerable extent in the film.

Following their whirlwind courtship and marriage, the straitlaced Lina McLaidlaw (for whom her parents have "laid" down the "law") grows increasingly suspicious that her beloved Johnnie is up to no good. Fettered in by her upper-class domesticity, Lina finds Johnnie's impulsive behaviour alternately charming and mysterious. And as she attempts to piece together his motivations and make sense of his emotional inconstancy, Lina's suspicions deepen until she has convinced herself that Johnnie is more than an enchanting if irresponsible reprobate: he is a murderer as well. Hitchcock presents the intensification of Lina's paranoia with the use of extreme close-ups and low-key lighting. In this regard the film clearly contains elements commonly associated with the film noir cycle, especially as this interpretation relates to the use of lighting and shadows. But as Michael Walker suggests, although "the link between the Hitchcock chaos world and the *noir* world suggests that

Hitchcock is more of a *noir* director than has generally been recognized," we need to take account of the fact that "Hitchcock is so strong an *auteur* that his films tend to be seminal [...] rather than derivative and [that] they have far more connections with one another than with any particular cycle or genre."[11] This is not to say that *Suspicion* has no allegiance to the film noir tradition, for the film certainly evinces cinematic elements consistent with the thematic and visual style of *noir.* However, there are also surrealistic qualities to the film that betray Hitchcock's personal touch far more than they reveal his allegiance to a particular genre. As in other Hitchcock works, the focus of *Suspicion* is on the subjectivity of the central character, and thus many of the atmospheric touches not only heighten suspense, but also deepen the emotional turmoil Lina is undergoing.

For instance, in one of the film's most celebrated scenes Johnnie carries a glass of milk upstairs to help an emotionally spent Lina fall asleep. As the scene unfolds the cinematic point of view is the spectator who has been privileged with a location near the top of the staircase as Johnnie ascends amidst ominous shadows. But the emotional point of view is clearly Lina who, though tucked away in her bed and unable to see her husband, imagines that the glass of milk he is carrying is poisoned. Hitchcock heightens both forms of suspense (the cinematic and the emotional) by placing a light bulb inside the glass to draw the viewer's attention to that object. The innocence of milk with its maternal and medicinal associations is confounded by the suspicion that it may have been contaminated. Though much remarked upon as indicating Hitchcock's fondness for gimmicks and visual trickery, the luminous glass of milk unites precisely those features that prefigure Lina's suspicion: innocence and evil. Ultimately, it is her uncertainty about Johnnie rather than anything about which she can be certain that takes her to the eventual pinnacle of her suspicion and apprehension.

Hitchcock sprinkles the story with a series of ambiguous developments and situations and keeps the viewer's suspicions firmly locked in Lina's perceptual and interpretive fields. This containment owes much to our general reluctance to question the reliability of the authorial voice. Thus, when Lina scrutinizes the events of her everyday life only to convince herself that she is destined to be Johnnie's next victim, the conclusion hardly comes as a shock. After all, the clues are obvious: Johnnie's clandestine sale of wedding gifts to pay off his gambling debts; secrets and lies about being fired from his job; his fascination with a local author's detective stories and the possibility of a lethal,

11 Walker, Michael. "Film Noir: An Introduction." In *The Movie Book of Film Noir*, edited by Ian Cameron. London: Studio Vista, 1992, p. 16.

undetectable poison; the taking out of a life insurance policy; the mysterious death of Johnnie's closest friend – who could blame Lina for her fears?

It is at this point that the issue of the film's conclusion becomes a matter of debate, for in a remarkable narrative twist the story resolves in Johnnie's favour. He is certainly a gambler and idler, but he is no killer. Moreover, in the film's closing scene he vows to go straight and become a conscientious drone in the capitalist hive. His inquiries about undetectable poisons, his fascination with murder mysteries, and his decision to furtively take out life insurance policies were motivated not by a plan to murder Linda, but by the contemplation of suicide, a turn of events that frequently strikes first-time viewers as abrupt and stilted. Perhaps those critics and observers who jeered the conclusion were inspired in their denunciations by Hitchcock's remark that a more sinister ending would have suited him better. The studio, he claimed, had vetoed his plans for a darker, malicious conclusion in which Johnnie is found to be the criminal Lina suspects. Hitchcock's concern about the ending was sufficiently intense, it is said, that when the film debuted in August 1941, he was prepared to disown the project should audience reaction be unfavourable (a preview audience had already laughed at a version of the picture that featured an even more improbable conclusion).[12] But audiences of the day apparently found the ending eminently satisfying. While it is possible that they were pleased to see that Johnnie Aysgarth's reputation was salvaged, they may have been more relieved to see Cary Grant redeemed. Hitchcock's suspicions about audience rejection turned out to be groundless.

Lina's suspicions, it turns out, were groundless too, mere fantasies fashioned from an overactive imagination. Johnnie was terribly misunderstood. True, he was a schemer, a gambler, a thoughtless rogue – but murder had never entered his thoughts. In the picture's closing moments, reconciled at last to the delusions of her mischievous mind, Lina must find a way to reorient herself to Johnnie, to put her previous fears behind her, and to overcome the illicit suspicions that have infected her thoughts.

The Uncertainties of Suspicion

That her suspicions were unfounded does not mean that the picture's central issue devolves to the facile observation that Lina somehow managed to get things wrong. The film does not merely preach truth above misapprehension, for this would mean placing Lina's subjectivity in the domain of the irrational and the feminine, while locating the solution to her problems in the world of

---

12 Spoto, p. 256.

rational masculinity. Of course, these associations are operating at one level in the film and recognizing this aspect of the gender politics of the narrative is important. But there are other elements central to the narrative that eclipse the issue of truth and falsity. Gender politics is an important aspect of the film's subtext, but we need to be careful to avoid the reduction of these dynamics to nothing more complex than the unmasking of error.

In the first place, Lina's suspicions are not all that suspect. Indeed, a major point of the narrative is missed if it is reduced solely to the view that Lina is emotionally unstable, or that her suspicions are produced from irrational impulses. Lina's apparent tendency to jump to conclusions may reflect certain of her insecurities in respect of her relationship with Johnnie, but it is unfair to usher her too quickly to the psychoanalyst's couch on that account. It is more valuable to recognize the way that insecurity and suspicion may often be linked, and to attend to the way that suspicion can symbolize fear and uncertainty. Suspicion may speak more to feelings of powerlessness than it speaks to the desire for control. Consequently, suspicion must be de-pathologized if other important elements in the film are to emerge.

Second, although *Suspicion* deals with a conventional binarism between masculine and feminine modes of perception, there is a depth to the central characters' relation that helps to disguise much of the subtlety of this dichotomy. This is the overarching question of the function of interpretation, for it is an integral aspect of the film that the heroine's efforts at understanding produce equal measures of confusion and logic. And it is the mundane nature of Lina's environment that assists in normalizing her uncertainty as a newlywed woman. Indeed, that Lina should grow suspicious even as Johnnie remains charmingly oblivious to the possible misconstruals to which Lina is inclined is readily normalized in the viewing experience.[13] Lina's introspection and Johnnie's sexually accented extroversion both serve to assist the orderly progression of the narrative by grounding its psychological poignancy in the ideology of gender relations. This ideological configuration is normalized both as the viewing experience and as the dynamic of power. Were the situation reversed – were Johnnie to exchange his extroverted manner for Lina's introverted suspicions – the picture would assume a peculiar quality indeed. How we understand another's behaviour is contingent upon our place in the hierarchy of social authority. The mode of suspiciousness that emerges is a function of desperation more than it is a function of gender identity.

13 Laura Mulvey's work on this theme is relevant. See especially her essay, "Visual Pleasure and Narrative Cinema." *Screen*, 16 (3), Autumn 1975.

Suspicion speaks not only of irrational impulses, then, but also of the problems of interpretation and about the urges that drive each of us toward sense-making. To break the film down into truth (Johnnie) and falsity (Lina) is to ignore the fact that it is precisely suspicion's power to affect our lives that Hitchcock explores with insight and sensitivity, irrespective of the truth values of those conjectures. Suspicion is an interpretive scheme conditioned by feelings of powerlessness, disenfranchisement, and disconnection. The content of the suspicion is thus secondary to the overall picture – not only the picture that Hitchcock filmed, but also the picture that Lina constructs for herself and for viewers in her interpretation of events. Had Lina's suspicions proved correct in the end, the subject would command our attention just as profoundly. We are, as Kenneth Burke notes, symbol-using and symbol-misusing animals.[14] Lina may misuse the symbolic tokens of her world in seeking to understand Johnnie's actions and behaviours, but she produces meaning, nonetheless. Every one of us constructs our interpretations of events through the manipulation of symbols, and we make meanings in this way to guide our actions.

This view of things suggests that what is especially provocative about *Suspicion* is that Lina's fantasies are no more outlandish than Hitchcock's plot. As viewers, watching events unfold from Lina's point of view, we are encouraged to side with her against Johnnie so that each piece of the cinematic puzzle contributing to his supposed guilt fits neatly into the overall picture of reality that Lina creates. Lina stands in for Hitchcock himself, providing us with a director's judgement in the ordering of events and the assignment of significance to some episodes over others. Along with Lina we construct the reality the film shows us.

This observation leads me to the view that some of the negative response to the picture's final moments may be doubly motivated. Not only were critics influenced in part by Hitchcock's own denunciations of the ending that the studio "forced" on him, but some critics also may have felt cheated, even disrespected. The sense-making power of the cinema is so encompassing that to have our constructed portrait dashed from its easel in the climactic movements of the movie is a jarring, disconcerting experience. Indeed, this discomfort speaks to at least some of the discomfort we associate with suspicion and its forbidding darkness. No one likes to be made a fool of, not Lina, as she grows suspicious of Johnnie, and not the filmgoer who feels betrayed by the film's dénouement. Hence the claim that the picture ends on an unsatisfying or unconvincing note is justified only if the viewer can demonstrate that some

14 Burke, 1966.

compelling and logical set of reasons entailed by the actual narrative forbids the conclusion to which we are treated. I doubt that this is possible. What strikes me as more to the point is that the finale precisely generates those feelings of mistrust that are embodied in the experience of being suspicious.

Although Lina's suspicions, as we learn in the end, are nonsense, at the same time, they are sense, for they provide her with a scheme for understanding events and behaviours for which she has no familiar interpretive framework. Non-sense is an evaluative concept speaking to the other's interpretations. As Lina reconciles herself to Johnnie, the viewer must reconcile him or herself to the fact that Lina's behaviour must be reframed to be more fully understood. Only in this way does the viewer avoid becoming trapped at a superficial level of critique.

Suspicion and Faith

This series of reconciliations that bring the film to its conclusion points to a further connection between two apparently disparate conditions enfolded within the narrative that is not so easily detected. This is the continuity between Lina's suspicions and her final optimism, a linkage between her suspicions about Johnnie and her eventual faith in his promise to reform. A connection can be drawn, in other words, between *two distinct ways of moralizing uncertainty: suspicion on the one side, and faith on the other.* In moralizing uncertainty, redemption and despair can be articulated concurrently.

What I am saying can be made clearer with the suggestion that suspicion is a form of faith, that both suspicion and faith rely on the power of the will to transcend the skeletal empiricism of facts and to embroider lavish patterns of significance from the flimsiest of threads. When faced with incomplete evidence we are also faced with choices. Should we believe, or disbelieve, and if we believe, what will we believe? When the evidentiary basis is shaky, what sort of belief will we entertain?

We may not always choose faith even though we choose to believe. This is because suspicion is faith's shadow, the dark underside of unsecured knowledge. Where faith promises redemption, suspicion augers destruction. In the beginning, Lina chooses suspicion, and it is only with her suspicions successfully quelled that she can look to the future with hope. Suspicion, then, is often a framing of the past, while faith is a reading of the future. In either case – suspicion or faith – we search for bridges to carry us over the abyss of not knowing.

For Kierkegaard, the leap of faith was one solution to the problem of these gaps, for although faith may be paradoxical – a choice without criteria, he argued – faith is the answer to the problem formulated by the conditions of our uncertainty.[15] The incompleteness of our knowledge compels us to the existential challenge of making a choice. As Kierkegaard argued, "faith begins precisely there where thinking leaves off."[16] At such moments of heightened indeterminacy, faith offers itself as a vehicle to convey us to safety. With faith in the ascendancy, the incompleteness of our knowledge no longer throws suspicion's shadows of doubt across our minds. Instead, it becomes a "mystery" pervious to the penetrating light of faith. Faith is a choice Lina makes in order to stave off the all-consuming torment of suspicion.

In taming her suspicions and bringing them under her command, Lina redirects her energies into an unfounded faith in the future. Put differently, in a cathartic release from her obsessions, Lina replaces her *unwarranted suspicions* about Johnnie's intentions with *unwarranted faith* in Johnnie's intentions. The same events and activities that were initially interpreted as evidence against Johnnie are reframed not so that they assume an adiaphoric function, but so that they emerge as testimonies to Johnnie's goodness and upstanding character. In the film's final images, Johnnie's willingness to forego the pleasures of his playful yesteryears signals the couple's entrance into a world of respectability and upper-class sensibility. This is made possible by several transformations, not the least of which is Lina's willing suspension of suspicion in favour of a willing subscription to Johnnie's promises. Lina's faith is the undoing of her suspicions on one hand, but it is also an extension, or a transformation of those suspicions, on the other. This continuity is easily overlooked, especially if our attentions are directed not to the problem of interpretation, but to questions of truth and falsity. *Suspicion* is a film most suited for the hermeneutic analysis of hermeneutics.

Indeed, suspicion is a kind of hermeneutic circle. One approaches the events for which an interpretation is sought predisposed to an understanding. This predisposition is then confirmed by the logic of subsequent interpretations. A great number of events that Lina might otherwise allow to pass without commentary are magnified by the interpretive scheme of her suspicions. When Johnnie's friend Beaky dies suddenly while overseas, Lina remembers a formerly innocuous comment Johnnie made that Beaky's taste for brandy would one day be his undoing. The intertextuality of Lina's thoughts brings Johnnie's comment back to her and inserts it in the newly forming text she is

15 On Kierkegaard's views on faith, see, for example, Kierkegaard, Søren. *Fear and Trembling* (orig. 1843), translated by Walter Lowrie. Princeton: Princeton University Press, 1941. Paul Tillich also sketches the outlines of a dialectical theory of faith in his classic treatise *Dynamics of Faith*, New York: Harper & Row, 1957.

16 Kierkegaard, p. 64.

mentally composing in which Johnnie plays the role of killer. Comments that were first interpreted as a friend's lament now become murderous foreshadowings – and potential threats to Lina.

But if suspicion is a semiotician's nightmare, the product of an overly interpretive mind, faith can be the termination of inquisition. Or, to put that differently, whereas suspicion is a continual questioning of the evidence, faith is a willing suspension of the inquisitive faculties. They are both modes of interpretation, but they differ in that whereas suspicion seeks the truth within, faith seeks the truth without. Hence there is a claustrophobic quality to suspicion and the questioning that it generates. This is made evident in the claustrophobic quality of Lina's life that prevails during the height of her suspicious thinking. But with faith there is an opening of windows, an optimistic dismissal of the minutiae by which she was surrounded. In place of questioning, there is blind acceptance. Lina abandons her hermeneutics of suspicion in deciding that Johnnie can be trusted. Johnnie, of course, has not really changed. What has changed is Lina's manner of dealing with the unknown.

These changes are important to a further understanding of the film. As with other of his works, in *Suspicion* Hitchcock reproduces the hegemony of heterosexualism in the production of the romantic couple. But it is significant that for the relationship to achieve stability it is Lina who must undergo a transformation, a shift from suspicion to faith, from darkness to light, from the past (what Johnnie has done) to the future (what Johnnie will become). Lina must deal with her suspicions by accommodating herself to Johnnie. Lina must suppress her emotions in service to Johnnie's putative ambitions. Her new life will hinge on the assurances he offers. Lina must completely change the belief system underlying her interpretive framework. For his part, Johnnie is required only to promise his intentions to reform.

It is noteworthy that as viewers we have no particular evidence to believe that Johnnie's promise to conform to the bourgeois lifestyle he has formerly rejected should be taken at face value. But as our cinematic point of view throughout the film has been Lina's, it is difficult to reject her faith out of hand. Some distance from the absorption with which we attend to the film is required to recognize the several layers of deception that appear to be mobilized against Lina – and against the viewer – in the picture's finale. Lina may seem foolish in accepting that Johnnie has at last discovered the roadway to economic and emotional responsibility. But this foolishness is attenuated somewhat by the viewers' humanity: each of us is inflicted by the human compulsion to believe. Johnnie's promises are palliatives of the moment, but Lina's desires are so strong that she is prepared to accept the medicine and move unquestioningly into the future with all of its uncertainties. Faith, not suspicion, now attends her.

In substituting faith for suspicion, Lina empowers herself, for if suspicion is the emblem of the powerless, faith is the symbol of the empowered. Both are strategies for dealing with the inevitable state of not knowing, yet faith makes a prize of ignorance, raising it aloft as an emblem of unconditional love. In that climactic moment in which she stands on the precipice of ignorance, Lina turns her suspicion around in her mind and finds faith is the opposite side to the coin of uncertainty. This becomes the currency with which she will purchase her future.

Suspicion, then, is an inverted form of faith, but how do we arrive at suspicion? Is it also a leap of faith, or, perhaps, a leap of despair? These are complicated questions, far more tangled than they may appear when expressed so simply. One of the dilemmas we face if we read Hitchcock's film merely as an exploration of Johnnie's odd behaviour and Lina's misguided attempts to understand him is that our efforts to interpret Johnnie's behaviour leave us inattentive to the real task: trying to interpret Lina's interpretations. Of course, Hitchcock provides plenty of material along the way to suggest that Lina is more right than wrong, but without such scenes the film would degenerate into a one-dimensional portrait of a disturbed mind. What is more to the point is that suspicion is not in and of itself a sign of pathology any more than faith is an indication of abnormality.

But here is another dilemma: Is faith an abnormality? Is faith a sign of pathological weakness, a symptom of our collective inability to live with uncertainty? This may be too strongly worded. Though uncertainty is one of the more conspicuous charms on the bracelet of postmodern fashion, it is neither a novel nor utterly nihilistic part of the ensemble. We must all face up to the fact that there are aspects to others that remain forever hidden from our view. To have faith that we can rise above petty suspicion, or to be suspicious about the sincerity of faith, amounts to pretty much the same thing: the world is largely unexplored and reconciling ourselves to the limitations of our individual perspectives is an act born of both courage and despair at one and the same moment.

Thus, suspicion is not merely a product of our perception; it is the mode of apprehension by which we make our perceptions meaningful. But suspicion only functions effectively to the extent that others can be brought into its web of intrigue; otherwise, the doubts and misgivings give way to paranoia, to obsessive thinking, and to social ostracism. Suspicion is a mode of interpretation that reinforces isolation. Hence in Hitchcock's film, we see Lina retreating ever further into a private enclave of foreboding and mistrust. We see self-absorption overtake her life rationally and emotionally. Her suspicions become all-consuming even as her day-to-day life becomes one of unbearable solitude. It is important to note that in taming these obsessions, and in coming to give herself over entirely to faith, Lina also provides us with a glimpse into the unspoken details of solidarity. Taking Johnnie at face value, taking Johnnie at his word, and taking Johnnie as one who is worthy of her self-denial are equally crucial parts of the experience of community life, especially the willing suspension of doubt that Lina engages in daily. And so it is with us. Unable to peer into the truth of another's intentions, we are forced to go on faith constantly. As the philosopher Knud Løgstrup has written:

> Regardless of how varied the communication between persons may be, it always involves the risk of one person approaching the other in the hope of a response. This is the essence of communication and fundamental basis of ethical life.[17]

Lina has reasons for doubting Johnnie; she also has reasons for having faith in his promises. And yet, whether she opts for faith or for suspicion, it is Lina who is making the choice, Lina who is seeing the world one way and not another. Compelled to decisions – decisions about her life with Johnnie, decisions about Johnnie's faithfulness, decisions about love and romance – Lina struggles to make the leap of faith and to leave suspicion behind. Hence her faith is indeed the medium of her salvation. Most viewers will say that it is Johnnie who is redeemed by the film's end, but Lina's redemption is the more compelling act of conversion in the final analysis.

---

17 Løgstrup, Knud. *The Ethical Demand*, translated by Theodor I. Jensen. Philadelphia: Fortress Press, 1971, p. 18.

INDEX

Ingram Content Group UK Ltd.
Milton Keynes UK
UKHW012207220623
423877UK00003B/9